THE
BLUE
AGE

THE
BLUE
AGE

HOW THE US NAVY CREATED
GLOBAL PROSPERITY—AND WHY
WE'RE IN DANGER OF LOSING IT

———

GREGG
EASTERBROOK

PUBLICAFFAIRS
New York

PublicAffairs
Hachette Book Group
1290 Avenue of the Americas, New York, NY 10104
www.publicaffairsbooks.com
@Public_Affairs

Printed in the United States of America

First Edition: September 2021

Published by PublicAffairs, an imprint of Perseus Books, LLC, a subsidiary of Hachette Book Group, Inc. The PublicAffairs name and logo is a trademark of the Hachette Book Group.

The Hachette Speakers Bureau provides a wide range of authors for speaking events. To find out more, go to www.hachettespeakersbureau.com or call (866) 376-6591.

The publisher is not responsible for websites (or their content) that are not owned by the publisher.

Print book interior design by Jeff Williams.

Library of Congress Cataloging-in-Publication Data

Names: Easterbrook, Gregg, author.
Title: The blue age : how the US Navy created global prosperity—and why
    we're in danger of losing it / Gregg Easterbrook.
Other titles: How the US Navy created global prosperity—and why we're in
    danger of losing it
Description: First edition. | New York : PublicAffairs, 2021. |
    Includes bibliographical references and index.
Identifiers: LCCN 2021016411 | ISBN 9781541742543 (hardback) |
    ISBN 9781541742550 (epub)
Subjects: LCSH: Sea-power—United States—History—21st century. |
    United States. Navy—History—21st century. | Trade routes—History—21st century. |
    Shipping—United States—History—21st century. | United States—History, Naval.
Classification: LCC VA58 .E27 2021 | DDC 359/.030973—dc23
LC record available at https://lccn.loc.gov/2021016411

ISBNs: 978-1-5417-4254-3 (hardcover), 978-1-5417-4255-0 (ebook)

LSC-C

Printing 1, 2021

to Ben Adams
who believes in books
vita excolatur

To multiply the harbors does not reduce the sea.

EMILY DICKINSON, 1871

CONTENTS

INTRODUCTION

IF THE ANCIENT MARINER COULD SEE US NOW

WAVES SLAP AGAINST THE HULLS OF CARAVELS ON AN INKY night, ships tracking each other via lookouts who watch for wakes and listen for the creak of wood against water. Commanders of the Portuguese fleet waited for a crescent moon so they could enter the Strait of Malacca in near darkness. Sailors whisper, knowing they will be punished for loud talking. Sound carries on a flat sea—should anyone on deck shout up toward the lateens, the cries might be overheard along the shores of this narrow passage.

Some of the sailors are nervous, knowing that within a few hours they may be dead or bellowing in agony as a surgeon hacks off a smashed limb. Others are eager to fight. The coming battle will afford the chance to win and return home in glory, claiming the reward promised by the throne—gold sufficient for a mere sailor to enter a gentleman's life of ease.

A navigator consults the heavens. He locates the bright star Canopus, known as Suhail to Islamic astronomers of old; measures the apparent distance from Canopus to other named stars by holding up his hand and using the knuckle of this thumb as a scale. The navigator consults a Chinese map many men died to obtain. He informs the captain their small fleet will reach the Sultanate of Malacca before daybreak. The captain orders marines to dress for combat.

The voyage from Portugal to the Strait of Malacca was timed to variations of ocean currents, which appear to mariners as colored rivers in the vastness of the water world, and to monsoon winds whose direction varies with the season.

The Portuguese have come from Lisbon, all the way down the west coast of Africa, around Cape Agulhas at the foot of the continent that is a mystery to Castile, to Kochi on the west of India, then across the Indian Ocean.

Merely reaching the location for the battle has been expensive, exhausting, perilous. Sailors died en route, and combat survivors will die on the voyage home, if there is such a voyage. From the start everyone knew that if half the complement ever saw Lisbon Cathedral again, the quest would be blessed of God.

The year is 1511, and these are not the first wooden ships to endure the hardship of a transit from Europe to what was then called the Orient. In 1498, Vasco da Gama was the first European to sail to India. By 1511, Spanish, Dutch, and other vessels have made the passage. Not long after 1511, Ferdinand Magellan would organize ships for the initial circumnavigation of our pale blue dot. Five carracks with 260 men departed Seville. Three years passed. A single vessel, with 18 men—a skeleton crew in more ways than one—returned to Seville. Their ship's log was one day behind, confirming the disputed notion that there existed an international date line.

In 1511 there will be war along the Strait of Malacca, a complicated multiple-party combat among the Portuguese, the local sultanate, the Dutch, the Ming Chinese, and the Venetians. Portugal will prevail, taking control of a water highway thousands of miles from home.

Those aboard local junks that ply the Strait of Malacca do not know of Lisbon's approaching fleet. Determining the specific location of ships at sea was a 3,000-year-old puzzle, from the Phoenicians through the late Cold War, solved only in the current generation by satellites and transponders. The instant locals sense a fight coming, they will race their junks to the nearest anchorage. When warships appear, most of what floats ends up sinking, including most of the warships.

For many centuries a trip down the Strait of Malacca was hazardous: pirates, boarding parties, armed ships of shoguns and royals were a constant danger because the water road between West and East ran through this contested channel, just as the water road to Athens of antiquity ran through the narrow channel at Artemisium.

Age-old kingdoms fought over the strait; navies of Renaissance Europe and Middle China fought over the strait; England devoted a hefty share of its collective wealth to establishing a fortress city at Singapore, to control the Asian entrance to the strait. In 1945 a powerful battle cruiser, *Haguro*, erred by steering into the Strait of Malacca. Soon the 927 men of the crew had gone to meet their ancestors.

THAT WAS THE STRAIT of Malacca in the past, war-torn and treacherous. Today the primary danger in these waters is collision caused by traffic.

The Strait of Malacca now suggests a Los Angeles freeway at rush hour, nearly as packed with ships as Interstate 5 is packed with cars. Now a lookout in the strait would observe reflecting off rippling waves in every direction the red, green, and white strobe beacons of merchant vessels. A warship would track the navigation beacons of dozens of large container ships, in addition to electronic signatures of tourist vessels, fishing boats, ferries, and privately owned yachts. The Strait of Malacca has become the busiest sea lane in the world, bearing more traffic than does the Strait of Hormuz, near the Persian Gulf. Nearly a third of international trade passes through the slender channel of the old Malaccan Sultanate, more than the share of trade traversing any other strait in the world. And today the Strait of Malacca has been peaceful for two full generations.

THE TRANSITION FROM FIGHTING on the waters to ubiquitous waterborne commerce is among the important events of our lifetimes—but unseen, happening at sea.

Battle for control of the riches of the ancient land of Malacca—now a state in Malaysia—was a small part of many centuries of blood on the waters. Those many centuries of maritime slaughter involved the British versus the Spanish Armada; the Venetians versus the Ottomans; Athens versus Sparta on the Mediterranean and its inlets; Athens versus the Persians; the British versus the French at Trafalgar and Chesapeake Bay and many other places; England versus the Dutch and the Danes in naval battles all three have forgotten; the thirteenth-century Mongols on two occasions sending invasion fleets against Japan; the Korean fleet versus the Japanese fleet at Noryang (seven hundred ships fighting 425 years ago—*seven hundred ships 425 years ago!*); the Japanese versus the Chinese in the Yalu River; the Russians versus the Ottomans and the Japanese; British privateers versus Chinese junks in the Pearl River delta during the Opium Wars; the Argentines versus the Brazilians at Juncal Island; the British versus the Germans in the Pacific and at many places in the Atlantic; the British versus the Germans at the Falklands; the Argentines versus the British at the Falklands; the Americans versus the British in many places, from Lake Erie to the East Indies; the Dutch versus the Portuguese off Brazil, India, and Malacca; the Americans versus the Spanish across much of the Pacific; the Americans versus the Japanese across the whole of the Pacific.

Twice, violent naval battles at the Falklands—desolate islands without resources or strategic significance, close to Antarctica. *Twice*, men boarded mammoth ships to fight over these barely inhabited atolls, and many never returned.

World War II in the Pacific began in no small part because imperial Japan wanted to eliminate America's ability to project power along South Pacific sea lanes. The World War II Battle of the Atlantic, engaging the merchant marine, destroyers, submarines, long-range aircraft, and the newest innovation in warfare—electronics—had as much to do with the liberation of Europe as did D-Day: itself mainly a seaborne event, involving some seven thousand vessels.

Vast movements of military forces occurred by sea long before thousands of ships supported the Allied units storming Normandy. In 1689, William and Mary landed in England with fifteen thousand soldiers carried by ship. In 1798, Napoléon landed in Alexandria with forty thousand soldiers carried by ship.

Theodore Roosevelt put the matter this way: "Throughout human history, there has been almost incessant warfare on the oceans." Yet during our lives, for the first time in human history, the oceans have been peaceful.

THROUGH CENTURIES OF BLOODY fighting, the waters also knew the constructive impulses of trade, exploration, and science. Thousands of years ago, mariners without maps or compasses rode ocean currents from the eastern coast of Africa to what is now Australia; similar one-way journeys atop currents may have taken ancient peoples to what are now the Polynesian islands.

Long ago, Arab navigators mastered the monsoon winds and ocean currents to travel from the Gulf of Oman to China and back, carrying far greater quantities than could be moved on foot and hoof via the Silk Road. They learned that currents have seasonal patterns and are distinct not just in speed but in color, chemistry— navigators sometimes tasted the local seawater—marine life, and nearby birds. They learned that some winds blow along predictable corridors according to cycles: the trade winds. The mariner who understood the signs and behaviors of the Atlantic's Gulf Stream, or the Indian Ocean Gyre, or the trade winds, could pilot a ship farther and faster than sails might suggest.

In the 1400s, sizable squadrons of three-mast oceangoing Chinese junks explored much of the western Pacific. In the 1800s, Royal Navy fighting ships mapped the globe's littorals, improving safety for every category of vessel. Science ships launched by a range of nations—such as the *Beagle*, Charles Darwin's brig-sloop— produced fundamental insights about nature.

Many Spanish treasure galleons sailed back and forth between Central America and Iberia, bearing the spoils of theft at a colossal scale; many British, Danish, Dutch, French, Portuguese, and Spanish vessels moved between Africa, the Caribbean, and the Americas in that most immoral of activities, slave trading. Nations such as England made heroes of criminals such as Francis Drake, whose specialties were carrying slaves by sea while staging piracy along the way.

WHAT MARINERS CALL "the blue water"—sea beyond the horizon—produced countless tales of discovery, bravery, savagery, and recklessness. Consider just one, the career of the sidewheel frigate *Mississippi*.

Construction of the *Mississippi* began in 1839 at the Philadelphia Naval Shipyard, which opened in 1776 to lay keels for challengers to Royal Navy ships of the line. *Mississippi* was among the first warships to be propelled mainly by steam (the ship also had sails) and to carry the formidable Paixhans gun, a cannon that fired exploding shells along a straight line, able to strike the side of a vessel rather than soaring past. Building of the *Mississippi* was supervised by Matthew Perry, a young US Navy officer who was to write his name into history by sailing through the Uraga Channel into Edo Bay, at Tokyo.

Launched in 1842, *Mississippi* spent time chasing pirates in what was then called the West Indies, before covering the US landing at Veracruz in 1847, during the Mexican-American War. After the close of that war, *Mississippi* churned across the Atlantic Ocean using paddle wheels to patrol the Mediterranean along the edges of the old Ottoman Empire. Then Perry, become a commodore, received a high-profile assignment: negotiate a trade treaty with Japan. Though at the time Japan and China might have seemed as distant as the constellations seem today, many nations were trading profitably with China. Few, however, were engaged in commerce with Japan, which resisted contact with the West.

Perry had the *Mississippi* and its escorts rigged for an arduous voyage. Departing in 1852 from the US Navy facility at Norfolk,

Virginia—today the largest naval base in the world—*Mississippi* churned over the Atlantic again, parking for a while at Madeira, in Portugal. *Mississippi* headed down the coast of Africa, rounded the southern expanse of that land mass (before there was a Suez or Panama canal, transocean sailing involved the southern tip of a continent), turned northeast across the Indian Ocean toward Hong Kong, then Singapore, then Edo Bay, arriving nearly a year after leaving Norfolk. The side-wheels of the *Mississippi* had churned the vessel roughly the circumference of the earth—easily done today by a jetliner, then an extraordinary challenge.

Perry's Japan mission led to trade and cultural exchange but also helped cause even more fighting between West and East. Metal hulls, screw propellers, oil-using engines, and new weapons far more destructive than a Paixhans gun made fighting at sea ever worse.

MILLENNIA OF COMBAT ON oceans, lakes, and rivers built up to the October 1944 Battle of Leyte Gulf between the United States and Japan. More than three hundred warships, many of them huge, and nearly eighteen hundred aircraft hammered at each other with bombs, torpedoes, and cannon shells weighing up to three thousand pounds.

Then suddenly—fighting on the blue water stopped.

Since Leyte Gulf, there have been only a few relatively brief fights among ships. At this writing, no naval combat of any kind has occurred in the twenty-first century.

In centuries past, fighting on the water was like the Battle of Jutland, staged in 1916, involving 58 battleships and battle cruisers (similar to battleships) plus 190 additional fighting vessels, leaving nine thousand dead and a significant portion of the national treasuries of Great Britain and Germany on the bottom of the North Sea.

So far in the twenty-first century, fighting on the waters has been like the 2019 day USS *Boxer* shot down an Iranian drone above the Persian Gulf. An international incident followed, with Washington, London, Brussels, and Tehran atwitter. But no one was harmed and nothing of value was lost—a computer-directed, unmanned missile blew to smithereens an autonomous eavesdropping device. The dead of Jutland, and a hundred other brutal naval battles, would call that progress.

During our lifetimes, there is still piracy, but its magnitude is nothing like in the past. Our lifetimes have coincided with the longest stretch of peace upon the waters since Thucydides. "Incessant warfare on the oceans" appears, at least, no more.

Why fighting declined on the waters is the first question of this book. What's happening on the oceans right now is the second question. What the future holds on the blue waters will be the final question.

WHAT'S HAPPENING ON THE oceans right now is that the current Long Peace at sea allows a huge expansion of trade—history's greatest such expansion by a considerable margin, even when rising global population is taken into account.

The global inflation-adjusted dollar value of trade more than doubled between 1994 and 2019, well ahead of the pace of population rise in the same period. Today's capacity of merchant ships to carry cargo (measured in deadweight tons) is three times greater than it was in 1980. Trade volume at the Port of Los Angeles has grown tenfold since 1985. By 2019, the family of nations had twenty-six ports that each handled more trade than the *total* amount of international commerce in 1960.

In early 2020, international trade declined because of the COVID-19 pandemic. The dip did not last. By August 2020, the United States set a record for containers of goods arriving at ports in a month. By early 2021, so many container ships were stuck in offshore queues waiting for dock space at American ports that some businesses could not keep shelves stocked.

The fantastic increase in ocean-borne trade is to most an abstraction, since the majority of people rarely observe the oceans. Container vessels bigger than the *Titanic*, ships upon which the global economy relies, can be seen only on the high sea or in harbors, which means few ever espy them. The undersea cables that carry the internet—most web communication and commerce is by ocean cable, not satellite—are not seen. Nor are the increasingly interlaced undersea fuel pipelines and power conduits that homes, offices, and schools rely on for electricity, oil, and gas.

Not all that long ago, ocean transportation was a fundamental experience for many, including Europeans emigrating to North America and Australia. Today, humanity knows the sea mostly by vacation vessels. Mainly we fly over the blue water—air travel is more convenient than boat travel for most, not just the affluent. Few people visit naval bases or working harbor quays, which are often closed to the public, in any case. Some harbors of the Mediterranean and Africa mix downtown café districts with ships and cranes. In most of the European Union, Japan, and the United States, the two types of places are separated: rare is the person who sees the physical evidence of action at sea.

The same obtains for blue-age infrastructure. Tourists don't take holidays to marvel at the expanded Panama and Suez Canals or the impressive ship channels of the Netherlands or tour important waterways such as the immense Soo Locks that connect Lake Superior with the lower Great Lakes. These and many other water-trade facilities have been renovated in recent years at a furious pace to accommodate more and larger ships. Harbor dredging has become an essential global economic activity—but most citizens of the United States and the European Union don't even know it occurs.

A GENERATION AGO, CHINA hardly built ships and was no player in global economics. Today four of the world's five busiest ports are in China, as is earth's most productive shipbuilding industry. In a single generation, China converted from a closed, state-controlled economic model that failed all except the Communist Party overlords to a market system based on ocean-borne commerce.

China's new commitment to ocean trade has improved the lives of hundreds of millions of ordinary Chinese. Vital for the human family—but not seen in the West—is that increased trade brought about rapid decline of global poverty. As recently as the 1970s, 50 percent of humanity lived in extreme poverty, according to the

World Bank definition. By 2015, extreme poverty was down to its lowest level ever, at 10 percent.

Nearly all the decline of extreme poverty occurred in the trade-focused nations of Asia. Max Roser, an economist at the University of Oxford, has noted that China's trade-based improvement of living standards in the last two decades works out to about 130,000 people escaping poverty *each day*. Roser calls this "the leading achievement in human history," greater than the Apollo missions, greater than the European Enlightenment, greater than independence for the United States or India.

Surely the reduction of Chinese poverty in the twenty-first century is among the leading achievements of history. Most Americans and Europeans don't even know it has happened. Instead, opinion polls show that by firm margins, Americans and Europeans believe developing-world poverty is getting worse.

China's antipoverty achievement could not have occurred without trade—and China is not finished. The country's Belt and Road Initiative, the most expensive public-works project ever (more costly in current dollars than the Manhattan Project) is mostly about ports and sea lanes, especially in the Indian Ocean, the Horn of Africa, and routes between Asia and Europe—subjects insufficiently appreciated by the United States.

The rise in international trade entails globalization, which millions of people say they don't like. But almost everyone in the United States and Europe benefits from the lower prices, improved consumer goods, and ample supplies that globalization provides, while the number of good jobs in the United States and Europe has risen, not fallen, during the period of globalized trade.

Through all centuries before ours, ocean commerce was confined to luxuries for the rich. Spices drew European ships across the world centuries ago because spices don't weigh much yet command premium prices from the well-off. Today the cargoes in ocean commerce are not silks and dyes for royal houses, rather, items intended to serve average people. Most oceangoing vessels bear clothing, electronics, and toys to stock Targets and Aldis, fuel or resources for homes and manufacturing.

Water transportation—cheaper than any other form of shipping—is the key to increased global trade. The growth in water commerce could not happen unless civilian vessels were unhindered by war on the seas.

PEACE ON THE WATERS is both invisible to most of humanity and tenuous. For decades the US Navy has been so strong that no other nation tried to contest its ensign. Recently, China has engaged in a clipped naval buildup. The saying "When you have a hammer, every problem looks like a nail" can apply to military affairs. Soon China will possess maritime hammers, and the world's oceans may begin to seem like nails.

The Russian Federation is improving its navy, while India, the United Kingdom, Japan, and other nations are adding warships. Destructive, almost continuous navalist military buildup was a distinguishing feature of the world from about 1500 to the 1950s. The English–German naval arms race that began in 1909 engaged the momentum of World War I. The reprise English–German naval arms race that began in 1936, coupled with Japan's preparations to sink the American Pacific fleet at Pearl Harbor, were major factors in the impetus for World War II. Should a new naval arms race commence, the impacts will be global and entirely negative. Americans ignore the prospect at our peril.

America's academic, political, and intellectual establishments, especially, ignore that prospect. All show concern with sea level rise, an acute problem, but neglect what happens upon the seas. The warships that for a century have defined much of America's role in the world; the ports, terminals, commercial vessels, and cargoes that define the contemporary global economy—few among the American elite seem interested.

Three-quarters of earth's surface is water. Much of earth's politics occurs on the blue water, and much of the human future lies there. Yet except for the US Naval Academy in Maryland and the Naval War College in Rhode Island, American colleges and universities rarely focus academic inquiry on events, trends, promise, and threats from the blue water, while only a few, such as the Lamont-Doherty division of Columbia University and the Scripps Institution division of the University of California, study the sea itself.

Political leaders are little better, consistently seeming ignorant of maritime issues beyond the budget appropriations for defense contractors in their states or districts. The mainstream media falter too. In the twenty-first century, the companies China Ocean Shipping, CMA CGM, DP World, Evergreen Marine, Hanjin Shipping, Hutchinson Ports, and Maersk Group have had more significance to the global economy than has Goldman Sachs. Yet there is scant media awareness of firms in that sentence other than Goldman Sachs, scant awareness of how international trade benefits the human family, especially by reducing poverty in the developing world.

This book will develop an understanding of naval power, ports, gantry cranes, and container vessels that is liberal both in the twenty-first-century political sense and in the eighteenth-century philosophical sense that was close to the hearts of America's framers. Literary figures, politicians, and editorialists of the United States and Europe would do well to reflect on this.

The liberal case for the US Navy is that rather than being used for conquest, this great fleet has in our lifetimes been used to maintain peace. Uneasy peace, to be sure—but ponder the alternatives.

The liberal case for ocean-borne trade is an amazing reduction of poverty in the developing world, twenty years with no inflation in the West, and higher material standards almost everywhere, even as jobs, overall, increase.

WE ARE LIVING IN the blue age. Many generations of our ancestors, up to our grandparents, could only have dreamt of a time when a guardian navy eliminated nearly all risk involving sea lanes, anyone anywhere can sell to or buy from anyone else, anyone anywhere can sail anywhere.

We are living in the blue age—and will miss it badly if it's gone.

PART ONE

WAR ON THE WATERS

1

A SCHOOL OF BIG FISH

THE USS *WASP*, AN ENORMOUS WARSHIP, TEEMS WITH IMPLE-
ments of combat—missiles, radar-guided high-speed cannon, attack
helicopters, jump jets that fly straight up, tilt-rotor aircraft that are
a hybrid of helicopter and airplane, and the new F35, the world's
most advanced supersonic stealth fighter. The ship carries a thousand US Marines dressed for amphibious assault. *Wasp* can, while
at sea, launch hovercraft that transport warriors and their supplies.
It can, while at sea, deploy utility boats that transport to shore the
fearsome Abrams tank, which no foe has ever bested in battle.

The *Wasp* is, alone, more powerful than any entire navy from
before the twentieth century—yet little known to Americans, like
much of the fleet. *Wasp* has supported humanitarian operations
and staged air strikes, but never fought another warship, and likely
never will. That today's warships are the fiercest ever, but not fighting each other, is one of the central facts of our blue age.

Aboard *Wasp*, I went to speak to the XO, or executive officer, the person who makes a ship run. Commander Javier Medina,
born in Puerto Rico, has a bachelor's in science and a master's in
public administration. He also had an office—not the corner of a

map room as the XO of an older vessel might have, but a white-collar-style managerial office with computers, file cabinets, and chairs for guests, or for sailors being read the riot act. On the wall, a flat-screen TV was tuned to CNN, airing a congressional hearing about impeaching the president.

Commander Medina had Wi-Fi access for his phone, as do most in the fleet most of the time. Today's US Navy vessels are sending and receiving such a bonanza of data, military and personal, that broadband is as much a factor as knots or caliber. For specific missions or when passing through crowded sea lanes, warships may go dark: moving mostly at night, listening to other ships but not broadcasting. If a captain announces "restricted communication"—cutoff of cell and internet connections, no ability to post on Facebook—there is an audible groan in ships' corridors.

I went to speak to the *Wasp's* physician, who showed me the surgical theaters and 400-bed infirmary—in battle, the giant vessel would receive casualties both from ashore and from smaller ships. Satellite links allow combat surgeons anywhere in the world to engage in real-time consultation with specialists at the Walter Reed National Military Medical Center, known to sailors by its former and catchier name, Bethesda Naval.

Then to the dentist's office, with three chairs. Marines tend to put off having their teeth checked until assigned to capital ships that, like the *Wasp*, attract topflight surgeons and dentists. Anyone who can fix combat dental injuries while an aircraft carrier rocks in the waves will someday make serious money doing suburban orthodontia.

In the dental wing was a sign adjoining an X-ray machine: IF YOU ARE PREGNANT TELL THE DOCTOR. Contemporary military vessels have many women aboard, including in command roles. The navy fight song still begins, "Anchors aweigh, my boys, anchors aweigh." But boys are only part of the complement. The 2020 US Navy was 20 percent female, low compared with the population but high compared with maritime history, as well as 17 percent African American, slightly above the population share.[1] The fight song once said, "Farewell to college joys, we sail at break of day."

Only officers feel nostalgia for college. Now, acknowledging the enlisted, the lyric is, "Farewell to foreign shores, we sail at break of day."

Down a maze of tight corridors, I met *Wasp*'s psychologist, who has a busy slate of personal therapy, including treatment for drugs and alcohol. Ship's counselors with postgraduate degrees in psychology or social work are now common on US capital ships. I arrived aboard not long after a *Wasp* sailor killed himself; in 2018, a three-star admiral named Scott Stearney died by suicide while on duty as commander of the Fifth Fleet, anchored in Bahrain. The navy's suicide rate for 2019 exceeded the rate for American adults as a whole that year—yet should be lower, since military members have ready access to no-cost medical care and psychological counseling and are under constant observation by officers trained to watch for emotional instability. Suicides shook the navy, leading to modernization of views toward mental health. Now there is doctor–patient confidentiality even during combat conditions, so asking for help does not appear on one's service record.

Lieutenant Troy Fairchild, *Wasp*'s tactical officer—in maritime ranks, a lieutenant is equivalent to a captain in the land services—says, "We've told parents to email the ship right away if they notice material or links on a son's or daughter's social media suggesting an issue. Once it would have been out of the question for a parent to contact a sailor's officer. Now we think, If something's wrong, who's going to know before anybody else? Mom, that's who."*

I met Lieutenant Tammy Spitzer on USS *Oak Hill*, another enormous warship. She explained navy sociology: "Not long ago young sailors had hardly any possessions. In port they slept aboard ship. Today, young sailors own cars and have apartments. Parking has become problematic at some bases. Sailors bring so much stuff to deployment that stowing it away is a problem. And they expect smartphone access."

---

* Throughout this book, quotations attributed to presidents or similarly well-known persons, or to organizations, are drawn from the public record. All other quotations are from interviews with me.

I talked with *Oak Hill*'s XO, Commander Kathryn Wijnaldum. After growing up in a rural town in Georgia, she was admitted to the Naval Academy in Annapolis, which in addition to being an officers' school—most US Navy leadership comes through the academy—is a highly selective liberal-arts college with literature in its core curriculum. College rankings are open to debate. That said, in 2021 *US News & World Report* ranked the US Naval Academy number six for liberal-arts colleges, tied with Bowdoin; ahead of such esteemed schools as Carlton, Middlebury, Vassar, Davidson, and Smith; trailing only Williams, Amherst, Swarthmore, Pomona, and Wellesley.[2] This result was a feather in the cap of the navy. Many high-status schools should be embarrassed that the military is doing well at education while much of upper academia unravels.

Wijnaldum, an African American, is a strict conservative on national security issues. We talked about international threats. Commander Wijnaldum cited a report from a Washington, D.C., think tank that contends American politicians are not concerned enough about maritime risk. She finds the international threat level more worrisome than I do. But that's easy for me to say, as she is the one who stands the watch.

Later, Wijnaldum emailed me the study from her ship's bridge.[3] Often we are too impressed by the pace of transitions in technology and culture. Change may be overestimated or simply inevitable. Still, I had to stop and whistle to myself on realizing that a high-ranking military officer who is an African American woman born in the deep South had used an internet connection aboard a fighting ship packed to the gunwales with advanced weapons to obtain and distribute the sort of intellectual treatise—harshly criticizing government—that would have been banned by most of the societies of history.

Visiting American warships, I became convinced it wasn't so much the flawless nighttime carrier landings; the nearly silent attack submarines with their demonically effective torpedoes; the lurking strategic submarines with their terrifying global-range nuclear weapons; the sophisticated sensor-fusion systems that allow navy ships and aircraft to know about every adversary; the arsenal of antiship, antiaircraft, antisubmarine, and land-attack missiles carried on submarines, surface ships, jet fighters and long-range aircraft; the at-sea logistical support (moviemakers think of war as guns and explosions—often, logistics is the high card); the insistence of navy leadership on planning to win, with minimum loss of US life, against opponents who don't care if their own people die; the enormous warships on which African American women give orders that buzz-cut white men follow. I became convinced the secret to the power of the US Navy was dentists and mental health counselors and TVs tuned to a channel the president can't stand. These things make you strong, not weak.

OUT ON THE OCEANS, politics, trade, and environmental issues matter more than naval hardware—but that hardware is the starting point for understanding the blue age.

The US Navy possesses eleven nuclear supercarriers, with four more planned.[4] A supercarrier can launch long-range strike aircraft, plus jet fighters, electronic warfare aircraft, and aerial tankers that refuel the others in flight. When sail gave way to propellers, coaling of warships dominated tactical planning; in World War II, running out of petroleum dominated plans; capital ships use up fuel rapidly. Nuclear power means a supercarrier can remain at sea for months or longer, with years between port calls for refueling. The United States has eleven nuclear supercarriers. All other nations combined have none.

France possesses the world's only nuclear-powered aircraft carrier that is not American. The French vessel is a regular carrier, not a supercarrier, able to launch only short-range aircraft. China, India, Italy, Japan, Russia, South Korea, and the United Kingdom have or are building aircraft carriers. None are nuclear supercarriers—all use conventional propulsion and have limited air wings. In 2020 France announced plans to build a nuclear-powered aircraft carrier that can accommodate long-range jets. If this happens, it will be the world's first direct competitor to America's ships.

In addition to supercarriers, the US Navy possesses ten assault ships, with at least two more in the works. *Wasp* is an assault ship.

To the eye, US assault ships are aircraft carriers, though they are not called aircraft carriers under the US classification matrix—maritime enthusiasts spend hours debating such hairsplitting distinctions as what's a destroyer versus what's a destroyer-leader. Unlike supercarriers, which are optimized for controlling large areas of the sky, assault ships are designed to take infantry and their supplies to an invasion while providing close-in air support. If there were war, American supercarriers would sink the other side's vessels and strike at its military bases, while American assault ships would land battalions and cover their movements.

An advanced warship simply designated *America* began, in 2014, the newest class of US assault ships; *America*'s sisters *Tripoli* and *Bougainville* will add further to the US lead in ships of the line. These three assault ships are bigger and more powerful and bear more aircraft than any ship any other nation calls an aircraft carrier.

Egypt, Brazil, South Korea, the Netherlands, and New Zealand have vessels in the assault-ship category, though they bear only helicopters, not the significantly more deadly attack jets found on *Wasp* and *America*. China is building several assault ships that may be the equal of *Wasp* and *America*, including their equal in deadly jets. France has three modern assault vessels and built two more on contract for Russia. Over the centuries, England and France sold high-end capital ships to Japan, the Ottomans, Brazil, and Russia when these nations were looking to step up in military prestige. Paris canceled its assault-ship contract with Moscow after the 2014 Russian invasion of Crimea and Ukraine. France later retailed those two very expensive warships to Egypt, a struggling nation that might seem to have better uses for large sums of public money.

Attached to the US Navy's sizable aviation wings are about thirty-seven hundred aircraft, including about two thousand long-range jets. No other nation has long-range sea-based jets, though China is working on them. The US Navy also possesses more advanced land-based naval jets than all other nations combined; again, China is trying to build such planes. Though most navy hardware is at sea, some resides on land, including at extensive navy-run airfields.

The navy's latest land-based combat jet looks like a big passenger plane that someone forgot to paint with United Airlines livery. Packed with the latest radars and other sensors, the jet launches antiship and antisubmarine missiles and can remain aloft in a contested area for many hours. Essentially it's a flying dreadnought.

All told, the United States has eleven nuclear supercarriers to none for the rest of the world; has almost as many assault ships as the rest of the world has assault ships and aircraft carriers (the nonsuper variety) combined; and has a larger naval aviation force than does the rest of the world combined.

FIGHTING SHIPS KEEP GROWING more sophisticated and deadly: the United States lead here is large as well. The F-35 stealth fighter carried by many US Navy vessels has no equal. The long-range homing torpedo fired by US Navy submarines has no equal. Electronic warfare suites used by US Navy ships and aircraft are tops, able to make formations disappear from radar scopes or (in recent use, deeply frustrating Russian and Syrian forces) make it seem as if a huge force were approaching from the opposite direction when in fact nothing is there. The Tomahawk land-attack cruise missile aboard many American warships has proven close to flawless—though the temptation to order this missile's launch has seduced Presidents Bush, Clinton, Bush, Obama, and Trump. Each time a Tomahawk is fired, diplomacy failed—which can't always be the other side's fault.

Every American supercarrier is equipped with catapults. France owns the sole non-American warship with a catapult; Beijing is believed to have a catapult-equipped vessel under construction. Catapults turn a ship deck into a moving airport, able to accommodate large or long-range planes. The United States has a near exclusive on this powerful feature. Without catapults, which are costly and hard to operate, aircraft carriers are limited to light, short-range jets.

America's newest class of supercarrier uses the first electromagnetic catapults on any warship. Electromagnetic catapults allow faster operation, require a smaller crew complement, and reduce risk to sailors by eliminating the presence of pressurized scalding gases. The new systems are an advance in naval power, and as usual, the United States leads.

Those versed in maritime issues were mystified in 2019, when President Donald Trump stood before a group of sailors to criticize the new catapults as "too complicated," demanding they be removed.[5] Electromagnetic catapults have fewer moving parts than steam catapults; reducing the moving parts is a long-standing objective of engineering. In below-deck terms, the new systems are simpler, not more complicated. During his peculiar discourse on catapults, Trump appeared to have absolutely no idea what he was talking about. The Chinese must have thought this as well, since China's aircraft carrier under construction seems, in satellite photos, to incorporate electromagnetic launch.

The speech at which the forty-fifth president rambled about electromagnetism occurred aboard the *Wasp*, when the ship was moored at the American base in Yokosuka, Japan. For this visit the White House demanded the navy place a tarp over the stern of the guided-missile destroyer *John McCain*, which has been forward-deployed at Yokosuka since 1997. (The significance of *forward-deployed* is taken up in Chapter 4.) Everyone other than Trump considers the three for whom the *McCain* jointly is named—two admirals plus their grandson and son, the Vietnam-era pilot and US senator—to have been highly accomplished men. But Trump is a draft dodger from a family of swindlers; he did not want to see a reminder that his rival, the youngest John McCain, was a hero from a family of patriots.

THE NEWEST SUPERCARRIERS, THE ones with the fancy catapults—*Gerald Ford* and *John Kennedy* under construction, two more in planning stages—are so awesome, sophisticated, behind schedule, and over budget, they may be the last supercarriers the US commissions.[6] The one supercarrier China is building is for prestige; a sister is unlikely. Soon this class of warship may go the way of the monitor and the flying barque.

Scheduled to slide down the ramp in 2027, the supercarrier *Enterprise* will be the ninth vessel to bear that storied name, eleventh if one counts the test-model space shuttle and Captain Kirk's starship. *Doris Miller*, scheduled launch 2028, will be the first capital ship commemorating an African American. Miller was a messman, cleaning up from breakfast when the Japanese attack against Pearl Harbor began. Standing in the line of fire without fear, Miller manned an antiaircraft gun and rallied his fellow sailors to fight back.

The decision to christen a magnificent vessel for a little-known enlisted man should open the door to renaming the supercarriers *John Stennis* and *Carl Vinson*.[7] Both celebrate rabid white supremacists who signed the 1956 Southern Manifesto demanding continued segregation of public schools. Neither Stennis nor Vinson served in the military; their primary achievements in life were promoting racial hatred. Both chaired military committees in Congress, the stated reason for the vessel names. But honoring sitting on a committee is like giving an award for most lunches eaten.

In 2020, the Pentagon began to face the issue of removing names of Confederate defenders of slavery from US Army bases. It is past time the names of defenders of Jim Crow be removed from US Navy ships. The *Vinson* and *Stennis* could become the *Frederick Douglass* and *Elizabeth Stanton*—those are names worth fighting for. Or the *Robert Smalls* and *Harriett Tubman*. Both were African Americans who had maritime exploits.

TODAY SEVERAL US NAVY vessels are titled not for the famous but for the little known. A new cruiser, the *Michael Monsoor*, bears the name of an enlisted man. Monsoor was a SEAL (the SEALs are the navy's special forces) who died performing a noble act. Names of warships are one indicator of a changing sociology at sea. The arrival of women on warships, including submarines, is another. The amphibious transport dock *San Antonio*, launched 2003, was the first navy vessel with separate accommodations for women and the first with bunks large enough to allow the occupant to sit up rather than being so tightly packed you slide in sideways. (Sailors call the latter arrangement "coffin ranks.") *Monsoor* and its sisters go the next step, with college-dorm-like sleeping areas, four sailors per room. The goals are improved conditions for enlisted personnel generally, privacy for women specifically.

The United Kingdom's new flattop, *Queen Elizabeth* (to crew, the *Big Liz*)—a standard aircraft carrier, not a supercarrier, still, the largest vessel ever in the Royal Navy—has five onboard gyms, four mixed and one reserved for women. How do we know? Because the social media officer of *Big Liz* tweeted that. Today warships of several nations have social media directors.

Current American supercarriers have berthings for the enlisted, with 180 bunks per area; the result is constant foot traffic in the dead of night, making it hard to sleep even when the ship isn't pitching. Beginning with the new *Ford*-class iteration, there are 40-bed berthings, creating at least some sense of isolation from the round-the-clock activity. These new supercarriers have Wi-Fi lounges, where crew members can use personal electronics without being furtive. Internet access is disabled within the berthings, so sailors don't lie awake staring at their phones.

Heads on the latest warships are unisex, no urinals. Naval architects are widening passageways. Aboard older vessels such as *Oak Hill*, people passing on a catwalk must squeeze tight against each other; submarine corridors are worse. This arrangement is far from ideal for mixed-gender crews.

AFTER THE SUPERCARRIERS AND assault carriers, the navy's leading vessels are ballistic-missile submarines. The United States has fourteen, about the same number as the rest of the world combined. The United Kingdom has four, Russia has four. (Russia also has old ballistic-missile submarines officially in service but in such poor repair they rarely leave port.) Russian spy ships attempt to track US ballistic-missile submarines whenever one departs from a base in the states of Georgia or Washington, but they are soon lost in the infinity of the blue water. Increasingly, miles of the Pacific and Atlantic are littered with hydrophones and sonobuoys used by the United States and Russian Federation in attempts to locate each other's ballistic-missile submarines.

These submarines are doomsday devices. Each of the US Navy's fourteen, plus each similar boat possessed by Russia, the United Kingdom, and China, could destroy most of the major cities of our world. That's each sub, acting alone: modern great-power doomsday submarines are much more horrifying than generally understood. Similar boats possessed by France and India, while not as powerful, still could do unthinkable harm. The United States is working on a new class of ballistic-missile submarines that will carry almost as many nuclear bombs and be even harder to find.

If ballistic-missile submarines of the great powers ever open their launch doors, the world will end. Should such machines exist? Because *The Blue Age* concerns the interactions among maritime power, seaborne commerce, and the need for governance mechanisms to protect the ocean environment, the who-what-where-how of the nuclear specter is beyond the book's scope. But a few aspects of nuclear deterrence bear on regular events at sea.

A memorandum of understanding signed by Washington and Moscow in 1991—not a treaty but observed as if it were one—stipulated the removal of tactical nuclear weapons from surface ships of both nations. Only ballistic (very long range) missiles remain based at sea, aboard the doomsday subs.

From the Cuban Missile Crisis of 1962 through the 1990 treaty that ended the Cold War (see Chapter 10), American and Russian warships carried nuclear torpedoes, tactical nuclear bombs, and, at one point, even nuclear cannon shells. The risk of accidental firing, or a field officer's ordering their use in an overreaction, was startling.

Today neither nation puts nuclear bombs onto vessels other than the ballistic-missile submarines whose purpose is deterrence. If navies of the United States and Russia fight, they will use conventional munitions.

China has not joined the American–Russian agreement to remove tactical nuclear warheads from ships but says that it abides by the restriction. So Chinese warships probably carry only conventional arms. But it's impossible to be sure, because there is no inspection regime for "trust but verify," as there are in mutual American–Russian naval interactions.

Because of the success of nuclear arms reduction treaties, the great powers now have about 85 percent fewer nuclear warheads than at the peak, which came in 1986—this reduction is among the most important positive facts about our world missing from public debate.[8] The treaty in force in 2021 limited the United States and Russian Federation to 1,550 strategic nuclear warheads, versus tens of thousands possessed by each side during the Cold War. The 1,550 warheads remain unimaginably horrific. At least the trend is in the right direction, with the weapons most likely to be fired by mistake eliminated. During the Cuban Missile Crisis, a Soviet tactical officer ordered his crew to arm a nuclear torpedo and load the weapon into a firing tube. Today a mistake that bad shouldn't happen.

Conventional military strength reduces the odds that nuclear war will occur, and the United States possesses tremendous conventional military strength.

In 1944 George Marshall, the American general later to sponsor the plan bearing his name, said, "Before the sun sets on this terrible struggle, our flag will be recognized throughout the world as the symbol of freedom on the one hand and of overwhelming force on the other." Both goals were achieved.

IN 2019, AS TENSIONS with China rose, *America* was repositioned from a previous home port in San Diego to the US naval base in Sasebo, close to China on a promontory of the Japanese home islands. Beijing could not have failed to notice the United States was moving an advanced invasion ship near its shore, nor failed to know that in 1940, the US Navy's Pacific Fleet was repositioned from California to Hawaii, to draw nearer Japan's shore.

In 2020 *America*, gleaming new, bristling with weapons, aircraft, and electronics, led a battle group from Sasebo through Chinese-claimed islands of the South China Sea. Later that year a pair of US supercarriers sailed through the South China Sea and simulated the launching of air strikes. Britain announced its aircraft carrier would cruise the Beijing-claimed waters of this sea as well.

About a decade earlier, the US Navy refitted four doomsday submarines so that instead of ballistic nuclear warheads, the large boats bear more than a hundred antiship missiles and conventional missiles for land attack. China has no way of knowing if one of these underwater arsenals loiters nearby, able to unleash clouds of precision munitions with short flight times to Chinese targets.

In 2020 the United States began renovating military facilities at Midway Atoll, roughly equidistant between Hawaii and the Pacific Rim. The navy base there, closed in 1993 as no longer required for US defense, was now being put back into service, to stage air support for any clash near China. In case anyone missed the point, in 2020, Air Force B-1 bombers remained aloft for twenty-four hours above the Pacific Rim, refueled in flight, bearing an antiship missile designed to sink the latest warships; this was a rehearsal for striking Chinese aircraft carriers in their home waters. Later the bombers flew all the way from South Dakota to the Black Sea, rehearsing launch of the new missile against Russia's fleet.

Imagine how Washington would feel if a powerful Chinese battle group sailed through the Channel Islands near Los Angeles, how London would feel if Russian bombers rehearsed attack runs off Scotland's picturesque Gare Loch, where the nuclear-deterrent force of the United Kingdom is based. Recent naval exercises by the United States and close allies, having such snazzy names as Baltops, Keen Sword, and Dynamic Mongoose, flexed muscle in waters vital to Russia and China. Imagine if China or Russia staged muscle-flexing exercises close to Florida or San Francisco.

THE US NAVY HAS about 150 destroyers and attack submarines. The category name *destroyer* sums five hundred years of sea-power thinking. Destroyers are the most common surface warships of current flotillas; some nations prefer frigates, which are similar in function but smaller and less expensive. Destroyer designs have converged to the point that the Western navies and China, India, and Japan use about the same basic blueprints.

The United States needs a large number of destroyers to keep the sea lanes open and to screen supercarriers at the nuclei of strike groups, preventing hostile vessels from approaching. Currently the United States has twice as many destroyers as China does and three times as many as Russia. China, which is building warships at a furious rate, is focusing on destroyers and frigates because having lots of these allows a navy to claim chunks of liquid blue real estate while screening ships of the line.

The phrase *attack submarine* may seem redundant—the designation means boats designed to sink ships or other submarines, as opposed to launching doomsday missiles. Some American attack submarines also carry the conventional Tomahawk cruise missiles designed to hit land targets. In 2017 the Russian navy demonstrated an ability to fire cruise missiles from a submarine toward a land target. There was rejoicing in the Kremlin, though the US Navy has possessed such hardware for a generation.

All of America's destroyers (and most other warships) employ gas-turbine power; all US attack submarines use nuclear reactors for propulsion. Nuclear-powered submarines are expensive; only five nations other than the United States possess one. A nuclear-powered submarine can traverse the seas for many months without being observed and without stopping for fuel or rising for air, which the reactors make from seawater via electrolysis.

From about 1970 to about 2010, the United States had a monopoly on nuclear submarines so quiet they were nearly impossible to locate; this was among the factors that convinced the Soviet Union to abandon the Cold War. But as Mr. Spock said to Captain Kirk, "Every military advantage is fleeting." Sonar and similar devices have gotten better at detecting pumps aboard a nuclear submarine; the pumps run continuously to prevent the reactor from overheating.

Some countries have improved their conventional-power submarines to reduce noise. In 2020, Japan launched the first diesel-electric attack submarine that employs lithium-ion batteries (the kind in laptops) rather than lead-acid (the kind in cars); the new batteries allow submarines to travel faster and farther without surfacing for air. To defend itself against the Chinese navy, Japan has quietly built one of the world's leading submarine fleets. Because the boats usually cannot be seen, they do not provoke the anti-militarism that is strong in Japanese politics. Sweden now builds an attack submarine equipped with a form of propulsion that has limited range but is nearly silent. Other nations could mimic the Japanese or Swedish designs.

Whether nuclear-powered attack submarines would dominate a contemporary naval battle is unknown, as they've rarely entered combat. If they do, for the moment the United States possesses a wide lead over the rest of the world in this category. And as contemporary naval strategists say, "There are two types of vessels, submarines and targets."

THE INVENTORY OF THE US Navy goes on at some length. Supply liners, amphibious-landing support ships—the United States has more of these than all other nations combined—hospital ships, oilers that transfer fuel at sea, many types of light combatants, high-speed sealift vessels kept in ready reserve because they burn so much fuel. The navy also has some of the strangest floating objects ever seen, including expeditionary mobile base ships that visually suggest a space-alien mothership from a bad science fiction movie.

Overall, the United States has nearly the same number of deployable modern naval vessels as do all other nations combined. It owns the only supercarriers, most of the world's assault carriers, most of the world's advanced naval aircraft, and most of the world's quiet nuclear submarines.

The cruiser *Monsoor* and its sisters represent a class that, at three ships, is too small to matter to the great-power equilibrium, but indicates the dominant position of the United States compared with other nations. *Monsoor*, *Zumwalt*, and *Lyndon Johnson* are at the forefront of all-electric drive. An onboard utility station generates power for electric propulsion—no crankshafts necessary.

One of the new cruisers is named for Elmo Zumwalt, an admiral whose personal cause was better treatment for average sailors; another for the former president whose first political cause was electrification of Texas hill country. Now the all-electric vessel bearing Johnson's name brings that outlook to the seas. The United Kingdom has begun building all-electric warships; all-electric container liners and cruise ships are not far in the future.

Electric-drive ships reduce pollutant discharge. Prodigious amounts of unburned propellants and waste oils follow the wakes of conventional-drive vessels. Low-emission propulsion is a necessity, considering the environmental harm caused by increases in ship traffic; all-electric is no panacea, but beneficial.

A warship built around a generating station could mount a rail gun, a device that would require copious kilowatts. Rail guns use magnetic fields to achieve dramatically more velocity and destructive force than cannons or missiles, plus very brief time of flight, an advantage as fast weapons proliferate. The rail gun has never worked outside a laboratory, but some analysts think this weapon will become practical. The US Navy's new cruisers have the voltage for this speculative technology. If rail guns succeed, the United States will gain years of sole possession of a new type of firepower, because China, Russia and other nations are not even trying to build this class of cruiser.

IT WOULD BE NICE to think no nation wants trouble, but there are lots of things that would be nice to think. For centuries, the seas were made violent to warships by battle, made dangerous to merchantmen and passenger ships by armed vessels seeking victims or booty.

Warships, pirates, and corsairs who were more or less operating under color of law—the US Constitution specifies that "letters of marque" may be issued to privateers to seize vessels in the name of Old Glory—prowled the oceans, gravitating to the Caribbean and the East Indies because there was much to seize.

Captured vessels were called *prizes*, this term used by courts of the past. Judges, kings, and parliaments awarded dollars, pounds, and francs for towing prizes to port. The crew hired by John Paul Jones was deeply embittered when Congress failed to confer prize money for *Bonhomme Richard*'s daring 1779 capture of British merchant ships near England, an event that shocked London and proved pivotal to the Revolutionary War. Ultimately, the sailors' descendants received their due in 1848, a timetable that was foot-dragging even by the notoriously low standards of the US Congress.

Admiralty law and maritime insurance became major industries because a high proportion of commercial vessels were taken as prizes, were sunk in battle, or simply went to the bottom because of hazards of the seas. Up to the present day, the sinking or grounding of a container ship, car carrier, bulk carrier, tug, or ferry is more common than you'd likely guess—nearly once per day, somewhere in the world, in 2018.

During the first half of the nineteenth century, the Royal Navy worked to stop the Atlantic slave trade while promoting what was by the standards of the time legitimate commerce—namely, colonial exploitation. During the second half of the nineteenth century, Britain's fleet began to oppose privateers who sought ships as prizes.

The naval arms race that commenced just after the turn of the twentieth century ended the Royal Navy's splendid isolation. Fighting that followed stained the waters with blood. Next came the American Century and US control of the oceans. American hegemony at sea made possible the flowering of international trade not in luxury items but in vast amounts of goods for average people, generating the prosperity, especially in Asia, that changed global poverty from rising to declining.

These basic points about maritime behavior and ships as prizes matter because the blue-age situation of having US warships practically everywhere, supported by satellites and supply bases, has been one of the best things that's ever happened to the world.

Many people do not like military organizations. The reasons to dislike them are self-evident, and we can dream of the day when no nation requires an army or navy. Many assume military organizations are always up to no good; a wide range of politicians and commentators in the United States simply cannot bring themselves to say the world is a better place because the American military mainly serves the global social whole.

Someday no nation will require an army or navy. Till that day comes . . .

I BOARDED USS *WASP* at Naval Station Norfolk in Virginia. The carrier had just returned from Japan, after the event at which Trump used *Wasp* as a stage. Like *Enterprise*, *Wasp* is a storied name. The current boat is latest in a line that stretches back to a schooner destroyed during the American revolution. The saying: "If you want peace, prepare for war." Eleven American vessels named *Wasp* have prepared for war.

Crossing the Pacific on the way home, *Wasp* drove through twenty-foot waves that tossed the ship so badly, cafeteria vending machines came loose and went flying, despite being bolted down like nearly everything on the high seas. Greg Baker, captain of the *Wasp*, told me that although he actually enjoys rough weather—not many agree, Winston Churchill dreaded ocean storms—he still gets seasick, and vomited during the squall.

Wasp displaces 41,000 tons. Just thinking about a 41,000-ton object steering into twenty-foot waves (the helm wants to face a wave at a forty-five-degree angle, not run parallel, to prevent rollover) might be enough to make anyone nauseated. During the storm, a twenty-five-ton helicopter began to slide off an elevator that brings aircraft from *Wasp*'s enormous hangar area onto the flight deck. Imagine trying to secure cables to a twenty-five-ton sliding object while an aircraft carrier pitches bow-down as it enters a tall wave, and you have imagined a sailor's day.

Baker is rare in being a capital-ship captain who did not attend Annapolis, having gone to Maine Maritime Academy, a public college that teaches seafaring but does not require graduates to join the military, as do the service academies. Throughout the electric utility industry, one encounters Maine Maritime alums, because the internal engineering of power plants is similar to the drive systems and gas turbines of most warships.

Arriving for refitting after a long tour, *Wasp* displayed rust streaks and scorch marks. Like many US assault vessels, *Wasp* has a well deck, which is essentially a flight deck plus water. The back third of *Wasp* is a cavernous hall large enough for battle tanks to move in: an oversized bulkhead opens to the ocean, when the ship is sailing. Opening the bulkhead of the well deck allows the landing craft used by US Marines to depart or arrive midocean. Thick, heavy chains lower the supply pallets needed by the marines to the landing craft, or winch back up damaged armored vehicles returning for repair. When the well deck is in use, bilge and ballast pumps work overtime to maintain the ship's equilibrium against the inrushing sea.

Along the well deck were sizable gashes where landing craft—always heavy, especially so if transporting the Abrams tank—slammed into the walls as *Wasp* lurched with seawater inside. Ponder what it takes to leave a sizable gash in plate steel.

"Everyone knows it's hard to put a jet down on an aircraft carrier," Baker says. "Bringing a hovercraft into a well deck is challenging too. *Wasp*, the hovercraft, and the seawater are moving at different speeds in different directions, and moving seawater imparts more energy than you might guess. It's quite a lot for the young person driving the hovercraft to handle."

Wasp was returning to Virginia after two years at Sasebo. That the United States and Japan engaged in an awful conflict across the Pacific and now the United States parks warships in Japan with the active support of the Tokyo government (and active assistance of Japan's navy) is another of history's ironies. *Wasp* was at Sasebo to help Japan feel secure against Chinese adventurism and to remind Beijing there was a powerful invasion ship much closer to China than any Chinese warship ever will get to American shores. When the even more impressive *America* arrived at Sasebo in late 2019, *Wasp* could come home.

Today the US Navy has facilities in many of the country's states, with large bases in California, Georgia, Hawaii, Virginia, and Washington. Though California is seen as a hipster heaven and

Washington a techie preserve, both have a heavy US Navy presence, owing to their positions commanding the Pacific. (In 1846, John Frémont named the strait that leads into San Francisco the Golden Gate because he saw this waterway, facing the golden setting sun, as a door to what's now called the Pacific Rim.) Beyond US states are major US Navy bases in Bahrain, Guam, Italy, and Japan, plus the Indian Ocean island of Diego Garcia.

Reaching Naval Station Norfolk, *Wasp* docked at the largest and most extensive maritime facility any nation has ever built. On one of my visits, four nuclear supercarriers and two assault carriers were moored there, along with destroyers and cruisers, support ships, the hospital ship *Comfort* (later to dock in Manhattan during the 2020 coronavirus emergency), oilers, amphibious support vessels, logistics ships, tenders, and visiting warships from other nations.

Part of the Norfolk base is a sizable facility for naval airplanes and helicopters; the thrumming of jet and turboshaft engines is ubiquitous. In the aviators' wardrooms and conference rooms, the *Top Gun* image was carefully adhered to. Navy aviators are slight (there is little space in a warplane cockpit), exceptionally fit, sharp-dressed and sport fashion haircuts, just like Tom Cruise. Jet pilots are officers, and a captain who flies may have the status edge on a captain of surface (most warships are surface), unless that captain holds a command—and most of the time, most surface captains hold no command.

Not far from Norfolk are more naval aircraft at an O'Hare-sized field in Virginia Beach. This master jet base, in navy lingo—the place supercarrier air wings go when not at sea—possesses the lovely name Oceana. Just as many contemporary American warships may, alone, exceed the power of entire navies before the modern era, Naval Station Norfolk and its sibling Oceana exceed, alone, the power of any other nation's entire navy in the world of today.

Norfolk, Virginia, has for two centuries been as important to global maritime issues as has Portsmouth, England. American and British warships fought off Norfolk in 1807 in a confused incident that helped trigger the War of 1812. Politics changed, and in 1940 and 1941, when the United States had not yet entered the war of wars, damaged British fighting ships limped across the Atlantic for repair at Norfolk, the very place the Royal Navy once opened fire.

In the summer of 1941, the British aircraft carrier *Illustrious* steamed to Norfolk for refitting, after staging a successful attack on Axis big-gun vessels at anchor in Italy. The Battle of Taranto was the first time carrier-based aircraft sank battleships; it would not be the last. While *Illustrious* was in Virginia being repaired, the captain, Louis Mountbatten, went to Hawaii to see Pearl Harbor and was horrified to learn that no preparations had been made against a Japanese carrier-based attack.

Lying at anchor side by side at Norfolk, supercarriers and assault carriers such as the *Wasp* appear nearly the same. Many well-informed people may not know assault ships exist, though these vessels are essential aspects of the contemporary global balance of power. Designed to support waterborne invasions, the assault carrier is a particularly American idea, since in the modern era the United States has conducted more amphibious landings than have all other nations combined.

Supercarriers evolved from the fleet carriers of World War II: big, extended-deck vessels with catapults to launch long-range aircraft. In that conflict, only the United States and Japan built fleet carriers. Every one of Japan's was sent to Davey Jones's locker, while the United States ended World War II with more fleet carriers than when the fight began; this was a core reason for the result in the Pacific theater.

Early in the Cold War, the United States added nuclear power to its largest carriers and dubbed them supercarriers. The Soviet Union tried and failed to match while other nations did not try, conceding this vessel class.

Initially, America's nuclear supercarriers were intended to fight other warships, as the earlier fleet carriers did. But when other nations withdrew from building blue-water fleets, American supercarriers were repurposed into strike weapons. The plan became that supercarriers would draw close to an enemy's shore (especially, to the northern approaches to Russia) and launch attacks deep into the interior.

Conceptualize the continental United States as a vast island—which it is, in geopolitical terms. An enemy approaching America's coasts to attempt an invasion would be exposed for thousands of miles of open sea while being opposed by a powerful navy backed by air power. For this reason, no adversary has landed soldiers on United States soil for two hundred years. Indemnity against threat of invasion is a primary aspect of American exceptionalism.

By contrast, from Veracruz in 1847 to D-Day in 1944 to Inchon in 1950 to many smaller operations, American armed forces arrive at foreign shores surprisingly often. If you live on a vast island, all military destinations look like beachheads to be stormed, however distant. This explains why the United States invests so much more in assault ships, dock ships, transports, and other vessels associated with amphibious action, while having a large military branch, the US Marines, dedicated to this end.

One hopes Egypt and France, the countries other than the United States with more than one assault carrier, do not plan to invade anyone. There is no strategic point in assault carriers unless your nation anticipates throwing soldiers and armor onto another nation's sands. For this reason, China looks askance at America's wide global lead in assault ships—and Washington and Taipei look askance at Beijing's beginning work on such vessels.

SPENDING TIME ON AMERICAN warships, I observed many quirks. For instance, on one bridge, a large chart headlined COMMONLY MISSPELLED WORDS—in naval annals, spelling mistakes have led to more than one misfortune. Quirks of the shipboard life are entertaining, but what struck me were the thoughts of officers and enlisted. Here are a few:

From Commander Bobby Rowden, XO of the *Donald McFaul*, who grew up in landlocked Montana and graduated from UCLA with a degree in political science. Rowden showed me around his ship after *McFaul* returned from eight months in the Persian Gulf. Named for an enlisted man and nominally a destroyer, *Donald McFaul* bears an elaborate system for shooting down medium-range ballistic missiles of the type possessed by Iran and North Korea. The system has never had a realistic test; ideally, never will.

Rowden says, "I hope the world always takes the US Navy for granted, because that would mean we are keeping things calm. If suddenly everyone wanted to know what the fleet is doing, that would mean something terrible was happening." By this reasoning, the less news from the Persian Gulf, the better.

From Commander Scott Wastak, a sharp-dressed naval aviator who has flown 120 carrier sorties above Afghanistan, Iraq, and the Mediterranean: Wastak holds a bachelor's in economics from George Washington University and did at tour at the Department of State as a political-military liaison. He says, "It's fair to ask whether we really need to allocate so much money to the military. The lesson of World War I and World War II was that America got behind because we weren't mobilized. The solution is—always be mobilized. If that prevents World War III, the money is well spent."

From Admiral John Richardson, chief of naval operations under Presidents Barack Obama and Donald Trump. Richardson grew up in tidewater Virginia and, like most future naval operations chiefs, attended the US Naval Academy. He holds a master's degree in engineering from the Massachusetts Institute of Technology. When China started building artificial islands in the South China Sea, Richardson sent warships to sail as close to them as allowed by international law.

Such freedom-of-navigation exercises were at the core of Royal Navy operations in the nineteenth century and are at the core of US Navy operations today. Freedom-of-navigation sailing by US warships near China, in the Black Sea, along the edges of the Persian Gulf—under Trump, called the Arabian Gulf on White House charts, to delete implied respect for Persians—asserts a right that is clear under law but murky in terms of realpolitik.

In 2020 the US guided-missile destroyer *Porter* made two freedom-of-navigation tours in the Black Sea: legal by international convention, but an obvious middle finger to Moscow. *Porter's* voyages were the rough equivalent of a Chinese guided-missile ship patrolling the Florida Keys, being careful to observe official boundaries.

I asked Richardson, what if the Chinese exercise freedom of navigation in the Gulf of Mexico or the approach to Puget Sound? His reply: "We can't believe in freedom of navigation only when it favors us. Any navy can sail close to our shores, if in accordance with international law." It is common for a Russian intelligence vessel disguised as a fishing trawler to lurk off Kings Bay, Georgia, where there is a US nuclear-missile submarine pen, watching to see if a sub departs toward open ocean. As long as the "fishing trawler" is in international waters, the United States takes no action.

DAVID HENDRICKSON, A PROMINENT American political scientist, wrote in 2018, "Freedom of navigation seems to mean the right of commercial vessels to transit the oceans without molestation, and no one objects to that." But around the South China Sea, Hendrickson thinks, "United States actions to vindicate freedom of navigation are paired with a strategy to extend military supremacy over China in its home waters, a posture that increases the risk of confrontation and that, as a consequence, threatens rather than supports the goal of openness."[9]

When the Royal Navy pressed for freedom of navigation in the nineteenth century, at one level it was performing a service to the global community by opening sea lanes; at another level, it was asserting British hegemony. Today's United States freedom-of-navigation tours both serve and disquiet the global community, owing to the same dual purpose.

US Navy hegemony is undeniable. That may not be enough to sustain the blue age.

2

IS SEA POWER OVERRATED?

FEW LOCATIONS OFFER THE WILD BEAUTY OF SCAPA FLOW, IN the Orkney Islands at the boreal tip of Scotland. A remarkable natural anchorage, the Flow is about twice the size of Cayuga, largest of New York's Finger Lakes. Protected from violent North Sea winds, Scapa Flow offers to mariners broad expanses of *roadstead*–places of gentle waves where ships can ride at anchor. The Vikings began mooring in Scapa Flow perhaps a thousand years ago, seeking relief from North Sea weather. During both world wars, Britain kept its fighting ships in this place, bobbing serenely on the cold, lambent water.

Scapa Flow has not been militarized for half a century; we can hope it will never be employed for battle again. Today naturalists seek out the wildlife and scenery. Scuba enthusiasts like the Flow because the water is clear and relatively shallow, ideal for recreational diving. Makers of specialized medical and scientific devices occasionally send teams to Scapa Flow, as along its floor is the world's best source of low-background steel.

This is metal forged before the open-air thermonuclear tests of 1951 to 1963. Hydrogen bomb explosions contaminated the earth's surface ore, and stores of metal, with radionuclides that are not necessarily harmful to people (smoke detectors employ radionuclides) but introduce false readings into hospital and laboratory equipment intended to measure radiation. Steel that lies on the floor of Scapa Flow was shielded by the lambent waters from atmospheric effects of the nuclear explosions; this metal can be employed to make instruments that are superaccurate.

The valuable steel on the seafloor is the kaiser's fleet, dispatched to the bottom to conclude the Great War.

The imposing big-gun vessels *Konig, Crown Prince Wilhelm,* and *Markgraf,* from the decade of warships called by Churchill "castles of steel," rest beneath the Flow, along with sunken wrecks of other fighting vessels. Dozens of expensive battleships, battle cruisers, and destroyers were scuttled at Scapa Flow in 1919. Their decks and bulkheads gradually are being broken up by divers seeking pristine low-background metal.

High school students are taught that the June 1914 assassination of Franz Ferdinand started the awful Great War. Robert Massie and other historians point to the Naval Panic of 1909, the moment England and Germany decided to channel sizable portions of their resources into dreadnoughts, the feared capital ships of the day. Once England and Germany spent far-fetched sums on castles of steel, governments and editorialists began itching to see them fight.

A famous photograph shows a line of battle cruisers, armed with thousand-pound shells, trailed by columns of coal smoke, leaving their base at Rosyth, Scotland, to head down the Firth of Forth toward the Battle of Jutland. Crowds cheered along the riverbanks. Many of the vessels and their brave crews were on the way to senseless destruction.

After the Great War culminated in a November 1918 armistice, wretched Germany allowed its armada—the High Seas Fleet by name, though never reaching the high seas—to be interned at Scapa Flow under British guard, pending resolution of Allied claims. Some months later, believing Treaty of Versailles negotiators were about to award the vessels as booty to the victors, German officers scuttled the ships. The contemporary equivalent of several hundred billion dollars' worth of national treasure sank in a few hours.

World War I is an oft-cited parable of nihilism. Other aspects of that conflict were less humane or more gruesome; no act exceeded the futility of the building, then scuttling, of the fifty-two large warships that went under at Scapa Flow. Unseen, like so much else that concerns the sea, warships on the bottom of the Flow remind us how easily men (then) and men and women (today) can be tempted by reckless plans of self-glorification.

Historical annals are replete with what Barbara Tuchman labeled "the march of folly." Maritime annals are replete with expensive fighting ships that accomplished nothing or even harmed their creators. (An inventory appears at the close of this chapter.) Are modern nations—especially the United States and China—doomed to repeat folly at sea? Will it be 1909 all over again?

Two seemingly contradictory contentions can be true at once. Sea power can be important and beneficial yet also dangerous and overrated. Most of this book will argue that advanced warships patrolling sea lanes chock with commercial traffic make the world a better place. This chapter waves a caution flag about how such a vision could go horribly wrong.

THERE HAS BEEN FAR too much fighting on six of the seven continents, going back too far, beginning at least thousands of years ago with clubs, arrows, pikes, and swords. Firearms were added to the expedients of slaughter, along with cannon and explosives, armor, aircraft, rockets. Human ingenuity that might have focused on crops or medicine turned instead to ways to kill and smash.

Whetted awareness exists of the too many battles that occurred on land. We observe the ruined structures and graves, know the politics of winning and losing armies. Townspeople on the edges of land battles remained behind to give witness. For land campaigns we build cenotaphs and hold commemorations.

The too many battles upon the waters mostly happen unseen by anyone except participants. Broken and burning, combatant ships sink, taking the victims, and the evidence for historians, down with them. Witnesses are rare. Nothing is left behind observable to the overwhelming majority of humanity that is almost always on land.

Soldiers' frays produce charred earth and monuments whose spires appeal to heaven; aerial confrontations produce crashed aircraft; sea battles produce ghosts, as if they'd never been.

Because fighting in the sky is a recent development, perhaps it is too soon to generalize. Fighting on land and at sea are ancient and, since antiquity, have shown different patterns.

Armies seek to conquer territory, seize resources, kill enemies real or imagined. Navies seek to control sea lanes for trade, to use blockades for political leverage or for pure cruelty. Conquered territory is occupied or returned; everyone knows what happened. Warships that fight at sea vanish: blockades vanish and are disremembered. The naval blockade is not a matter confined to yore: NATO blockaded Libya in 2011, Russia blockaded Ukraine in 2014. Already these savage actions—the purpose of blockades is to impose collective suffering, punishing the average for decisions by the elite—are largely forgotten. Happening on the waters, they left no evidence.

Perhaps we don't need to care about armies and navies fighting anymore, as in the last two generations, all forms of great-power conflict—land, water, and air—have declined.

This may seem hard to believe considering the tenor of the news, but frequency of war, intensity of war, and casualties from war are in long-term diminution, according to the Stockholm International Peace Research Institute, which tracks the awful statistics of combat.[1]

Across the world, a person's chance of dying in battle is the lowest it has been in human history.[2] The chance of dying in war isn't just lowest-ever in the rich nations—it's the lowest-ever in Asia, in the Western Hemisphere, in most of Africa, in the subcontinent, even most of the Middle East.

Spending for war is in long-term decline as well. Adjusted for population growth, global military spending since 1990 is down 17 percent; in the same period, per-capita spending on education and health care rose almost everywhere. The World Bank finds that since the 1970s, military spending dropped from 6 percent of global GDP to 2.1 percent, a reduction that soars into the trillions of dollars.[3] Global investments in education and health are up by trillions of dollars through the same period.

That the world has for decades been spending less on war and more on schools, colleges, and hospitals suggests a hopeful narrative rarely heard.

At this writing (Northern Hemisphere autumn of 2020) there has been no tanks-against-tanks battle in any nation since 2003, no large air-to-air battle anywhere since 1991, no major naval battle anywhere since 1982.

Coming chapters will explore in detail why great-power war is fading. Telling, here, is that the relationship between navies and economics is more pronounced than the relationships between armies, aircraft, and economics. Less fighting on land or in the air means less destruction and fewer atrocities but doesn't necessarily bring economic benefits. Less fighting on the oceans means more trade, which benefits almost everyone.

Lack of fighting is always a good: deaths avoided, destruction averted, citizens can live as they please rather than in terror or conscription or both. But lack of fighting on land does not, in itself, encourage nations to trade with each other. Lack of fighting at sea does, and historically, nations that trade are more prosperous, more tolerant, and more open.

LET'S TAKE A BRIEF step back. Much of our understanding of the ancient world centers on the Mediterranean Sea, where a diminutive ocean forged the cultures of Phoenicia, Athens, Sparta, Carthage, Egypt, Canaan, Assyria. Trade on the Mediterranean brought groups into contact, causing both battle and productive exchange.

In the ancient world, about 95 percent of transfers of goods happened across the waters of the Mediterranean. The retired admiral James Stavridis, who earned a PhD in international relations from Tufts University and was top commander of NATO in the first term of the Obama administration, noted in his fascinating 2017 book *Sea Power* what seems to be a natural constant: from antiquity to the present day, 95 percent of items in commerce move by water.[4]

Why the 95 percent rule is so, and what this may bode for the future, will be explored in Chapter 6. Suffice for the moment to say that water has always been the essential of large-scale trade.

Historian Lincoln Paine showed in the magisterial 2013 book *The Sea and Civilization*, about antiquity, that the challenges of commerce and exploration to be had upon the seas were for several thousand years at the cutting edge of developments in engineering, economics, academics, science, and government. Any brute with a club could organize some other brutes to raid the next village. To sail to the next continent required thinking and planning—indicators of civilization.

On the waters of the Mediterranean in ancient times, the good and the bad of human ambition met the demands of vessels, weapons, and astronomy. For as far back as records exist, cargoes upon the Mediterranean were enticements for profitable trading or larceny. As vessels (many rowed by slaves) began to transport valuable goods across the Mediterranean, warships began to seize or sink them or blockade their access to safe harbor.

Fighting became exceptionally intense yet seemingly invisible since there were few witnesses. Centuries before the birth of Julius Caesar, more than 300 warships clashed at Aegospotami, along the Aegean, in the climax of the Peloponnesian War. The Athenian and Spartan fleets that met at Aegospotami in 405 BCE were, to that juncture, the most complex and expensive creations of human society since the Pyramids. Ancient land battles such as Thermopylae are taught by historians and celebrated by writers and artists; Aegospotami, a more sweeping and important clash, left no impact on Western consciousness, because the ships sank, their legacies forgotten and their victims ghosts.

Archaic conflict between Carthage and Rome is remembered for Hannibal's elephants, but the battles that determined the outcome between these societies occurred on the waves of the Mediterranean. There are many similar examples from the ancient world.

Conflict on the Mediterranean escalated to the 1571 Battle of Lepanto, on the Ionian Sea, where nine hundred sailing ships and galleys rammed and boarded each other, leaving fifty thousand dead and years of immiseration ahead for Austria, Venice, Spain, and the Ottoman Empire, which bankrupted themselves to join the battle. By the time of the world wars, hundreds of big-gun vessels and submarines fought each other on the Mediterranean, eventually joined by aircraft and missiles.

Visit the Mediterranean today—it's a placid vacation spot, among the lovely places on our great spinning world. Throughout history its waters often turned red, usually because of the desire of nations to control trade. Shed, the blood dissolved into wet salinity, leaving no memorials, only ghosts. Today, fighting on the Mediterranean Sea is as rare as once it was common.

IN GEOGRAPHIC TERMS, THE Mediterranean may be considered a microcosm of the seven oceans; in historical terms, a microcosm of naval war and waterborne trade. During antiquity, both fighting and trade on the Mediterranean increased as the centuries passed. Across the seven oceans the pattern would repeat at global scale, fighting and trade intensifying with the centuries, leading up to the many phases of worldwide naval combat that will be detailed in Chapter 10.

Probably no one of the ancient Mediterranean basin thought its brutal level maritime conflict someday would spread across the globe. This is well to keep in mind as we think, today, that the seas won't return to flames. The expansion of maritime conflict is a warning of how going down to the sea in ships can backfire.

The year 1511 confrontation described in this book's introduction saw Portuguese caravels take on a sultan's war elephants over access to the Strait of Malacca, to control trade in what was then called the East Indies. In 1598, perhaps six hundred warships of the Sengoku, Ming, and Joseon feudal structures fought off what's now South Korea, mainly over Japan's desire to dominate Korean Peninsula trade. Around the time the Netherlanders were negotiating with the Lenape for what's now Manhattan, English and Dutch vessels were attacking each other in the East Indies, mostly over trade. The Dutch won and for more than three centuries beginning in

1602 mostly controlled what's now Indonesia—immoral colonization, to be sure, accomplished using wooden ships sailing thousands of miles. From 1665 to 1667, England and Holland turned the seas off Europe and the Caribbean crimson in an event hardly anyone remembers—the Second Anglo-Dutch War, again fought over trade. Again the Dutch won, though in a concession to finalize the Treaty of Breda, New Amsterdam was renamed New York.

Later in the Seven Years' War, Britain, France, Russia, Austria, Portugal, Spain, Peru, Sweden, the Moghuls, several German states, many colonies of European nations, the Iroquois Confederacy, and the British East India Company—a profit-making venture turned formal belligerent—fought across the continents, including along the area hauntingly called the Spanish Main (the Caribbean and coastal Gulf of Mexico). Armies marched, but the proliferation of warships made the scope of the Seven Years' War possible.

Much of the American Revolution was fought on the Chesapeake Bay and Lake Champlain, the climactic Battle of Yorktown being for the most part a maritime engagement. French warships chased away the Royal Navy, checkmate for British soldiers cornered at Yorktown.

Off England in 1779, John Paul Jones and a motley band aboard the outdated *Bonhomme Richard*, the name a sly reference to Benjamin Franklin, encountered *Serapis*, a marvelous new capital ship with a disciplined crew and a huge advantage in firepower. That motley band prevailed after Jones maybe did or maybe did not shout to the British commander—historians are divided—"I have not yet begun to fight." From today's perspective, the striking part is not that the superior *Serapis* was bested by an outgunned old boat but that *Serapis* was escorting forty-four merchant vessels from Sweden, bound to British ports. More than two centuries ago, large formations of commercial ships were moving between nations.

Jones was a gifted commander entangled by the lust for glory long among the drawbacks of sea power. He ended up fighting the Turkish navy in the Black Sea as an officer of Catherine the Great, a commission Jones accepted not caring about the cause, just to hold another command in battle. Before his death in 1792, Jones had been living in poverty in Paris, writing to the monarchs of Europe, asking please for a few ships and a quest.* A century later, in 1897, when Teddy Roosevelt was named assistant secretary of the navy and was striving to make the United States a maritime power, he reinterpreted the captain's tormented life as a symbol of American destiny. And was right.

TEDDY WOULD SHOW, WITH a book published at the callow age of twenty-four, that the War of 1812, a formative event of American history, was largely a naval confrontation. An attack by British ships against the harbor fort at Baltimore resulted in the "Star-Spangled Banner." Innovative designs by American shipwrights enabled vessels such as USS *Constitution* ("Old Ironsides") to defeat Royal Navy men-of-war viewed as kings of the sea. Because the Great Lakes could not be reached from the ocean—later the Saint Lawrence Seaway would change that—warships fighting on those waters in the War of 1812 were constructed along the lakes' shores, with cannon and naval stores dragged long distances through wilderness. In 1812, Congress authorized warships purpose-built to travel around Africa, cross the Indian Ocean, traverse the Strait of Malacca, and assault British commerce near what is now Java.

Many had marveled that tea from China came all the way to North America in the holds of English and Dutch sailing vessels. At Boston in 1773, tea that came all the way from China would be among the proximate causes of a revolution. By the outbreak of the War of 1812, the United States knew that merchant shipping in the East Indies near the Strait of Malacca was a soft spot for the British Empire, whose fleet had been tied down opposing Napoléon. Two hundred years ago, long before engines drove ships and vitamins kept sailors healthy, ocean fighting on the opposite side of the world was integral to American geopolitical thinking.

---

* Evan Thomas, *John Paul Jones* (Simon & Schuster 2003), does a terrific job of evoking the world of wooden ships in the eighteenth century and the part of Captain Jones's legacy that began after his death.

Wrestling for sea lanes of the Mediterranean, especially the straits that access the Black Sea, was primary casus belli of many awful fights, including the Crimean War—a conflict little reflected on today because it seems irredeemably stupid, yet essential to understanding the blue-water politics of Eurasia. Control of the straits at the Dardanelles and Bosporus has been a theme of history backward to the Greek legends, forward through the 1945 Yalta Conference, and continuing to the Russian assault against Ukraine in 2014. The Crimean War involved England, France, Russia, the Ottomans, Greece, and parts of what are now Italy and Austria. The conflict inspired changes in warship designs—screw propellers, metal armor, really big guns—that would trigger naval arms races across the world, including South America, where in the nineteenth century, poor nations with low living standards devoted vast sums to battleships to please their corrupt leaders.

THE EGOS OF KINGS and kaisers and South American tin-pots wishing for impressive battleships to strut aboard should not be underestimated. That warships may be built to please political leaders is a disturbing underside of the history of navalism.

Edward VII (king of England leading up to World War I) and George V (king leading up to World War II) liked to wear admirals' uniforms at public appearances.* Neither man ever earned this rank, simply awarding the distinction to their own names, along with chests of medals conferred for imaginary acts of valor. They paraded about like little boys playing dress-up.

England gave admiral of the fleet uniforms as gifts to Kaiser Wilhelm II and Czar Nicholas II. Both of these vicious little boys wore the costumes in public, and no one dared mention the medals were fake. The kaiser formed a collection of admirals' uniforms from Britain, Denmark, Russia, and Sweden, choosing one to don on his very large yacht or when stepping out to the theater. After

---

*The strange desire of kings and emperors to dress up as admirals and strut around the decks of ships is detailed in Robert Massie, *Dreadnought* (Ballantine, 1990).

Japan sank the battleship *Prince of Wales*, Emperor Hirohito, a vicious little boy whose cause in life was slaughter of the helpless, appeared to his war council in an admiral's uniform.

By the modern era, royals generally did not wear army uniforms, yet still donned naval regalia. Why did the sea cause monarchs to crave fake valor?

Henry V may have led his dear friends into the breach at Agincourt, but that was 1415. Most monarchs learned to avoid the battlefield, since in land combat, persons of importance get captured or killed. When planes took to the sky, kings knew they'd look farcical in goggles at the controls and that if they tried to fly, they'd crash. But a monarch in a glittering uniform could stand on the deck of a dreadnought and be photographed grandly ordering "full speed ahead!" without any risk or exertion.

Civilian politicians felt the same pull. Winston Churchill was delighted when named First Lord of the Admiralty in 1911, as the position gave him control of *Enchantress*, an extremely large yacht with immoderate staterooms, valet staff, and an exceptional wine cellar. Until war broke out, Churchill spent much of his time relaxing aboard *Enchantress* in the glorious Aegean, close by the whiskey rail and entertaining, at public expense, patrons who could advance his prospects. Eric Geddes, a railroad executive named Britain's Sea Lord in 1917, began to swan about at court events in an admiral's uniform, though he never served in the military. Britain still has an official who is addressed, presumably without laughter, as Sea Lord. As I write this, the Sea Lord is one Tony Radakin. Your Lordship, here is the jewel-encrusted trident!

The vanity of leaders, often a factor in the growth of maritime power as a tool of war, remains today. Russian president Vladimir Putin, who likes to be photographed on guided-missile ships, seeks to restore his nation's fleet because imposing navies are associated with great-power status. In 2020, Putin revived a tradition not seen since the czars, staging a naval parade past the docks at Kronstadt. Putin sat in a monarch's gilded chair, waving to passing destroyers with crews on deck at attention in dress whites.

Through the centuries, warships beloved of kings and dictators were used to fight other warships, to bombard ports, to control sea lanes, to escort unarmed vessels, to seize unarmed vessels, and to blockade.

The blockade is among the unseen aspects of maritime events, often affecting life on land without the obvious mayhem that characterizes a clash between armies. Blockades are one of the ways in which warships can be abused—a reason to be skeptical of praise for naval power, including the praise this book offers.

Blockades were common in the days of the Phoenicians, Venetians, and Ottomans—every Mediterranean port faced this problem. A blockade can cause terrible damage by stopping commerce, especially in food and medicine, without anyone being shot by an arrow or a firearm. The place blockaded may not seem to be at war, but the effects of war are present.

England's 1713 acquisition of Gibraltar prevented that rock and its narrow channel from being used for a one-stop blockade of everything from Spain to Egypt. During the Revolutionary War, British ships staged blockades of Boston and New York City. When Napoléon tried to control the economy of the continent, his ships blockaded approaches to England and its allies. The French despot complained that because the new United States was neutral in his "continental system" dispute, American merchant vessels cherry-picked trade with Russia. Napoléon's 1812 invasion of Russia, the largest military action prior to the twentieth century, was to chasten Moscow for defying the blockade—as even centuries ago, waterborne trade was essential to national power.

Through the Great War period when German submarines were sinking merchantmen bound for the British Isles—a bloodied but futile attempt at open-ocean blockade—the Royal Navy executed a ghoulishly effective cordon against the Central Powers, preventing foodstuffs from reaching Germany, Austria, and their allies. An estimated 750,000 German civilians starved to death during the Great War. The cause of that conflict was callous Prussian militarism. The result was a humanitarian horror, average people dying of hunger while the Junkers dined on veal.

From the November 1918 armistice to the June 1919 Treaty at Versailles, Britain maintained the blockade of the Axis—such that thousands of Germans, Austrians, and Turks died of preventable starvation *after* their governments surrendered. This shameful action by the Royal Navy is not mentioned at that service's many ceremonies of self-celebration. Desire for more farmland, so the nation could not be starved again by water blockade, became a force in German politics of the interwar period. (The relationship between modern agricultural science and reduced fighting on the oceans is a topic of the next chapter.)

The successful Union blockade of the Confederacy was as important to the result of the American Civil War as were the land battles. The South took desperate measures attempting to break the blockade to receive goods for Europe. These measures included the first military use of a submarine, in 1864, to sink a Union sloop that was preventing access to Charleston harbor; the submarine also sunk.

An international convention signed in 1856 at the conclusion of the Crimean War appeared to ban most blockades: one goal was to reduce suffering by average people. Rather than change their ways, governments changed their terminology. When Union warships cut off access to Confederate ports, Abraham Lincoln, a lawyer by training, was careful never to say the Confederacy was subject to a blockade, as under the 1856 agreement, only sovereign nations could be blockaded, and Lincoln contended the Southern states were in rebellion rather than sovereign.

Chile declared war on Bolivia and Peru in 1879, a sea conflict that left no impression on United States thought, though is discussed in South America to this day. The first action of the War of the Pacific was a naval blockade of a Peruvian port. Chilean gains in that confrontation left Bolivia landlocked, a terrible disadvantage in a world of waterborne trade.

US blockades against Japan were one cause of fighting in the Pacific in World War II. When President John Kennedy ordered a blockade during the Cuban Missile Crisis in 1962, JFK, like Lincoln, did not use that term. He instead declared Cuba was subject to a "quarantine," because at the time, commentators were saying that civilized nations do not blockade each other's hungry civilians.

In the 1990s the United Nations allowed strict sanctions, including a naval blockade, against Iraq. The UN blockade caused awful suffering for average people, while Iraq's Baathist privileged continued to bathe in splendor.

Since 2007, Israel has blockaded Gaza, the longest naval blockade of modern centuries. Israeli actions cause food and power shortages, unemployment, and hopelessness among Gaza youth, while having no impact whatsoever on the corrupt Hamas tyrants who are the blockade's ostensible target. The International Committee of the Red Cross has classified the Israeli blockade of Gaza a violation of the Geneva Conventions. The great powers stand idly by.

Contemporary blockades like the one against Gaza happen more often than many realize. Russia, loser of the Crimean War, violated the spirit of its own 1856 agreement in 2014 by blockading some of the very places over which that conflict had been fought. In 2018, Russia further blockaded Ukrainian access to the Sea of Azov, which connects to the Black Sea.

That Russia's 2014 and 2018 blockades were forbidden under agreements signed by Moscow went unmentioned by Presidents Barack Obama and Donald Trump and by most leaders of Europe. Lack of condemnation of the Russian blockades around Crimea and the Israeli blockade of Gaza are among recent examples of Western leaders and public opinion seeming unaware of significant events on the waters.

America wields the most naval power, yet American political and media leadership appears to possess disturbingly little knowledge of the subject. Perhaps the lack of teaching of naval history at most top US colleges and universities has real-world consequences. In many public-policy areas, obliviousness to history can lead to terrible misunderstandings of current events. For maritime issues—whether regarding navies, trade, or ocean governance—not knowing history may cause today's mainly good situation to revert to being mainly bad.

THESE OBSERVATIONS ARE RELEVANT as regards Alfred Thayer Mahan, a nineteenth-century navy captain and maritime theorist, beloved by Teddy Roosevelt, whose opinions played a role in the worst wars of the twentieth century. Mahan had the good sense to die in 1914, at age seventy-four, before the worst wars of the twentieth century could demonstrate that much of what he contended was wrong. Yet one still hears Mahan's name spoken deferentially in Washington, D.C., Beijing, and London. In 2020 Admiral Shen Jinlong, chief of China's navy, said, "Those who do not command the sea are commanded by the sea," a line straight out of Mahan.

Born in the Hudson Valley in 1840, Mahan captained small US Navy vessels during the Civil War and the War of the Pacific. He did not distinguish himself.[5] There were repeated instances of ships under Mahan's command striking other vessels or shoals, or "wedging" into quays—docking so hard they can't move. After poor grades on the bridge, Mahan transferred to the Naval War College, whose teaching halls and parade grounds, overlooking Narragansett Bay, are among the most pleasing campuses in the world. For the remainder of his life, other than to gaze upon the majesty of Narragansett Bay, Mahan avoided the sea.

At the Naval War College, Mahan met thirty-year-old Theodore Roosevelt, a visiting lecturer. Teddy had recently published his *Naval War of 1812*, a book that has stood the test of time. Roosevelt's volume devoted considerable page length to wind-tacking in the age of sail and to cannon weights that were then the measure of naval firepower. (A ship of the line in the War of 1812 could throw 425 pounds in a broadside; by 1944, Japan's *Yamato* could "throw" 27,000 pounds.) Roosevelt made the fundamental point that during the War of 1812, the army of the United States did not fight well, but the young nation's navy subdued the Royal Navy from the Great Lakes to the Atlantic.

Teddy expanded his analysis to contend that through history, land fighting has received too much attention, naval fighting too little. Later as assistant secretary of the navy, still later as president, Roosevelt pushed for the United States to build battleships and colliers to acquire sea power with global reach.

To sell his vision of a mighty American fleet, Roosevelt rehabilitated John Paul Jones in terms of reputation: in 1905, he had Jones's bones exhumed from a Paris cemetery and reinterred at the chapel of the Naval Academy in Annapolis. Always press-conscious, Roosevelt arranged extensive media coverage of the warships sent to fetch Jones home. Public support for a battleship fleet rose. To add intellectual heft to his arguments, Roosevelt drew attention to Mahan's 1890 book asserting naval force is the bringer of great-power glory.

That volume, *The Influence of Sea Power Upon History*, would end up praised by kings, politicians, and editorialists for generations. Kaiser Wilhelm II, on the throne from 1888 to 1918, ordered copies made available on the conn of German military vessels. Churchill kept Mahan's work in his many offices. After death, Mahan grew into a revered figure at the US Naval Academy, the Britannia Royal Naval College in Dartmouth, and now the Dalian Naval Academy, where Chinese cadets and young officers study.[6]

Like John Keynes or Kenneth Galbraith or Marian Wright-Edelman, Mahan became a name to drop in the halls of government—dropped by officials who have, one suspects, scant idea what these thinkers contended, just that they are associated with gravitas. In 2008, I interviewed Michael Griffin, then administrator of the National Aeronautics and Space Administration. Griffin introduced himself as a Mahan aficionado and said, "We need to apply the theories of Alfred Thayer Mahan to the control of outer space."

Mahan's theories were three. First, that naval force is the essence of great power. Second, that fighting ships need not be deployed—after all, Mahan himself was a bust on the waters—rather, it could float at anchor, frightening other nations with the mere act of existing. Third, that if sent into action, a navy should concentrate all force into a single, decisive melee.

As the Boston University historian Cathal Nolan showed in his superb 2016 book *The Allure of Battle*, "decisive battle" was what monarchs wanted to hear: they should spend vast amounts of other people's money on an armada that would justify their own admirals' uniforms and seek one earth-shattering confrontation in which brilliant strategy composed over cognac would lead to quick, total victory and the admiration of history. Going into Pearl Harbor, the leaders of Japan, Nolan writes, entertained "spectacular delusions" about a quick, decisive victory, because they believed Mahan. German leaders in 1914 and 1939 cultivated similar delusions, often from Mahan.

Scheming for "decisive battle" at sea, Nolan contends, allowed dictators and royals to drift in a dream world. No theorist made the fairy tale sound better than Mahan did. The problem was that actually following Mahan's formula led to fiasco. The Kaiser's Germany, Nazi Germany, and imperial Japan—the nations that employed Mahan's formulas—ending up in flaming ashes.

WHAT HISTORIANS DUBBED THE Naval Panic of 1909 commenced when Germany—rising in population and industrial output compared with England and France—began to build dreadnoughts the nation seemed not to need. England, already devoting too much money to these ships, vowed to increase naval production even more.

To Germany, it appeared London wanted to be so strong on the water as to blockade the North Sea, rendering Germany landlocked. To England, it appeared Berlin's only reason for a ruinously expensive warship program would be to cover an invasion fleet headed for the British Isles. A self-fulfilling prophecy of war began.

Germany's desire for battle cruisers stemmed in part from the childish fantasies of Wilhelm II, one of the kings who played dress-up with admirals' uniforms. Egging Wilhelm on was Admiral Alfred von Tirpitz, a devotee of Mahan. Tirpitz became head of the German navy a few years after *The Influence of Sea Power Upon*

History was published. Repeatedly he told the kaiser the book held the secret to how Germany could achieve *Weltmacht*—world power.

Tirpitz was a classic chicken hawk: he thought others should fight and die, yet he himself never experienced combat. Once World War I was afoot, Tirpitz followed the Mahan doctrine by keeping the German fleet mostly in port. The German naval officer class quickly realized the concept allowed them to live ashore in safety, attending balls and the symphony, while infantry suffered in the trenches. When the one German attempt to force a decisive naval battle, in June 1916 near Jutland, failed to break the British blockade, the kaiser's superexpensive fleet remained at anchor till the armistice, after which it sailed to Scapa Flow and met its fate beneath the waves.

Unable to make Mahan's theoretical notions work in the real world, Tirpitz pressured the kaiser to allow unrestricted submarine warfare against American merchantmen. This decision, taken in winter 1917, brought the United States into the Great War. As German chancellor Theobald von Bethmann-Hollweg left the abnormal midnight meeting at which Wilhelm II authorized unrestricted attacks on US civilian ships, Bethmann-Hollweg declared, "finis Germania." So it was. By drawing in the United States, strongest nation in the world, Mahan's theories converted German military advantage into utter ruin.

For decades scholars have dissected the strangeness of Neville Chamberlain's flying to Munich in 1939, hat in hand, to kiss Hitler's ring and hand him the Sudeten region of what was then Czechoslovakia. Yet appeasement policy began in 1938, with a conference at which the British government agreed to release Germany from the Treaty of Versailles naval limits. Given the green light by London, Hitler conceived a pure Mahan strategy, with the ominous label Plan Z, of building supergiant battleships, aircraft carriers, and long-range cruisers, all of which never would leave port: the ultimate fleet-in-being, to use Mahan's terminology. Only a few Plan Z vessels were launched, and considering the sums of money that would have been required, the scheme was always an exercise in unrealism. That Hitler was so enthusiastic for this scheme suggested the grip Mahan had on leaders' minds.

Japan's emperor and his war counselors often discussed Mahan, whose treatises were found on Japanese capital ships of the period. Following Mahan's lead, the Imperial Japanese Navy built two supergiant battleships, the largest in history—then kept them in port, neither ever sinking another vessel. The sea-power challenge Japan mounted against the United States, beginning at Pearl Harbor, followed Mahan to the letter, concentrating force into a decisive battle. The result was Japan's cities smashed and unconditional surrender.

One could argue that because US power would have overcome Germany and Japan regardless of what military tactics these countries employed, the fact that German and Japanese strategists were disciples of Mahan does not discredit the thinker's work. But the reality that there have been three real-world tests of Mahan's ideas, and all three led to national fiasco, is not what might be called a petty inconsistency.

THE INFLUENCE OF SEA POWER UPON HISTORY, the book that romanced Teddy Roosevelt and aggressors of both world wars, concluded at the year 1783. In other writing, Mahan sang praises for Horatio Nelson's victory at Trafalgar. But the battle happened in 1805, and at any rate, Trafalgar did not end the Napoleonic Wars, which dragged on despite the "decisive" navalist win. Mahan's backward-looking theories did not reckon with screw-driven ships, armor, turbines, oil power, exploding shells, armor-piercing shells, underwater torpedoes, air-launched torpedoes, naval aviation, sonar, magnetic and high-frequency detectors, and other innovations available by the 1940s, to say nothing of precision-guided ordnance, jets and helicopters, homing torpedoes, nuclear reactors, ducted propellers, satellites, and digital technology. Mahan's thinking was confined to a heroic age of sail that engaged the imagination but no longer existed in the real world.

But autocrats wanted to hear that they could build stunningly expensive ships, have their pictures taken on the decks, then use the ships to demand that other nations kneel. What leaders *want* to hear can be more powerful than any declaration of fact. In the fading days of the Ottoman Empire, rich purses of national treasure were spent on dreadnoughts so that Mehmet V could stand aboard a boat as mighty as any owned by the king of England. Burning money this way never made sense. But the point was that it was the kind of thing autocrats *want* to hear.

That Mahan's ideas are to this day what certain types of leaders want to hear is why this section has ventured into the seemingly esoteric question of the result of a nineteenth-century naval analyst's words in castles and palaces.

Today, Alfred Thayer Mahan is admired in China. Officers of the Chinese maritime force—officially the People's Liberation Army Navy, the existence of an organization called the Army Navy being delightful—are required to read *The Influence of Sea Power Upon History*. A documentary about how the upstart Tudor fleet brought great-power status to England in 1588 by defeating the Spanish Armada in decisive battle is shown on state-controlled Chinese television, followed by a talk-show format discussion of the genius of Mahan.

Sea trade has always mattered, but through the period of the world wars, conquest at sea could seem more important than trade at sea. From the start of the twentieth century through about 1940, the share of the global economy that was trade held at around 10 percent.[7] By 2019, just before the coronavirus took hold around the world, about $21 trillion*—about 25 percent of the world's economic activity—was international trade, the preponderance moving by sea. This social transition alone knocks out Mahan's belief that fighting would always be the essence of the sea.

From 1990 to 2019, the current-dollar value of global trade increased to 2.5 times that of the year 1990. Global population rose 30 percent in the same period, placing the gain in global trade far ahead of population rise. Should China make a Mahan-style move,

---

* All money references in this book are converted to 2020 US dollars.

the harm to international trade will send the entire world spiraling backward.

If a diabolical calculation once suggested Germany and Japan might come out ahead by bringing bloodshed to the seas, today's calculation shows that war at sea would cause global economic depression. (More on this in the next chapter.) It is imperative that Mahanian fantasies be discarded and the cycle of naval war not repeat.

TWO SEEMINGLY CONTRADICTORY CONTENTIONS can be true at once. It can be true that the power of the US Navy, obtained at dear cost, benefits the world by policing the waters, and also true that too much money has gone into warships, including American warships, that may tempt nations into avoidable conflict.

This book began, and will end, by endorsing a strong US Navy as a positive for nearly all the nations of the world—as a force for general prosperity and for reduction of developing-world poverty, improving billions of people's lives in ways that do not necessarily meet the eye.

But it is important not to go overboard, if the pun may be excused. Historically, warships have done more harm than good. This pattern may repeat.

The auspicious circumstances of our moment—American sea power allows nearly all nations to benefit from global trade—could in a single day become awful circumstances, if the United States and China (or any combination of the many contemporary nations now investing in maritime buildup) go to war on the blue water. Sea power is at once vital and overrated. It can both prevent terrible things from happening and cause terrible things. Even as the United States cheers on its fleet, Americans should remain skeptical.

Here as a short course in skepticism is an accounting of big, expensive, powerful warships that proved overestimated, concentrating on the late nineteenth century to 1945, the period of naval arms races that helped instigate consecutive world wars:

Dreadnought, launched by England in 1906, kicked off global competition for a new class of expensive capital ships with the design parameter of a few very large guns. (Previous ships of the line had lots of small and medium-sized guns.) Royalty in several nations spoke in hushed tones of *Dreadnought*'s supposed invincibility, wanting their own versions so they could be photographed aboard. Yet *Dreadnought* never fought another capital ship and was so useless it was sold for scrap only a decade after being commissioned.

Yavuz Sultan Selim, built in Germany in 1913 as the dreadnought *Goeben*. Cornered in the eastern Mediterranean by a British force at the outset of the Great War, *Goeben* made a dash to the Bosporus, essentially claiming asylum. Germany gave the vessel to the Turks as a gift to entice the Ottoman Empire to join the Central Powers, which proved a ruinous blunder. Renamed *Yavuz Sultan Selim*, the vessel was Turkey's flagship all the way until 1950, the last *Dreadnought*-class vessel in the world. Like so many other expensive fighting ships, *Selim* never won a battle.

Friedrich Wilhelm was one of four seagoing battleships built by Germany just before the turn of the twentieth century. Used mainly as a flagship for Wilhelm II to strut on. Sold in 1910 to Istanbul. Despite cost-no-object construction, *Friedrich Wilhelm* was outclassed by small Greek vessels at the 1912 Battle of Elli during the forgotten Second Balkan War. That *Friedrich Wilhelm* and its siblings were expensive and looked impressive was what mattered to kaisers and sultans.

Dunkerque and sister ship *Strasbourg*. France's fast battleships, an advanced class, built at great expense. Neither ever sunk another vessel; both scuttled to prevent them from falling into Nazi hands.

Bayern and *Baden*, two super-dreadnoughts launched during the Great War. The most expensive ships ever built for the kaiser's fleet, they helped drive imperial Germany to insolvency; neither ever sunk another warship. *Baden* ended its days as a gunnery-practice target for the Royal Navy.

Rio de Janeiro / Sultan Osman I / Agincourt. A dreadnought ordered by Brazil in 1911 from the British shipyard at Newcastle-upon-Tyne. Later Brazil canceled the order; England sold the ship to the Ottoman Empire, which renamed it. When war broke out in 1914, *Sultan Osman I* was in trials off England. Winston Churchill, head of the Royal Navy, ordered the vessel seized and renamed *Agincourt*. London's seizure of a battleship belonging to Istanbul was another reason the Ottoman Empire sided with the Central Powers. Never fighting, the thrice-named craft was scrapped in 1922 after an existence that consisted exclusively of political machinations.

Hindenburg, among the last battle cruisers built. Available during the Great War but kept in port per adherence to Mahan doctrine. Never fired on another ship, existed primarily to be scuttled at Scapa Flow, though *Hindenburg* lent its name to the 1937 rigid airship disaster.

Hood, a battle cruiser commissioned by England as the Great War ended. Through the 1920s a flagship and source of British national pride because it was unusually large and handsome. The only warship *Hood* ever destroyed was a French battleship helpless at anchor during the treacherous 1940 British surprise attack on London's ostensible ally. In 1941 *Hood* faced the *Bismarck*, the sole time it was given fair battle, and sank in minutes.

Bismarck, depicted by Nazi leaders as an unsinkable super-battleship. Sortied once, destroyed the *Hood*, three days later joined *Hood* in Davey Jones's locker.

Tirpitz, sister ship of *Bismarck*. Spent World War II seeking places to hide—the perfect ship to bear the name of the chicken hawk Alfred von Tirpitz. Sunk by British bombers while beneath camouflage nets in a Norwegian fjord.

Yamato, Musashi, and *Shinano*. The three largest warships of World War II; the first two were super-battleships, the third a super–aircraft carrier. All had extensive, well-stocked onboard apartments for senior naval officers, who tried to keep the vessels out of battle, officially in obedience to Mahan, actually to preserve senior officers' personal luxuries.

Yamato, almost twice the size of any American, English, or German battleship, never sank another vessel; only fired its gigantic guns (shells about the weight of a car) a few times. In its first action, *Yamato* came about and ran the moment lesser ships gave battle. In its second action, the battleship went under before even firing in reply.

Musashi, similarly huge, used its gigantic guns only for protection against American dive-bombers; in flames early in the only battle it ever tried to join. *Shinano* stayed in port until World War II was almost over, then was sunk by an American submarine on the Japanese vessel's first sortie.

Prince of Wales, England's top battleship entering World War II. Never sank another vessel. Sent to Singapore in 1941 by Churchill, who said the vessel's greatness would "overawe" the Japanese, *Prince of Wales* was destroyed by those same Japanese during its first action in Asia.

Nagato, the last dreadnought built by Japan. Never sank another vessel, spending most of World War II in hiding, per Mahan. *Nagato*'s fate was to be the target of a US atomic test in 1946.

Richelieu, a French super-battleship, never sank anything, but set some sort of record by being under the control of France, then Germany, then the United States, then England all in the same war. At various points British forces fired on the ship or assisted it. *Jean Bart*, a sister super-battleship, had a similarly strange résumé. In 1942, *Jean Bart* attacked American warships and, a year later, asked to sail to the United States for repair. In 1956, *Jean Bart* played a comic-opera role in the joint British-French-Israeli assault on the Suez Canal, testing its mighty guns then retiring after finding no targets.

Roma, lead ship of three large Italian battleships during World War II. Never fought another ship; was sunk by Nazi aircraft in retaliation for Rome's withdrawing from the war.

Stalingrad-class battle cruisers. Even after aircraft carriers showed battle cruisers obsolescent, Stalin demanded an impressive warship carrying his name—a ship he could be photographed on. Immediately after Stalin's 1953 death, all *Stalingrad*-class ships under construction were canceled.

Iowa, lead ship of America's fast battleships of World War II. These four vessels are generally considered the finest battleships ever, with the best mix of speed, firepower, armor, fire-directors, and reliability. None of the four ever sank a capital ship. At the Battle of Leyte Gulf, *Iowa* spent a full day using its enormous engines to steam at flank speed in the wrong direction. Its sister *New Jersey* holds the distinction having been decommissioned then recommissioned four times.

Vanguard, in service in 1946, the last battleship sent down the slipway by any nation. *Vanguard* had heating for Arctic operation and air-conditioning for the tropics. Never fought, used by Elizabeth II as a 45,000-ton heavily armed yacht. ("Duchess, won't you be a dear and come for a nice ocean voyage on my battleship?") Scrapped 1960.

Because this list is mainly big-gun vessels, perhaps it proves only that time passed the cannon-based ship by. For two hundred years, cannons were a feature of warship design because on water, a large, heavy cannon may be moved, while on land, moving large cannons via treads or railroad cars proved ineffective. As seaborne aircraft grew practical, even the longest-range naval cannon were outclassed: the vessel carrying the large guns could be sunk from the air before it drew close enough to give battle to the vessel carrying the aircraft. Once seaborne aircraft and sea-launched missiles could hit targets inland, big guns on ships also ceased being first-choice implements of bombardment. The battleship and its cousins became vestiges.

But other types of expensive modern warships have proven worthless too. Argentina invested a chest of national treasure in the aircraft carrier *Veinticinco de Mayo* (Twenty-Fifth of May, which is Argentina's National Day). It went into combat once, in 1982 at the Falkland Islands, intending to provide air support for Argentine soldiers ashore. Warned that a British nuclear submarine was near, *Veinticinco de Mayo* skedaddled back to port and never came out again, falling into disrepair. Engines no longer functional, in 2000 *Veinticinco de Mayo* had to be towed all the way across the Pacific to meet its fate at a scrapyard in India.

DURING THE PERIOD WHEN billions of dollars, pounds, marks, yen, pesos, and francs were invested in fighting ships that proved to be of little value, lots of people thought battleships were invincible. Today lots of people think aircraft carriers are invincible.

3

WHY FIGHTING ON THE BLUE WATER STOPPED

NEAR THE ISLANDS OF SAMAR AND LEYTE IN THE PHILIPPINES, October 1944, thousands of years of carnage on the blue waters built to a cataclysm. Every kind of naval destruction that is possible occurred. Giant warships fired cannon from turrets the size of elementary schools, lofting shells so enormous the recoil could shove a battleship sideways. Submarines and destroyers launched torpedoes, aircraft dropped explosives—many of the planes using the harrowing dive-bombing technique in which they do a full-power plunge toward a target. Ships shot back at the aircraft using machine guns, repeating cannon, and half-ton shells that threw clouds of shrapnel. Fighting took place on the open ocean, along shorelines, in and out of coves. Troop carriers landed soldiers on beaches as ships fired at them and cannon from other vessels replied. Japan's mystery-shrouded mega-battleships appeared, America's vaunted fast battleships veered through the water at speeds that would have made Admiral Farragut gasp. Light, medium, and large aircraft carriers were present. For days the Battle of Leyte Gulf raged as the Pacific Ocean changed from pacific to a "sea of thunder," in the words of historian Evan Thomas.

This awful confrontation brought utter defeat to the navy of imperial Japan, signaling that the United States was certain to win the final phase of the war, though huge numbers of civilians—Japanese under falling bombs, Chinese and Southeast Asians under Japanese colonial oppression—still were to die till Tokyo cried quarter. The mega-battleship *Musashi*, on which, in 1943, as millions of his own people suffered, Emperor Hirohito wore an admiral's uniform to a ceremony of self-glorification, sank at Leyte Gulf on October 24, a sinking that symbolized both Japan's foolhardiness in believing Mahan theories of sea dominance and the moral outrage of imperial Japan's desire to subjugate and slaughter the helpless.

As the last smoke from the Battle of Leyte Gulf drifted away, the last oil slick dispersed, and the final corpse disappeared beneath the waves, thousands of years of bloodshed on the blue water came to a close.

Since October 1944 there has been only sporadic combat at sea, nothing close to the "almost incessant warfare on the oceans" that characterized the previous three millennia.

Leyte Gulf was the final time an all-out naval battle was staged on our pale blue dot. May this statement always remain true.

Why has fighting at sea declined so dramatically? Can we prevent this scourge from resuming? That naval fighting has gone from "incessant" to rare is among the important, unnoticed aspects of contemporary society. Unnoticed in one sense because it involves the deep-blue-sea areas most women and men never personally observe; in another because it requires awareness of what is *not* happening. What is *not* happening may be as important as what is. But what *is* happening produces pictures that can be used to stoke fear; what is *not* happening does not.

AN OBVIOUS ELEMENT OF declining great-powers combat is the arrival, first, of nuclear weapons, second, of nuclear weapons carried by long-range ballistic missiles that cannot be stopped. Bombers flying toward cities, as happened at Hiroshima and Nagasaki, might be shot down. But no country possesses an antimissile system able to intercept more than a handful of warheads incoming from space. Because of ballistic missiles the United States, United Kingdom, Russian Federation, and France can threaten any nation with obliteration via strategic missiles; China, India, Pakistan, Israel, and North Korea, which have atomic weapons but lack intercontinental-range missiles, can threaten neighbors with horrifying loss.

Nuclear deterrence is creepy in the extremis but has discouraged war. The most potent deterrent is the ballistic-missile submarine, for which the United States holds a large lead in numbers and technical quality.

Keith Labbe, an Annapolis graduate and a retired US Navy lieutenant, served on the *Maine*, a ballistic-missile nuclear submarine that can launch up to 336 doomsday warheads to almost any location on earth. Labbe says, "Before nuclear deterrence, nations feared each other. Now they fear war itself. No rational person thinks it is possible to win a nuclear exchange. So far at least, the most awful of weapons, ballistic-missile submarines, have been under the control of rational people."

The Federation of American Scientists tracks patrols by doomsday submarines and finds that the United States usually has more at sea than do all other nations combined. When Labbe was aboard the *Maine*, each deployment—below sunlight depth, listening but broadcasting nothing, hoping no launch order ever is received—lasted six to seven weeks. Labbe says, "The fresh food ran out quickly, and UHT milk, the kind that can be stored without refrigeration, having strawberry UHT on Lucky Charms made you long for dorm food."

I asked Labbe a question I always ask officers who serve around nuclear warheads—if the order came, would you? Labbe said yes: "If it was real—we confirmed the order was not a spoof—every US submariner would launch even though millions would be killed by this action. You'd know the order would not be coming unless your family and friends were already doomed. You'd think, 'My family is gone, are we going to allow the people who did this to become the tyrants of the world?' And you'd know the order to fire would be coming from a presidential authority who wouldn't be sending that code unless the United States was down to its last resort."

By "presidential authority," Labbe means whoever has the doomsday-button levers now that the president and vice president are dead. Whether any person in any nation should have such buttons can be debated. In our world, a range of persons in several nations do.

Labbe says he accepted nuclear submarine duty because he believes ballistic missiles deep in the sea, moving randomly and nearly immune to preemptive attack, avert war. If nuclear weapons were only on land, in missile silos or at air bases, there might be a temptation to strike first. Having them underwater and constantly changing position tells any leader that a nuclear first strike will fail. At least, any rational leader.

MANY TIMES IN THE past, a development has been said to mean no more war. The rifled barrel (predecessor to the repeater rifle), the Maxim gun (predecessor to the machine gun), movable artillery, poison gas, long-range bombers, cruise missiles—when new, these and other weapons were thought so awful they could never be used. But they were used. Nuclear bombs are too awful to use. Will that stay true?

When he was president, Jimmy Carter, a former navy officer who had been the XO of a submarine, joined the Soviet Union in signing the treaty called SALT II, which aimed to reduce strategic nuclear weapons. SALT II begat an arms control regime now called NEW START. At the end of the Carter presidency, the United States and Soviet Union possessed about 54,000 nuclear bombs, according to the Federation of American Scientists; today the total is down to about 9,900. In 2009, Barack Obama won the Nobel Peace Prize for advocating elimination of nuclear explosives.

Full elimination of nuclear arms might backfire by allowing great-power fighting to resume—but the smaller the inventory, the better. The 1,550 strategic warheads allowed to the Russian Federation and United States by the latest treaty might comfortably be reduced further, as long as most such bombs are aboard ballistic-missile submarines that remain hard to find.[1] (Strategic warheads are the worst kind—there are also short-range, relatively small nuclear bombs.)

For now, nuclear deterrence clearly discourages war. In the short span from 1947 to 1971, India and Pakistan attacked each other three times. Later, both acquired doomsday weapons. Though there have been incidents, general combat between these nations has stopped.

ANOTHER ELEMENT IN THE decline of battle is the close of the Cold War, which fostered many proxy conflicts, coupled to the last of colonialism. Not needing to defend colonies reduces the chances of armed conflict. Had France not tried in the 1950s to hold colonies in Southeast Asia, for example, the Vietnam War never would have occurred.

Less visible is the decrease in lust for land as a national, an aristocratic, or an individual objective. For thousands of years, until the industrial era, nations could add wealth mainly by seizing land and attendant resources; nobles could enlarge wealth mainly in the same manner. Average people needed sizable tracts of land too. Colonization in many places, including what's now the United States, was powered by desire for land. In what's now Ohio, Vermont, California, Oklahoma, Oregon, and other places in North America, average people wanted land they could farm or graze animals on because this was their best hope of decent income.

As the industrial era progressed, people learned that wealth could be produced as well as seized, first by industrial means and now by intellectual. These methods render stealing from other nations by war less attractive and reduce the need for land.

At roughly the same time that wealth through production rather than plunder became appealing, the relative value of manual labor went down. A long-standing goal of colonizers was to attain forced labor. In recent generations, unskilled labor has become less a necessity to despots and aristocrats.

Forced labor still exists in too many places, and in the United States, there is a lively market for educated persons, often Indian nationals, who enter on category H visas to fill tech jobs without benefits or assurance of residency status—a kind of white-collar indenture. But in general, the incentive to seize acres and enthrall laborers is declining. This change reduces the stresses that led to war.

Fighting at sea was often about permitting or denying control of land, labor, and markets. With land and labor less important, while markets in most cases are held open by World Trade Organization regimes, war at sea grows less tempting.

The effect of diminished need for land is pronounced regarding agriculture. It has become fashionable for well-fed Westerners who live in comfort to censure the Green Revolution farming techniques that saved billions of lives.* But not only do Green Revolution seeds and crop techniques make possible the sharp reduction in malnutrition seen in almost every nation's current generation, by producing more food and fiber from about the same amount of land, high-yield farming ended the centuries-old enticement to attack in order to eat.

Germany and Japan behaved so immorally during the second world war that it's hard to think about either in detached fashion. Set the awful immortality aside for a moment to consider the land dynamics.

Coming into the 1930s, since around the founding of the Holy Roman Empire, German-speaking peoples sought grain and other foodstuffs from as far away as North Africa. Imagine moving hundreds of tons of grain across the Mediterranean by wooden ship in the year 800, when Charlemagne was crowned! And for at least several centuries, Edo Japan imposed (brutal) reproduction control because there wasn't enough rice, or enough trees for construction and heat, trees being to preindustrial economies what silicon chips are to the tech era.

------

* For the counterargument to chic nonsense about high-yield crops, see Robert Paarlberg, *Resetting the Table: Straight Talk About the Food We Grow and Eat* (Knopf, 2021); Paarlberg is a Wellesley College agronomist.

Old Japan and the thousand-year Holy Roman Empire were more or less stable in part because population change was slow. In the nineteenth century, this dynamic changed a lot—and cataclysmic war followed closely. From about 1850 to the 1930s, the populations of Japan and Germany roughly doubled, upped by the beginnings of industrial output and science-based medicine. After centuries of roughly stable supply and demand of food and raw materials, Germany and Japan suddenly needed far more agricultural products. Both looked to conquest as the means to obtain the land and resources they desired.

Today high-yield agriculture can solve the food problem while high-tech industry can produce money that buys whatever resources are needed. In the 1930s these things weren't possible; war resulted. These things became possible; war declined.

During the Great War, Germany knew starvation caused by naval blockade; by the 1930s, Germany wanted to seize the fertile agricultural areas of Poland and Ukraine to feed itself. The German population of the present day is 45 percent higher than of the 1930s, yet everyone is well fed and expansionism has ceased being an imperative. Today, high-yield farming supplies bounty while market economics generate the currency to buy whatever must be imported, and no blockades impede commerce.

This basic dynamic—gaining land is no longer essential to increasing food production—applies to many parts of the world, including South America and the Indian subcontinent. A few regions still suffer malnutrition, intolerable in this well-off age, or food insecurity. Overall, farm production almost annually increases faster than population, disproving Malthus.

Since 1960, the world's population has grown 135 percent, malnutrition has declined, yet the number of acres in cultivation has risen by only one-third. The ability of less land to feed more arose because crop yields skyrocketed. Wheat yield is up 200 percent since 1960, for example.[2] Two hundred percent better harvests, 135 percent more people, equates to less food scarcity—and less war.

A similar situation applies with raw materials. When fossil fuels, ores, and other primary resources are sufficiently plentiful, it is cheaper to purchase them than to seize them by conquest. On the day Joe Biden was sworn in as president, petroleum was in such oversupply that US gasoline pump prices were lower, adjusted to current dollars, than when Buddy Holly was performing. During the 1970s, Western analysts talked about going to war to commandeer oil fields. In the contemporary market, petroleum is so inexpensive, all you need is a tanker to pick it up, and with two exceptions (Iran and North Korea), no blockade will impede the tanker. Primary resources may be strained someday. For now, they offer no incentive for conquest.

Today, military and paramilitary force mean less to national, and to individual, pursuit of wealth than they have at any other time since the early Bronze Age pharaohs. Nations and the very rich no longer need to seize by force: to purchase with cash is easier.

A SOMEWHAT SIMILAR TRANSITION applies to persons under arms. From ancient times roughly through the 1950s, population was indispensable to military power—men (sometimes boys) to form battle squares, swing swords, die as cannon fodder. The rise of German-speaking population relative to English-speaking and French-speaking unsettled the European balance of power in the run-up to both world wars, because Germany could mount ever-more divisions. The rise of the Japanese-speaking population unsettled the Pacific Rim balance of power in the run-up to the second world war, as Japan acquired sufficient manpower to attempt conquest of China and Southeast Asia.

Today economic productivity, not waves of fusiliers, drives the leader status of the United States, the European Union, China, and a few others, while technology is the amplifier of martial prowess. Massed infantry on land, or thousands of vessels on the water as occurred on D-Day, probably will not happen again.

Add to these causes the rise of the multilateral organization: the United Nations, the World Health Organization, the World Bank, the World Trade Organization, the International Organization for

Migration, the International Monetary Fund, the Organization of American States. Former Pentagon official Rosa Brooks wrote in 2016 that the advent of the United Nations means "militarily powerful states are far less free to use overt force to accomplish their aims."

Large international institutions may be stultified or plagued by corruption, but all rose in stature during the same period great-power combat became less likely. This cannot be just some weird coincidence, especially considering the big three international institutions were founded before the decline of war, not as a result of it: the World Bank in 1944, the United Nations in 1945, and the World Health Organization in 1948.

GENERAL INFLUENCES DISCOURAGING WAR are joined by circumstances specific to combat on the seas.

First is the rise of satellites or, to polish the metaphor, the launch of satellites. Prominent naval surprise attacks—the Dutch raid on English docks in the River Medway in 1667, the British naval attack on Copenhagen in 1807, "damn the torpedoes" at Mobile Bay in 1864, Manila 1898, Port Arthur 1904, Pearl Harbor, others—occurred because defenders had no idea large contingents of warships were bearing down.[3]

Much of the Battle of Jutland, the largest naval confrontation of the Great War, involved the Royal Navy trying to figure out where the High Seas Fleet was. For hours British warships could not find German warships that were close, huge, noisy, and emitting tall plumes of high-visibility coal smoke, yet could not be located. Much of the Battle of Leyte Gulf involved American spotters trying to figure out where the Japanese aircraft carriers were. For hours a brawny squadron of US vessels raced in the wrong direction because admirals lost track of the Japanese main force, which included the two biggest ships in the world.

Centuries of sea fighting involved uncertainty about the other side's vessels, disposition, and location. Often the captain wishing to join battle found battle difficult to join. Reconnaissance satellites have changed that.

The early models covered only small areas of the earth and lacked real-time features—canisters of film were dropped back into the atmosphere to be caught, taken to intelligence bureaus, and painstakingly analyzed. By the 1980s, improved satellites sent reasonably prompt data on the positions of Russian warships, their smoke plumes, and even voiceprints of their radio calls. The US Navy's many satellites for these purposes had *Avengers*-movie names like White Cloud, Ranger, and Intruder.* By around 2000, real-time optical and radar data was broadcast from space directly to Pentagon bureaus and deployed units. In recent years, Russia, China, and India have attained similar orbital technology—though never with a name as good as White Cloud. Real-time optical data is Horatio Nelson's dream come true. Think of Nelson standing on the forecastle squinting with his one good eye into a cracked spyglass, versus a flat-panel screen of real-time images.

Coverage of the vastness of the oceans is not without flaws. In 2019, US and British naval units needed two days to locate an Iranian oil tanker that turned off its transponders in the Persian Gulf. (Modern ships have devices similar to airplane transponders, which electronically announce location, course, and speed.) But in the main, ships are more visible than ever before. The United States and Japan began in 2020 a joint program to place in orbit dozens of relatively low-cost small satellites to provide continuous coverage of maritime activity, including flight paths of naval missiles, around the South China Sea.

As recently as 1996, when China staged a campaign of intimidation against Taiwan, the Taipei government had little clue about the movements of Chinese naval forces. A few years later, the United States patched Taipei into the network of US surveillance satellites. In 2020, Taiwan began construction of a fleet of fast-action minelayers. If at some future juncture Beijing were marshaling ships for an invasion of Taiwan, leaders there would

---

* Development of the navy's ocean surveillance technology is described in Marc Ambinder, *The Brink: President Reagan and the Nuclear War Scare of 1983* (Simon & Schuster, 2018), a meticulously researched account of Cold War tension.

know within hours and would deploy the fast-action minelayers to booby-trap sea lanes between the nations. Plans like this are hardly foolproof but make war less likely, since now the great powers possess information about each other's mobilizations and force dispositions.

In coming decades, hypersonic projectiles that move extremely fast, or tiny robot submarines designed to sneak up while a large, crewed submarine creates a diversion, may provide a deadly bolt-out-of-the-blue when the horizon appears clear as seen from space. Overall, the arrival of real-time reconnaissance satellites, plus surveillance drones and electronic warfare aircraft that scan long distances, lowers the risk of maritime combat.

Hollywood exaggerates the power of technology—spy agencies cannot read license plates from orbit—but modern satellites do remove much ambiguity from a nation's knowledge of the opposition. One relic of the Cold War, a treaty allowing NATO and the Warsaw Pact nations to fly unarmed photoreconnaissance aircraft through each other's skies, lapsed in 2020, made unneeded by improvements in satellites.

Not that long ago, reports about locations and movements of maritime forces, compiled by spotters using binoculars, were written out by hand, coded, transmitted, decoded, then plotted in chart rooms, where officers pushed tokens around map tables. New real-time sensor-fusion systems combine satellite data with drone images and scanner information from ships and planes. Supercarriers launch their own radar-dome aircraft, similar to the Airborne Warning and Control System (AWACS), while the navy has begun to field long-range, land-based surveillance jets with advanced sensors. Military technicians at Silicon Valley–like stations get the updates in minutes instead of hours.

Greg Baker, captain of the *Wasp*, says, "Every year there is less uncertainty about what the other side has and where their forces are. Less uncertainty reduces the temptation to war."

WHATEVER MAY HAPPEN WITH hypothesized armaments such as rail guns and hypersonic missiles, new conventional weapons are sufficiently powerful that nations may conclude there is no point in fighting at sea.

In 1982, the United Kingdom and Argentina declared war over a small group of islands near Antarctica known in London as the Falklands, in Buenos Aires as the Malvinas. That anyone would fight for remote islands without strategic value, populated primarily by herds of sheep, shows the march of human folly. Argentine dictator Leopoldo Galtieri ordered an invasion to divert attention from domestic repression and his bottomless incompetence. English prime minister Margaret Thatcher wanted to show she was more manly than most men.

British and Argentine warships and aircraft met in the sole naval battle of global consequence in the span from Leyte Gulf in 1944 till this writing. Both sides expected something along the lines of a staring contest. Instead, the brief battle was a bloodbath.

Using acoustic homing torpedoes, a British nuclear-powered attack submarine blew up Argentina's big-gun cruiser, drowning 323 men. Gleaming British destroyers and frigates were sunk by Argentine planes that flew straight through supposedly airtight defenses. Several bombs hit British vessels but failed to detonate, owing to an error in setting fuses; had these munitions gone off, the Falklands War would have rivaled the 1781 Battle of the Chesapeake as England's worst defeat at sea. And in an outcome that shocked experts, a French-built antiship missile sank the destroyer *Sheffield*, a new model equipped with the latest self-defense weaponry.

David Wroe, a US Navy captain, says, "The Falklands fighting was far more costly than either side expected." Wroe grew up on Cape Cod and, as a boy, was fascinated with sailing. He graduated from Holy Cross with a degree in political science, rose to command a guided-missile destroyer in the Persian Gulf—a water body where every captain is on edge. Wroe says, "Since 1982, navies have worried that if what happened near the Falklands is what happens when guided missiles and homing torpedoes are used, the first day of a major naval battle will be awful like nothing has ever been awful."

In the years after 1982, antiship missiles and homing torpedoes have grown more deadly as range, speed, guidance, and destructive power have improved. Torpedoes now may have two or more homing mechanisms; if one is electronically defeated, the next takes over. Some nations, notably China, have fielded long-range antiship missiles that can be fired from land, without an attack aircraft having to approach the target.

A measure of the decline of fighting at sea is that since 1955, just two vessels have been sunk by submarines—the Argentine cruiser at the Falklands and an Indian frigate destroyed by a Pakistani sub in 1971. While the torpedoes have stayed in their tubes, the prevalence and deadliness of these weapons keep rising. Today's navies have hundreds of lethal, fast, nearly silent homing torpedoes aboard submarines, surface ships, airplanes, and helicopters, and soon, aboard flying drones and robot mini-subs too.

Unlike in the movies, ships and submarines cannot use evasive maneuvers to escape homing torpedoes. There are some countermeasures, but war games by the US Navy and other navies show that in most cases, a targeted vessel does not know the torpedo is approaching till a few seconds before the explosion. If even a small portion of the world's inventory of homing torpedoes is launched, the result may be "awful like nothing has ever been awful."

One reason the Falklands battle was more destructive than expected is that most modern warships have little armor or use aluminum where once was steel. During the period of dreadnoughts, the thickness and positioning of steel were paramount concerns, leading to distinctions such as armored cruiser versus protected cruiser. Beginning around 1970, aluminum was substituted for steel to increase ships' speed and stability; air defenses were thought to have become so good that nothing would hit a modern warship. Obviously, an incorrect assumption.

The 1982 battle caused a trend back toward steel, sandwiched around composite liners that block shrapnel. Great-power navies also responded by arming warships with computer-controlled, radar-directed electric cannon that in theory will shred any object that gets close. Some sailors call the new guns R2-D2s, because they resemble the cute Disney robot. Having walked in front of an R2-D2 on a US warship deck, your author can assure you it is not cute to be in the sights of an autonomous weapon powerful enough to blow the shielding off a supersonic object.

The combination of new kinds of armor and computer-controlled point-blank defenses has never been employed under real-world conditions, so whether they will keep ships afloat is anyone's guess.

Fighting at sea is further constrained by the coalition building the United States has emphasized for a generation. Coordination among allies, or even one nation's own martial branches, has not been a theme of history. During the Napoleonic Wars, several professed coalition members pursued different objectives, with little synchronization. The Balkan Wars of 1912–1913 were so disjointed than in the midst of the conflict, Bulgaria switched sides and attacked its allies. As late as the February 1945 Yalta Conference, the American, British, and Soviet offensives into Germany were not coordinated, the Big Three's general staffs engaging in almost no exchange of information.[4] When in 1979 the United States attempted a military rescue of hostages in Iran, the raid failed primarily because the air force, army, marines, and navy did not harmonize actions. Everyone has heard the saying about a house divided against itself. For centuries, this problem made military alliances more vulnerable than they might have been.

In a policy change that began in the 1980s, the US military has reduced interservice rivalries while the Pentagon and Department of State have formed close defense coalitions with NATO, Japan, and other nations. When COVID-19 broke out on the supercarrier *Roosevelt* in 2020, causing international headlines, this happened just after the ship made a show-the-flag stop at Da Nang—port city of a nation the United States tried, in recent memory, to bomb back to the Stone Age. In 2018, Japanese warships made a show-the-flag visit at Cam Ranh Bay, an anchorage of a nation Japan not so long ago brutally repressed. Like the *Roosevelt*, the Japanese warships were greeted by pomp and local dignitaries.

The biennial Pacific Rim naval exercise called RIMPAC, sponsored by the US Navy for coalition building, involves warships of many nations—NATO countries, Australia, Brunei, India, Indonesia, Japan, Malaysia, Mexico, New Zealand, the

Philippines, Singapore, South Korea, others. US-sponsored naval exercises in the North Atlantic are similarly well attended. In 2019, when China announced a joint naval exercise, only Russia and Iran were willing to join, Iran solely with coastal patrol boats. For all of America's manifold faults, governments of many nations want to be involved in US projects, because to most of the world, America = Success. Only a handful of nations voluntarily associate with the petty tyrants at the top of China and Russia, a realpolitik the leadership classes of these societies would do well to muse on.

Coordination among Western navies, in contrast to China and Russia facing the world largely alone, militates against war. "Britain, Canada and the Netherlands have better navies than most people realize," says Baker, of the *Wasp*. "We are close in operational terms with the Japanese and Norwegian navies. In the past, there were alliances, but when battle started, each went its own way. Now the Western militaries are well connected. That makes the risk of fighting decline."

China and Russia know that no powerful nation is operationally linked to their militaries. Russia's only allies are Syria and Venezuela, which is like having negative allies. China, largest of countries, is without a military affiliate. Beijing has been romancing Bangkok, offering roses, chocolates, and diesel submarines, in hopes of having at least one regional ally. What does Beijing's lack of allies say about how much the world despises the Chinese Communist Party? That question aside, the Chinese navy, even as it expands, remains vulnerable. This should reduce the chance of an ocean war that ends the blue age.

Pique might increase the chance. Until 2016, China was invited to RIMPAC. US Navy and People's Liberation Army Navy forces sailed side by side. Arrival of Chinese warships at Pearl Harbor, the departure point for the exercise—marching bands playing, honor guard at attention—was a hopeful sign about the future. But in 2018, with Beijing–Washington tensions rising, China was disinvited from RIMPAC, even after details such as codes and IFF frequencies (what militaries use to avoid accidentally firing at friends) had been exchanged. This was a little like disinviting your bestie from a Sweet Sixteen on the morning of the party. For the 2020 RIMPAC, China did not receive an engraved invitation, though Vietnam found one in the mailbox.

The Naval War College, with that glorious view of Narragansett Bay, enrolls midcareer officers from nearly every maritime force in the world—in part so they can learn for themselves that opposing the US Navy is senseless, so why even try? The primary exception: officers from the navies of China and Russia do not attend.[5]

Small in themselves, these slights could result in accretion of political anger that might have been avoided. The more the Chinese and Russian navies are involved with the US Navy, the better. The United States is the one in charge—and so ought to act graciously.

TWO OTHER FORCES LESSEN the peril of naval war, though an unhappy end could loom.

One is the high value, to most nations, of waterborne trade. Chapter 2 noted that about 25 percent of global economic activity is trade, mostly through ocean commerce. This represents almost as much GDP as the decline associated with the Great Depression. If fighting resumed at sea, causing waterborne trade to end, that would trigger a second depression.

On the eve of the Great War, about 10 percent of the global GDP was trade via ocean commerce. That was a large amount (because the global GDP is large) but not a depression-level sum. Germany before both world wars, and Japan before the second, might have believed that conquering, enslaving, and stealing would produce value after the costs of fighting were subtracted. No nation could believe this today—at least, no nation with rational leaders.

A country strong enough to start a great-power war could not benefit from stopping global trade. Blockades and sea battles that bring down one-quarter of the world's economic activity would harm the aggressor as much as the victim.

"Suppose we decided to fight China. What would victory even look like?" asks Derek Reveron, a professor of national security at the Naval War College. "How would the United States come out ahead in such war, even if every battle was a clear win for us? How would China come out ahead, even if winning the battles?"

Nuclear deterrence changed the great powers' relationship with war by adding the fear that survivors would envy the dead. The contemporary globalized economy adds the possibility that victor would suffer as much as vanquished. Today, for the first time in history, there is international dependence on the blue water.

Traditionally, rising powers enter conflict with established powers. This was the situation of Germany relative to England before the Great War, of the Qing China relative to Joseon Korea, of Rome relative to Greece in the Iron Age. Other examples abound. But there has never been a great-power relationship similar to the one entered into, since about 2000, by the United States and China. Both nations rely on each other economically. Win-win outcomes can be imagined, as can lose-lose outcomes—but not an outcome in which one defeats the other without doing itself extraordinary harm in the process.

Chinese diplomats like to speak of "win-win cooperation," which often decodes as, "China gets its way." But aspects of American diplomatic rhetoric decode as, "United States gets its way." Just because Beijing likes the phrase *win-win* does not make the view wrong.

Ronald Reagan purportedly said of the Cold War, "Somebody's going to win and somebody's going to lose." Of the blue age, Reagan would say either everybody wins or everybody loses.

"EVERYBODY WINS" IS MORE likely if the US Navy remains the big fish of the deep blue sea.

Spain, Portugal, old China, imperial Japan, kaiser-era Germany, the ancient Phoenicians, the ancient Greeks, Renaissance Venice, colonizer-era Netherlands and Denmark, nineteenth-century Brazil and Argentina, the Mediterranean-era Ottoman Empire, Ming China, Great Britain—these and other nations sought hegemony over the waters. Today the United States actually has the global ocean hegemony of which many previously dreamt.

Political science views *hegemony* as a dirty word, assuming that unchecked power will be abused. So far, American hegemony over the oceans has not been abused: rather, has been employed to keep sea lanes open, to prevent fighting, and to protect vessels of all but a handful of flags. Across today's world, US warships act as guardians for merchant ships—including commercial vessels of nations in competition with American business interests.

This is not the first time a naval force placed global interests ahead of its own. During negotiations for the Declaration of Paris, the 1856 agreement that ended the Crimean War, the Royal Navy agreed to surrender its long-claimed authority to stop neutral vessels and search for contraband. This was, the historian Paul Kennedy has written, "an incredible gesture by the world's strongest naval power."

Through the second half of the nineteenth century—a period when England did terrible things as a colonizer in India, South Africa, and elsewhere—the Royal Navy did noble things by protecting neutral shipping while mapping the shoals of the world and allowing mariners of every nation access to the maps. Around this time Parliament repealed the Navigation Acts of 1651, rules that kept commercial vessels of other nations out of English-controlled ports. Not only would the Royal Navy protect other nations' vessels; those vessels could dock where they pleased. Noble aspects of England's nineteenth-century behavior set in motion the laisse-faire global trading philosophy that, by our lifetimes, expanded as never before, improving living standards while reducing poverty.

The latter phase of Royal Navy hegemony, from 1856 to roughly the world wars, was a period in which the strongest naval force was a friend to nearly all nations. So far, the period of US Navy hegemony has been the same.

"Along shipping lanes, the United States national interest is almost always the same as the interest of other nations," says Captain Wroe. "Nations want to trade, the United States Navy makes it safe to trade. If we let down our guard and there were major fighting at sea, the entire world would be harmed."

4

THERE'S ALWAYS A BIGGER FISH

IN SUMMER 1992 A HUGE FLOTILLA LED BY FOUR AMERICAN supercarriers—the most powerful fleet to move anywhere in the world since the US Navy approached the Japanese home islands— sailed across the GIUK Gap. That stretch of brine, whose initials stand for Greenland, Iceland, and the United Kingdom, is a nautical choke point between the vastness of the Atlantic and the relatively confined waters around Scotland, Scandinavia, and Arctic approaches to what is now the Russian Federation.

Just before the main force turned north to enter the GIUK Gap, a decoy contingent turned south toward Africa. Movements were scheduled so the decoy group would be seen by Russian reconnaissance satellites, which at the time had limited scope, while the main force could sail unobserved. Today the main force would be continuously tracked. US satellites pass over most of the oceans at least once a day, with radar to peer through clouds. China's Chang Guang Satellite Technology agency is about halfway through a plan to orbit a constellation of 138 small spacecraft that will inspect almost every patch of earth up to five times daily.

Feints like the one used in 1992 are associated with battle. When Allied bombers approached the Axis in 1943 and 1944, a diversionary group might break away just before the primary attack, to distract defenders. In 1992, not only was a very large naval strike force headed toward America's adversary, it was employing a warfighting tactic.

Moscow knew no actual attack was coming. But the movement of the large fleet conveyed the message that the American navy had become able to do to Russia what no navy had ever been able to do to any nation. Until roughly the 1990s, no country's ships had been capable of sea-launched deep strikes. Now US naval aviation had long-range jets plus long-range weapons: tanker planes lofted from supercarriers added attack radius. A new type of vessel, the fleet-defense cruiser, equipped with a new type of radar and long-range antiaircraft missiles, meant Russian bombers that Moscow thought could sink American warships instead had no hope of getting near them.

The fleet's 1992 maneuvers were to ensure that Moscow—in turmoil as the Soviet Union imploded, the Commonwealth of Independent States doing little better—saw proof the United States could wield a degree of waterborne power no nation had ever possessed.

Moscow further knew its forces could not threaten the US interior in the same way Russia was menaced. The Soviet navy had no supercarriers, no advanced air-defense cruisers. With Russia geographically disadvantaged to begin with—its ships can reach open ocean only by passing through bottlenecks, while America has thousands of miles of open-ocean direct access—the US naval lead had become overwhelming.

A common belief is that Moscow agreed to end the Cold War when the Politburo accepted the United States was so far ahead in wealth and science there was no chance Russia ever would catch up. The naval aspect is overlooked. Positioning a vast fleet in Russia's ocean backyard drove home to Lenin's descendants that their position was hopeless.

Before both world wars, Germany's kaiser and führer were obsessed by "encirclement": enemies in each land direction yet no assured access to the blue water. During the Cold War, the Politburo was fixed on the notion the Soviet Union had been encircled. Hollywood presents Russian leaders as either evil incarnate or jovial drunks. A nuanced view is that, knowing Germany, their worst foe, failed utterly at sea, Russian leaders fear the same fate. Moscow worries about encirclement in a way the United States, with affable neighbors and a bonanza of open-ocean coastline, never has.

The 1992 exercise that sent a fleet traversing the GUIK Gap was saber-rattling, and rattling of sabers can result in war. Here, the result was peace. Seeing the overwhelming naval power arrayed against it, Moscow defunded its navy for many years, diverting rubles to coastal patrol and icebreakers. In 1994 the sole super-carrier Russia tried to build was canceled while in dry dock, the never-seaworthy hull broken up for scrap.

The US Navy is a war machine. Yet in this and other cases, a war machine brought peace, which, as the next chapter will detail, opened the door to global prosperity through trade.

SAILING A BATTLE FLEET into Russia's backyard represented a change in philosophy by the navy.

At the founding, the framers hoped the United States would possess no uniformed services—no standing army—and would hold only a maritime force composed essentially of private contractors. Most of the framers opposed standing armies, which can be used to oppress citizens. (The Chinese Communist Party likes a standing army for the same reason the framers did not: soldiers can oppress civilians.) Initially the thinking was that militias would be raised in emergencies—the Constitution vests the power to raise armies with Congress, not the White House—while maritime problems would be contracted out. Congress would tell privateers what they might and might not do on the waters, promising payment for enemies sent to the bottom or prizes towed into port.

Hope that "these united states" would not need a military lasted about a decade. In 1798, Congress established a Department of War to manage the raising of temporary armies and a Department of the Navy to maintain a standing force of warships. Armies, mainly using weapons most men were familiar with, such as rifles and light cannon (which then functioned like big rifles), and tactics most men knew, such as enfilade and defilade, could be raised and drilled quickly, or so the thinking went. (Later as infantry units acquired armored vehicles, rockets, and radars, the thinking obviously changed.) Navies, on the other hand, require capital investments spaced out over years. Warships must be built well in advance, even when the horizon is calm; crews must have long periods of training.

The framers and their immediate lineage reasoned that unlike armies, a navy would be hard to employ to oppress citizens—especially when the United States ended at the Ohio Valley, and most Americans lived beyond the range of the best naval gun.

It was not long till presidents began to task the new Department of the Navy with assignments far from home. Once opposed to a permanent navy, Thomas Jefferson, after being sworn in as president in 1801, almost immediately dispatched frigates and marines to North Africa to put down the Barbary gangsters—the "shores of Tripoli" moment. Soon the navy was aggressive across the globe. But there seemed then, and seems today, only little risk that the navy could be employed to oppress the nation's own citizens.

In 1946, after American forces defeated fascism and imperialism and came home, President Harry Truman sought to cut the navy in budget and significance, believing aircraft and missiles could fill the global power-projection role. Truman's advisers thought ponderous warships smacked of wood and sail, compared with supersonic fighters and shiny rockets. The small part the navy played in the Korean and Vietnam conflicts seemed to show its day was done.

In the White House, Jimmy Carter conceptualized the navy as strictly a defensive organization to prevent violation of the Monroe Doctrine. The US Navy, Carter thought, should be a regional force that defends borders, no longer traveling the world.

Taking the Oval Office in 1981, Ronald Reagan surprised Washington with several new views, among them a reversal of Carter's policy. Reagan switched the primary tactic of the navy to forward-deployed—present far across the oceans.[1] Under Reagan and his successor, George H. W. Bush, navy warships annually simulated taking up positions necessary for two military goals. The first was to bottle up the Russian navy in the same basic area where German surface ships had never been able to stage a breakout during the world wars; the second, to conduct carrier-based bombing strikes deep in Russian territory. To boot, the navy forward-deployed across much of the globe, whether near adversaries, allies, or neutrals.

Most of the military forces of history were primarily for defense of borders; border defense remains the primary role for most nations' forces in the present day. The United States has almost never faced a close-by military challenge. Exceptionalism favors America in so many ways; one of the overlooked ways is that the strongest nation in history need not defend its land borders and shorelines, such defense for many nations being a dunning cost. Conceptually, the US military has almost always been an expeditionary force—intended to operate over the horizon. This is a national luxury.

Many argue that today's US military has too much over the horizon. David Vine, a professor at American University, counts 119 US military installations in Germany, a nation that can defend itself.[2] For Japan and South Korea, Vine counts a total of 209 US military facilities, a number that's awfully high and a dagger pointed at China—the United States would be fearful if any potential adversary had so many military facilities so close to America. On the larger canvas, US involvement in the endless-war conflicts of the Middle East and Afghanistan should conclude.

But even if the US military retrenches, a forward-deployed navy still makes sense. Gary Roughead, a retired admiral who was chief of naval operations from 2007 to 2011, says, "Land and air forces can win disputes, but it is the navy that keeps disputes far from our shores." Eight decades have passed since the last military attempt against American soil, at Hawaii in 1941. Keeping disputes far from our shores looks better all the time.

REAGAN'S DECISION TO SWITCH warships to forward-deployed necessitated distant logistical support. Bases were acquired or expanded. Today the navy has two in Japan, one in Bahrain, one at Guam, one at Diego Garcia in the Indian Ocean. These are the large bases; there are others, including a new base on Crete. Just as the US Army has too much presence in Germany, the US Navy could be leaner.

American naval facilities on the remote island of Diego Garcia, whose legal status is disputed, symbolize the blue age. At all points of the compass from Diego Garcia, there is naught but ocean— more than a thousand miles to land in any cardinal direction. Yet because of the degree of American force kept there, Diego Garcia commands the Indian Ocean. The Strait of Malacca, on which China depends for trade with the European Union, has for centuries been a choke point going east; Diego Garcia makes the strait a choke point going west as well. US naval planners observed how the confines of the North Sea, and of the Turkish Straits, constrain the Russian navy in a way the US Navy has never experienced. For the moment, with the Chinese navy opposed in the Indian Ocean, Beijing's forces are delimited too.

In 2018, the US Navy changed the name of its Pacific Command to Indo-Pacific Command; in 2020, Congress shifted money toward this new subdivision. That same year, a US supercarrier conducted exercises with Indian warships in the Strait of Malacca, then sailed across the Indian Ocean basin showing the flag at major harbors.

Also that year, the Department of State and the Pentagon signed an agreement with New Delhi to share the highest-level US surveillance satellite data with the Indian military. Included are real-time locations of Chinese warships and precise topographical data. The United States has a little-known organization, the National Geospatial-Intelligence Agency, devoted to creating high-resolution, three-dimensional images of the entire earth. Cruise missiles and other "standoff" munitions need detailed topographical information to achieve bull's-eye accuracy. The US military has possessed such information for a generation. Now the United States is sharing the data with India, and it is obvious to Beijing who the Indian missiles may be targeted at.

After the US announcement of an Indo-Pacific Command, France and Germany declared new military policies regarding the region. Such declarations would seem far afield for both nations but not perhaps in a time of blue-age trade. The Berlin government's 2020 document, *Leitlinien zum Indo-Pazifik*, declares a German national interest in "international order" around the Strait of Malacca. That same year, France created an ambassador to the Indo-Pacific, quite an unorthodox diplomatic portfolio. The prospect that French, German, and Chinese forces might eye each other through gunsights on the Indian Ocean would have seemed impossible even a few years ago. No more.

To military strategists, increasing US emphasis on the Indian Ocean makes this expansive water body—so important to history, so little studied in the West—a twenty-first-century flashpoint as ominous as the South China Sea.

America's many wars and battles in Afghanistan, Iraq, Libya, Sudan, and Syria were preceded by the establishment, in 1983, of Central Command, a Pentagon organization focused on that region. Before Central Command in 1983, American strategy had little to do with these countries: once a command was funded to intervene in the region, US military activity there soared. If you have a well-supplied and powerful Department of Hammers, you are likely to perceive a sudden upwelling of nails. This happened with Central Command and the Near East, and could happen with the Indo-Pacific Command and the Indian Ocean.

American and Chinese moves in the region may become self-reinforcing. In 2017, Beijing inked a deal with the government of Sri Lanka to take over a natural harbor at Hambantota, on the southern edge of that island nation. China will improve Hambantota's port and terminals, which will be good for trade, while acquiring an Indian Ocean fortress to rival America's at Diego Garcia. China got Hambantota under the terms of a ninety-nine-year lease. The ninety-nine-year lease Britain obtained for Hong Kong in 1898 numbered among the "unequal treaties" causing China's century of humiliation. Now China has the clout to impose unequal treaties on others.

Who will control the Indian Ocean throughout the twenty-first century—the United States? India? China? A demilitarized international coalition focused on trade and fisheries? A seafloor environmental preservation regime? Do not discount the latter possibility.

WHATEVER ELSE THEY ARE, expanded American naval bases across the world exemplify the philosophy of forward deployment. As recently as the early 1970s, the US Navy had no regular presence in the Middle East; now the Fifth Fleet is based at quays along the Persian Gulf. The 1967 and 1973 Arab–Israeli wars were fought without any permanent American forces in the theater. Now the navy base in Bahrain looks a lot like Florida, while a sprawling air force base in Qatar looks a lot like Texas.

The navy's Strike Group Five—a supercarrier, an Aegis air-defense cruiser, destroyers, other ships, and many aircraft—anchors near Tokyo. Cuba wants the United States to quit Guantanamo Bay; Japan wants Strike Group Five to stay, because this constrains China.

Strike Group Five is forward-deployed to conduct attacks around the Pacific Rim at a moment's notice. One can argue whether this policy is defensive or provocative. One cannot argue that no power in world history had the wealth, matériel, and person-nel to station such potent forces so far from its shores, simply as a precaution. Spain bankrupted itself trying to forward-deploy in roughly a quarter of the world; Germany, the Netherlands, and Portugal threw in the towel at about a fifth of the world. The nine-teenth-century Royal Navy was the only previous maritime force to aspire to a fighting-forward strategy on a global basis, and this strained England's treasury even in flush times.

"Our concept of fighting forward, no other nation is attempt-ing that," says David Wroe, the destroyer captain. "True global forward deployment is so complicated and expensive, most of his-tory's great powers didn't even try. But today, no matter where you go on the waters of the world, the US Navy is already there. It's complicated. It's expensive. And it discourages war."

THERE SEEMS AN OPEN-AND-SHUT case that the Monroe Doctrine (1823) and Roosevelt Corollary (1904), both enforced by the US Navy, are other American policies that discourage war.

The near-complete absence of armored columns or carpet bombing from the Western Hemisphere is almost never remarked on—Americans, Mexicans, Brazilians, and others do not seem to wonder why the hellish slaughter that ravaged the other hemisphere never came here. The taken-for-granted absence of major war from an entire hemisphere is one barometer of how the positive effects of the blue age are overlooked.

The Monroe Doctrine forbade Europe from holding colonies in the Western Hemisphere. The Roosevelt Corollary said that if nations in the other hemisphere had disputes with governments of the Western Hemisphere, America would resolve such disputes. At the time, England, Germany, and Italy were threatening Caracas about repayment of a debt and sent dreadnoughts to blockade Venezuela. The United States chased the European battle fleets away, then persuaded their capitals to accept a financial haircut, ending the dispute peacefully. For the century since, warships from Europe and Asia have with only a few exceptions steered clear of the Western Hemisphere. They know where they're not wanted and, more to the point, know the United States has the muscle to enforce our rules.

Since the 1823 and 1904 naval policies imposed by American edict, there has been only occasional nation-versus-nation fighting across the Western half of the world, compared with generations of brutal war in the other half. For the Cold War proxy battles in Nicaragua, Chile, and Honduras, the United States bears some blame. Colombia long was riven by simultaneous narco war and ideological war; Costa Rica, by a brief civil war; and elsewhere in Central and South America, various forms of cyber war and "asymmetrical" tensions. But the Crimean War, the two world wars, the Korean and Vietnam wars, the Middle East and North Africa wars—long, horrific episodes of massacre and destruction—had no parallels in the Western Hemisphere.

Through the young twenty-first century, there has been no military-versus-military fighting anywhere in the Western Hemisphere.

Any force wishing harm to the hemisphere would have to get past the US Navy. Half the world mostly at peace—and we take this for granted.

Some economists argue the two US doctrines have slowed development in South and Central America. This theory will be put to the test as China has begun to invest in those regions. Whoever proves right, the Monroe Doctrine and Roosevelt Corollary rely, for their war-discouraging effect, on the navy's making it impossible for armed forces of Eurasia to operate in the Western Hemisphere. Indigenous movements can; foreign militaries cannot.

LEADERS OF MANY NATIONS would like to wield American-style global power. Contemporary China wants this option power, which would require a great navy. Since Russia about a decade ago gave up its hope of European Union membership, turning cold to the West, the Kremlin has resumed longing for the kind of maritime power that great nations possess. Russia's moves against Crimea and Ukraine were seen in the West as owing to Putin's ego. To the Kremlin, they were an attempt to fulfill centuries of Slavic desire for year-round access to warm waters.

In 2016 India joined the select club of nations that own ballistic-missile nuclear submarines, when *Arihant* became operational. Though not as powerful as any US *Ohio*-class ballistic submarine, *Arihant* and its sister *Arighat* could, alone, destroy the major cities of China. A Sanskrit word, *ariant* translates to "slayer of enemies." Whether rising navalism by contemporary nations is a response to world events or an attempt to manipulate them, more naval power is happening.

In defense-budget politics, the tactic is called threat inflation—make the opponent sound like a colossus. Threat inflation pleases Pentagon empire-builders and defense contractors. In media, the tactic is called alarmism—make every headline seem the end of the world. Roughly since the 2010s, threat inflation and alarmism have been applied in Washington, London, and Canberra to naval issues, as contractors seek money and news organizations seek "holy cow!" stories, the more negative the better.

Often, nations overestimate each other. The fine 2019 book *Appeasement* by the historian Tim Bouverie contends that a primary reason Neville Chamberlain bowed low to the führer in 1938 was that the British cabinet believed Germany had already mobilized. In fact, Germany would not be ready for war for another year—its 1938 position was a bluff. Had London invoked the Treaty of Versailles in 1938, Bouverie showed, Hitler would have been arrested by his own officers; millions of deaths would have been averted. But England believed Germany was stronger than it was, overestimating a foe.

Today one hears China spoken of by American commentators as an invincible colossus. The 1938 analogy is apt, for Chinese society is rife with contradictions, instability, and internal discord—far more unsteady than American society is, even the 2020 America of riots and political venom.

For example, the immensity of China's aging population is little grasped in the West. America has 50 million citizens older than sixty-five; China has 200 million. China is on to track, by the middle of the century, to have more senior citizens than the *entire* population of the United States.

From a national-resources standpoint, older citizens consume much more than they produce. With each passing year, a larger portion of China's wealth must be diverted to underwriting the old. Currently China's debt as a percentage of GDP is lower than America's. But the Chinese ratio of debt to economic production is rising faster than the similar ratio in the United States, suggesting America's arrears are manageable, whereas China's are taking on a life of their own—just as many millions of Chinese file for pensions.

The upside is that older people tend to be wise and to oppose war. Japan, the oldest large society in our world, consistently places its weight behind international peace initiatives. On the eve of the US invasion of Iraq, the Pew Research Center found older Americans less likely to favor military action than were younger citizens.[3] If Chinese citizens obtain a meaningful vote—which may not happen, given Chinese Communist Party totalitarianism—it is likely the aging cohort will counsel the young to embrace the Confucian goals of diplomacy and coexistence over martial solutions.

Nevertheless, threat inflation by the military-industrial complex and alarmism by journalists have conjoined to make China sound as if it were engaged in a super-shocking arms buildup, especially in terms of the blue water.

CRAVING PESSIMISM, EDITORS LOVE the scare story of Asian naval might, though they would be horrified if the United States responded by dispatching a few Chinese warships. In recent years the *New York Times*, *Wall Street Journal*, and *The Atlantic*, among the most important publications in the West, have embellished China's military power, seemingly in search of negative headlines.[4]

Media heavy breathing aside, there is no doubt the Chinese presence on the oceans is growing in the military and commercial sectors. Contemporary Chinese submarines are superior to the clunkers they supplant. Destroyers China began launching around 2015 are similar to their US Navy counterparts in possessing vertical launch tubes for missiles (deceptively important) and electronically steered radar (flat panels rather than whirling dishes), potent features American warships had to themselves for a generation. New Chinese destroyers employ gas-turbine propulsion rather than antiquated boiler systems. At the turn of the twenty-first century, China did not sail any modern destroyers. By 2020 it had about half as many as the US Navy had, a significant increase in a relatively short time.

Stephen Wrage, a professor of political science at the US Naval Academy, says, "China has improved its ability to build ships of all types." In 1990, when China took initial steps toward market economics, the country launched 3 percent of the world's new ships; today, 40 percent. *Tripoli*, America's newest assault carrier, took about three years to build: in 2019, China completed an almost-as-good assault carrier in six months. Most industries feature either labor or capital. Shipbuilding requires both, and China has both, allowing for fast production.

America and Europe have nearly dropped out of commercial shipbuilding. The result is fewer skilled-labor jobs in the traditional shipbuilding cities of United States, England, Germany, and Scotland—but more employment at the shipyards of China, India, Taiwan, and South Korea.

In 2014 the rock musician Sting (birth name Gordon Sumner) premiered a musical, *The Last Ship*, about the disappearance of working-class shipyard jobs for welders in Wallsend, England, where Sumner grew up. The musical's songs concern longing and loss—often what artists feel when they reflect on childhood. But there could be a second musical titled *The New Ships*, about how maritime production in Asia is lifting hundreds of thousands of workers from poverty to a middle-class standard. As in so many cases, Americans and Europeans hear about decline (Western shipbuilding employment) but don't hear about improvement (median income in India and Asia).

China is launching ships so fast there's barely enough champagne to smash against the bows. The International Institute for Strategic Studies calculates that at the turn of the twenty-first century, the United States was outbuilding China seven to one on warship displacement. (Vessels can be rated by displacement or by several measures of tonnage; usually the distinctions matter only to specialists.) By 2017, China was launching about 50 percent more warships by displacement than the United States was, and the margin continues to increase in China's favor.

Quality still favors the United States. China's two aircraft carriers, *Liaoning* and *Shandong*, have no catapult, rather a "ski jump" that arches upward. Ski-jump takeoffs limit an aircraft carrier to short-range jets. *Liaoning*, an obsolete design, is strictly a junior-varsity ship—in US Navy nomenclature, it would be a light carrier or a "jeep."

President Xi Jinping attended, in late 2019, *Shandong*'s first departure from port, at Hainan Island. Hainan is the southernmost province of China, near the disputes of the South China Sea, to which *Shandong* deployed after the Xi-attended event. Considering a presidential sendoff was given an aircraft carrier that the old Royal Navy system would have called second-rate—not fit to face the adversary's best—should Beijing someday launch an aircraft carrier equal to any in the US Navy, likely this would occasion fireworks in China and a fresh round of threat inflation in Washington.

Hainan Island represents the shortness of memory. Until the awful morning of September 11, the Hainan Island Incident, occurring April 2001, was expected to be the worst thing that happened that year. An American signals-intelligence plane flying along the boundary of international airspace near Hainan naval base was clipped by a Chinese fighter jet scrambled to warn the plane off. Both aircraft crashed. The American crew survived; the Chinese pilot died. Politicians and think-tank types in Washington expressed outrage that China would impede a lawful flight in open airspace. The US action was roughly as if one of Beijing's signals-intelligence planes had flown right against the boundary of international airspace off Virginia, trying to gather intelligence on the naval base at Norfolk.

Following the Hainan Island Incident, many thought a cold war between America and China would begin. A short time later 9/11 dawned, altering America's priorities, while China decided to focus its economic activity on export income and its martial activity on espionage at US universities and laboratories. Two decades have passed. The underlying dynamic of the Hainan Island Incident remains and could restart at any time.

FOR NOW, CHINA'S GROWING nautical force is intended for the nation's environs, not as a blue-water navy like America's. In 1996, when the Chinese government made a play to intimidate Taiwan, President Bill Clinton sent aircraft carriers into the Taiwan Strait, and that was the end of that. Backing down, Chinese leaders viewed the result as yet another humiliation. Although it may be a long time—if this ever happens—before China's navy could threaten the Western Hemisphere, the day is not far off when a new Taiwan Strait confrontation would look very different from the one in 1996.

Because Beijing–Washington relations soured in 2018, the United States has sold advanced munitions to Taiwan, including a late-model homing torpedo that can destroy a submarine even at depths once viewed as secure. Perhaps such sales are justified. Imagine how Americans would react if China supplied advanced torpedoes to Cuba.

THE SOUTH CHINA SEA, the place China's emerging fleet is optimized for, has, to China, approximately the cultural significance the Gulf of Mexico has to the United States. But America is blessed with many natural harbors—if the Gulf of Mexico were blocked by a foe, both oceans still would beckon. China has only a few natural harbors, and they funnel ships toward the South China Sea.

Geography is a strategic weakness for Beijing, whose maritime ambitions face a substantial geographic disadvantage compared with the United States, chosen among nations. The United States can corner Chinese warships into the relatively small South China Sea, which looks an awful lot like the North Sea where Britain twice boxed in modern German navies, or use air and sea power to close the Strait of Malacca, choking off China's ability to trade. There is no similarly confined ocean area that China could attack to incapacitate America. This makes the South China Sea a must-have, to Chinese thinking.

So far these waters are mostly peaceful—for which China receives no credit in the West. Speaking in 2019 in Singapore, General Wei Fenghe, a top Chinese defense official, noted that about 100,000 vessels transit the South China Sea annually. Combat among these ships is unknown, and when sailors declare emergencies, China reacts quickly. (Rapid assistance to vessels in distress is considered a mark of responsible stewardship.) American and British contingents show up in the South China Sea proclaiming they will protect freedom of navigation, Wei said, yet China already protects freedom of navigation there, and nothing has gone wrong. This viewpoint is never reflected in Washington and London speechmaking or on the pages of these capitals' newspapers, General Wei concluded, making his points with some force.

The trouble is that Brunei, China, the Philippines, Taiwan, and Vietnam have intersecting claims in the South China Sea. International law generally allows a nation to ban warships within twelve miles of its shores, and to exercise exclusive economic rights (fishing, prospecting) within two hundred miles of shore. In the South China Sea, exclusive economic zones overlap in crazy-quilt fashion, creating disputes with no obvious solutions. In almost every case, Beijing's proposed solution is to give China control.

Ocean chemistry and temperatures make fishing grounds off Indonesia among the world's finest. Beginning around 2015, as the Chinese navy acquired heft, Beijing sent warships or coast guard cutters to harass Philippine, Vietnamese, Indonesian, and Malaysian fishing operations in the area. Offshore natural gas in the Pacific Rim, especially in Vietnamese waters, is vital to economic growth for young nations that want average people to enjoy access to reliable electricity, equally significant as a low-carbon fuel for climate-change progress. China has been harassing natural-gas platforms too.

In response in 2020, Manila, which previously said it would withdraw from a "visiting forces" memorandum that allows US Navy units access to Philippine facilities, declared that the US units could remain. Australia and India signed an agreement to open their docks and logistics facilities to each other's navies. Australia and India are not adversaries but don't have much in common either. The agreement acknowledges their mutual need to keep at the ready enough maritime force to discourage China.

Battle is the daunting risk, but the offshore component matters as well. Gary Roughead, the retired admiral, notes, "In previous centuries, nations had no offshore infrastructure. Now nations are investing in capital-intensive deepwater oil and gas platforms and in wind turbines. Offshore energy facilities are expensive to build but can be destroyed at low cost using standard maritime weapons." Chinese warships sailing close by practically say, *Nice little drilling rig you've got there. Shame if anything should happen to it.*

Ocean wind turbines built so far have been anchored to rock, mostly off Britain, Denmark, and Germany, which have expanses of relatively shallow coastal water where dropping a support shaft is practical. The East Anglia Array, under construction in waters off England, should produce from wind about five times the output of a large coal-fired power station; no fuel will be required and no greenhouse gases emitted. General Electric, which has considerable experience with turbines in the form of jet engines and industrial power plants, installed at Rotterdam in 2020 an enormous wind blade—about the height of One Financial Center, a Boston skyscraper—as a prototype for planned North Sea wind farms.

Offshore wind-generated electricity is good news for the environment and for naval gunners. As colossal rock-anchored wind turbines become familiar along coastlines—perhaps joined by floating wind platforms—they will provide clean energy but also represent what tactical officers call soft targets.

Some technologists believe there could be intertidal power generators; the endless, moon-driven movement of tides would spin dynamos to supply zero-emission self-renewable kilowatts. In principle the chemical gradient between saltwater and freshwater could be employed to generate electricity: this zero-fuel energy source is found across the world. Tidal power, floating wind turbines, and salt-to-fresh kilowatts offer an appealing energy future—but the seaborne facilities would be super expensive to build and easily smashed by torpedoes.

Israel and Saudi Arabia have offshore desalinization stations. More nations may, if freshwater rather than petroleum becomes the scarce liquid of the mid-twenty-first century. Desalination plants are like deepwater gas platforms—they take years to build, minutes to blow up. If electric drive replaces the internal combustion engine in cars, buses, and trucks, lithium will be needed to make the batteries. Land deposits of lithium are few, and the mining involves exploitation of workers in Bolivia and elsewhere. Lithium can be refined from seawater by machines rather than low-wage labor. The machines would be expensive, tempting naval targets.

AS ECONOMICS MOVES OFFSHORE, the incentive to create islands, and thus stake claims to national control of ocean waters, will rise.

China began to construct landfill around the Spratly Islands, a small chain with disputed national status. The United States and Philippines protested; Manila had a strong claim, while America, whose own capital is built partly on landfill, had only a peevish claim. In reply to China, Taiwan started developing another tiny archipelago, the Pratas Islands. The Pratas would make an excellent location to install antiship missiles intended to sink the Chinese navy if it were approaching Taiwan. This puts the islands (or are they atolls? reefs? outcroppings?—more in Chapter 8) among places where the blue-age peace might end.

If the filled-in Spratly Islands are recognized as territory, this would have the effect of extending China's exclusive claims through most of the South China Sea, as a circle may be described around each nationally owned islet. The Beijing government distributes ocean maps with nine dashed lines, indicating what China considers its historical rights in the South China Sea. The maps are offensive to all Pacific Rim governments other than China's. The nine-dashed-lines concept is sufficiently touchy that in 2019, Malaysia forbade theaters from showing the DreamWorks children's movie *Abominable*. One may wonder how a cartoon about a talking snowman became a political lightning rod. To please the Beijing Communist elite, DreamWorks, which is owned by NBC Universal, included a schoolroom scene in which the nine dashed lines are shown on a blackboard and referred to by the teacher as a settled question. Outrageous? Sucking up to Chinese dictators is a prominent activity in corporate America. Just ask Disney or the NBA. Malaysia banned the movie to prevent schoolchildren from glimpsing the image.

Most of the sea area confined within Beijing's nine dashed lines is not contiguous to China, being closer to the Philippines, Vietnam, or Brunei. A better name for the waters within the nine dashed lines would be the South of China Sea, since that's where the area is located.

China's Foreign Ministry declared in 2020 that the Chinese have controlled the South China Sea for "thousands of years," predating the modern concept of exclusive economic zones. Because in customary water law, prior claims may be superior to new laws, the word *historical* matters in this context. But China did not inform other nations of its water claims—a long-established step in diplomacy—until 1948. That is late by the standards of maritime assertions. For instance, it was in the 1820s when Colombia and Venezuela informed other nations of their claims in the Gulf of Venezuela. China's assertion of control over the South China Sea based on a distant historical right only recently enunciated is as if Italy said, "The whole Mediterranean belongs to us because once the Romans were kings there."

From the standpoints of Vietnam, Brunei, and the Philippines, the South China Sea moves are a Chinese power grab. For the United States, the situation are not as clear-cut. Beijing's assertions, justified by a past presence, are not meaningfully different from claims the young United States made in 1784 about fishing rights east of Canada. The new nation based those rights on the historical presence of whalers out of New England harbors. If historical rights to water were once recognized for the United States, why shouldn't they be recognized today for China? Current rules, including the Law of the Sea (see Chapter 9), don't give a clear answer.

CHAPTER 1 NOTED THAT under Donald Trump, the White House, for political reasons, called the Persian Gulf the Arabian Gulf. The South China Sea is another example of how names for bodies of water can be freighted with politics.

Between the west coast of Japan and the east coast of China is an area of water—a really big lake or, to cartographers, a marginal sea—that maps usually label the Sea of Japan. South Korea wants these waters to be known as the East Sea, as the term Sea of Japan is a reminder of Japanese atrocities against Koreans, Chinese, Filipinos, and Malays. North Korea wants these same waters called the Eastern Sea of Korea, to emphasize the interest of Korean peoples.

Some nations, including Vietnam and the Philippines, object to the marginal sea due south of Hong Kong being known as the South China Sea. Why not some other name—perhaps, the Gulf of Hong Kong? Politically, using the name South China Sea lends credibility to Beijing's project of filling in artificial islands there. If the name were Sea of Vietnam or Gulf of the Kinh, China's island-building project would face stiffer headwinds.

The Atlantic Ocean is so named owing to a Greek phrase of antiquity for "the place where Atlantis is." The place where Atlantis is began at the Pillars of Hercules, now the Strait of Gibraltar. Imagine if, today, a dispute arose over what to call the Atlantic Ocean. Should the name honor the Old World or New, the south or the north, the white or the brown, legends or actuality? There would be no clear answer, any more than there is for the South China Sea.

AMERICA'S ABILITY TO PLACE formidable strike groups in the waters near China, while China cannot return the favor, is not without downsides for the United States. China's new land-based antiship missiles threaten US capital ships in a way no missile on US territory threatens any Chinese warship. China has engineered torpedoes specifically to sink supercarriers. No torpedo has ever struck a supercarrier, so what might happen is unknown. It's unlikely to be pretty.

A remarkable feature of the balance of power is this: Chinese missiles costing a relative trifle might smash a supercarrier worth billions of dollars, while China has no priceless vessel the United States could threaten as reprisal. As a result, in a crisis, the supercarriers might withdraw beyond the range of Chinese land-based missiles, leaving smaller ships without the aid of America's big sticks.

This has led to recent changes in US Navy thinking. One is to cut back on the service's corvette, a lightly armed vessel capable of unusually high speed and designed to keep sea lanes clear of piracy. Funds subtracted from the corvette program will be put into a new class of frigates possessing the type of firepower needed to fight warships.

Another change is that the marines will reduce tanks and heavy equipment that would be used in D-Day-style landings, while adding antiaircraft and deep-strike munitions. Antiship missiles will

be retrofitted onto vessels once intended solely for logistical support, such as the new *San Antonio* class of dock ships. (Dock ships
move close to an invasion to provide supplies and a place where
the wounded can be taken; *San Antonio* dock ships are the world's
best.) The current marine focus on urban fighting in failed states
will be replaced by preparation for great-power combat. Beijing
can hardly have failed to notice that the new emphases are aimed
squarely at China.

In 2018, Trump withdrew the United States from the
Intermediate-Range Nuclear Forces Treaty signed with Moscow
in 1987. Following Trump's lead, the Russian Federation withdrew.

An outgrowth of the 1980s nuclear-freeze movement, the treaty's primary language prevented NATO and the Warsaw Pact from
aiming intermediate-range nuclear missiles at each other. Eliminating these weapons was a win for humanity. A side title banned
land-based, conventional-warhead, intermediate-range missiles, the
type that threaten ships. Because at that time there was no naval
competition between the West and China, the treaty's side title
seemed to matter only to the United States and Russia. Washington
and Moscow signed the 1987 deal; Beijing did not.

Around 2010, China realized it could design a new generation
of land-based antiship missiles without violating any international
compacts. The best move would have been to get China to sign
the accord, forestalling an arms race in land-based antiship missiles.
Instead the United States dropped out of the Intermediate-Range
Nuclear Forces deal, in the process freeing the Russian Federation
from its promises. Now, if Moscow wants, battlefield nuclear-tipped
missiles can be returned to eastern Europe, while all nations may
develop advanced land-based antiship weaponry. The dissolution
of the 1987 accord is the sort of news that rarely draws notice in
today's media cycle yet signifies more than the gaffes and insults
dominating that cycle.

IF CHINESE LAND-BASED ANTISHIP missiles work (like so much
contemporary technology intended for water warfare, they've
never been tried in realistic conditions), this would represent both

a military and a political risk to America's magnificent super-carriers. The military risk is obvious. In theory the US fleet's layered defense of air-defense cruisers and automated cannon would shoot down any Chinese projectiles. If they did not, a relatively cheap weapon might sink a $5 billion vessel at the cost of up to five thousand lives, a supercarrier complement. Relatively low-cost antiship weapons now under development in several nations, including swarms of mini-missiles that might overwhelm point-blank defenses, may be cost-effective against big, expensive targets.

Mao often said he didn't care how many Chinese died in war because there would always be millions more. Even if that was a bluff, the Chinese military is accustomed to mass casualties, while the United States reacts to military losses with horror. For this reason alone, loss of a carrier would harm the United States much more than loss of a carrier would harm China. As regards super-carriers, for the United States these vessels exist partly to convey prestige: if one is sunk, the whole project would miscarry. Since no other nation possesses any vessel as expensive or important as a supercarrier, only the United States runs this blowback risk.

Supercarriers and nuclear weapons engage a special hazard. Because any use of nuclear weapons against a nation's territory would kill huge numbers, no sane leader could believe a limited nuclear exchange would not spiral out of control. But suppose a single nuclear warhead were fired at a supercarrier strike group in the open ocean. Warships would sink, including one of the most valuable ships in the world; no city would be damaged. The single-warhead nuclear strike against a US supercarrier would represent an outlandish gamble—but is perhaps the only first-use scenario that might allow an aggressor to obtain some concession from the United States without engaging the gears of doomsday.

Here's the scenario: China fires a single small nuclear warhead at a supercarrier strike group far from land. American vessels and their crews are obliterated, but civilians are safe. China tells Washington that if the United States yields regarding something important—perhaps, stay out of the way on Taiwan—Beijing would pay reparations and never take the same step again. Would the United States chose this option or choose general war?

Students of history know what's being described is an update on the Pearl Harbor attack. In late 1941, the Japanese war cabinet hoped that stunned by a sudden loss, the United States would agree to withdraw from the Pacific Rim in exchange for gestures from Japan. Obviously the plan was a total failure. But failed ideas have a way of recurring.

Cost and potential vulnerability may mean the day of the supercarrier soon will end. Wrage, the Annapolis professor, says, "Historically the top leadership of military organizations has not abandoned obsolete prestige weapons until compelled to do so by a calamity."

In all large organizations, whether government or corporate, wishing away problems is more common than is addressing them. On the eve of the Great War, analysts warned that a newfangled weapon, the seagoing submarine, imperiled the Royal Navy's beloved prestige weapon, the big-gun battleship. Rather than adjust to a new reality, some in the British admiralty hoped that gliding beneath the waves could be declared piracy so that captured submariners could be hanged as common criminals. Today's weapon that is beloved by American admirals—naval aviation off the wide-deck carrier—has never failed in combat. But it may be better to move on from supercarriers before they emulate the battleship.

WHILE AMERICAN AIRCRAFT CARRIERS are the best and China will soon enter this space, Russian aircraft carriers are a standing joke.

In 2016 the Russian Federation sent its sole carrier, a rustbucket called *Admiral Kuznetsov*, to participate in one of the many fruitless Syria campaigns.[5] The voyage of the *Kuznetsov* was a Monty Python routine. Smokeless propulsion is essential to military stealth—it's been decades since a US Navy warship emitted smoke. (Like smokeless gunpowder, smokeless propulsion makes you harder to spot, while not impeding your own view.) Sailing toward Syria, *Kuznetsov* belched tall columns of dark fumes from a low-grade fuel called mazut, which the Russian navy buys on the cheap, perhaps using internet coupons. The blackened pillar was visible for miles. No Western navy employs mazut: the baking soda that children use to propel toy boats would be superior. Tugboats accompanied *Admiral Kuznetsov* from Russia to the Mediterranean because the mazut propulsion system was so unreliable.

During operations, two of *Kuznetsov*'s jets crashed trying to return to the flight deck. The rest were waved off and flew on to airports, avoiding their own carrier. The ship broke down altogether in the English Channel on the way home. It was the first time a Russian aircraft carrier participated in combat, and *Kuznetsov* failed to do what American aircraft carriers had been doing for seventy-five years to that juncture.

Events such as this make it tempting to dismiss Russia as a maritime pretender. Moscow's fleet, however, is growing in response to reawakened Russian desire for great-power status. Early in the Cold War, there was competition between the United States and Soviet Union to build nuclear-powered surface vessels similar to battleships, armed with batteries of missiles rather than big cannon. Both sides mothballed such warships, which were of little use owing to inaccuracy of missiles of the time. Recently Moscow sent back to sea two of the old nuclear cruisers, refitted with digital electronics and precision-guided missiles. Imposing and all but decorated with a bend sinister, the ships make perfect backdrops for photo ops.

The super-submarine Hollywood invented for Moscow in the 1990 box-office smash *The Hunt for Red October* was far more impressive than the clanking, unreliable boats sailed by the actual Soviet Union of that year. In moviemaking terms, the *Red October*, captained by Sean Connery, was a *MacGuffin*-class submarine. By contrast Moscow's new *Yasen*-class submarine is all too real, quiet, and capable. It is possible the US–Russia naval tensions that seemed to conclude with the end of the Cold War will resume.

Japan's fleet is improving as well, through the addition of modern guided-missile destroyers and the commissioning, in 2017, of a helicopter carrier for antisubmarine warfare. In 2020, China tried to slip a submarine into Japanese territorial waters: the anti-submarine helicopters gave challenge. China wanted to know if an undersea intrusion would be detected. Japan wanted China to know it now has the equipment to sink Chinese visitors.

That encounter ended quietly; the next may not. Across the Pacific Rim, nations are aware that the blue age may be in jeopardy.

ALTHOUGH THE END OF the blue age could arrive through battle on the waters between the United States and China or Russia, these are not the most likely outcomes. Ocean combat seems more probable between China and Vietnam.

Because the West views the unhappy saga of the Vietnamese fight for independence as concluding with the 1975 American withdrawal, few remember China invaded Vietnam in 1979, triggering what one hopes will always be the final Indochina war. Leading up to the 1979 invasion, China had tried to dominate Vietnam for a millennium: bad feelings between the nations remain to the present day, while American–Vietnamese emotions have gone from frozen to warm. One measure of those feelings: a 2020 newspaper editorial denounced Chinese ambitions in the South China Sea while praising the United States as a force for good throughout the region. Where did the editorial appear? The *Hanoi Times*.

Through roughly the last decade, Vietnam has become prosperous, China has become assertive, and the offshore natural gas fields near Vietnam have become valuable. Though Vietnam spends about 2.3 percent of its GDP on defense, not an unusual figure—the global average is 2.1 percent, America spends 3.2 percent—Vietnam's economy is roaring at a recent gain of 7 percent annually, treble the output increase of the United States.[6] If a nation's economy gets bigger quickly, the same level of military expenditures buys a lot more. As regards Vietnam, much of the new purchasing power is disbursed to shipyards.

Twenty years ago, Vietnam had no navy; today, it possesses about thirty modern warships, all intended for use in the place Beijing calls the South China Sea. In 2019, Vietnamese frigates sounded battle stations as they warned Chinese warships away from a reef Hanoi claims, in the place Hanoi calls the East Sea. China withdrew, supposedly after a "go ahead, make my day" gauntlet was thrown.[7]

Though the Vietnamese national personality is sweet, a century and a quarter of resisting French, Japanese, American, and Chinese invaders hardened the mindset of the nation's military, which knows it overcame the world's strongest power and does not fear the world's next-strongest. And for all the sorrow America inflicted on the Kinh, don't be surprised if someday the US Navy fights to defend them.

VIETNAM'S SITUATION IS ALSO the situation for India—strong economic growth allows for a larger military without the defense-budget share increasing. Indian military expenditures have been stable at 2.4 percent of GDP, but GDP has been rising at 7 percent. Much of the new money goes to warships, which India is building more briskly than any nation other than China.

Once based on creaking obsolete vessels purchased from countries that no longer wanted them, India's navy has changed to state-of-the-art. It's not just that India now possesses a nuclear ballistic-missile submarine with the disturbing name *Slayer of Enemies*—a boat built at an Indian shipyard. New Delhi's polysyllabic *Visakhapatnam*-class stealth ship, scheduled to sail sometime in 2021, is expected to be the equal of American and Chinese vessels in its category. The ships' armaments—based on patents from or partnerships with British, French, Israeli, Russian, and US defense contractors—represents a greatest-hits of contemporary naval warfare.

The US Navy's decision to declare an Indo-Pacific Command reflects both the rise of India as a maritime power and US desire for a second level of containment of China: should the People's Liberation Army Navy break out of the South China Sea, it could be stopped at the Indian Ocean. Such "defense in depth" has been a favored concept in war colleges for generations. An aspect of this strategy is that the United States now supplies India and Australia with its latest land-based flying dreadnought, the large jet that can monitor sizable areas of ocean, then launch antiship and antisubmarine missiles. Beijing knows that placing these formidable weapons in the hands of America's regional allies makes the Indian Ocean a treacherous passage for Chinese warships.

In 2020 there was a short but violent ground clash along the China–India demarcation zone quaintly named the Line of Actual Control; both sides blamed the other. (There has never been formal negotiation to finalize the China–India border: and better to jaw-jaw than war-war, regardless of whether Churchill really said that.)[8] Following the 2020 clash, New Delhi showed displeasure by sending its aircraft carrier to patrol the South China Sea. If, after some dispute with the United States, Beijing showed displeasure by sending its aircraft carrier to patrol the approach to Long Island Sound, this might cause war fever. Also in 2020, India protested that the World Trade Organization favors China by ignoring its attempts to manipulate international currency values, while penalizing India for manipulation.

By population China is the world's leading state, India the world's second state: for number one and number two to shoot at each other has been alarmingly common through the centuries. Both China and India have fast-expanding trade, both have fast-expanding militaries, both eye the Indian Ocean as central to their expectations.

Nirmal Kumar Verma, a retired admiral and chief of naval staff for India from 2009 to 2012, closely follows the annual speeches of China's defense minister and political general secretary, attended by throngs dressed alike. "Not long ago," he says, "these speeches were cautious about foreign affairs, respectful toward the concerns of other nations. In recent years the language has become belligerent. China knows she has a powerful navy now. Will she be foolish enough to test the United States? Or might she test India?"

A primary difference between China and India, Verma thinks, is civilian rule: "In all successful nations, the military is subservient to civilians. This is one of the lessons of history—nations with civilian rule succeed, nations with military rule collapse. The British were so successful partly because their military was subservient to civilian governments. Britain left this concept in India, where the military accepts that it is subservient to elected officials."

In China there are only sham elections. The military is not restrained by civilians, it is the armed wing of the Communist Party. Should party leaders want to veer into what Karl Marx denounced as Bonapartism—military adventures for personal glory—neither elected officials, nor laws, nor public opinion would constrain Chinese armed forces.

Kathleen Walsh, a US Naval War College professor who specializes in China and India, notes, "From about 1990 to about 2010, China was liberalizing. Now it's a dictatorship. Dictatorships always fall apart, and are prone to lashing out as they do." If China lashes out, the place may be the Indian Ocean.

AS I WRITE THIS paragraph in 2020, the US Navy has 295 vessels in what it calls battle force, either steaming or able to cast off on short notice. (Even nuclear-powered ships *steam*—the reactors make steam. All but a few modern warships steam in one sense or another.) The figure included 5 aircraft carriers underway in various parts of the world and many "forward submarines" positioned in the straits and other sensitive maritime areas. The navy reveals specifics on the locations of surface ships; since the whole point of submarines is that you don't know where they are, secrecy is practiced regarding subs.

On that 2020 day, the 295 available warships exceeded the total for battle-force warships for all navies of the rest of the world combined. Is it enough?

On V-J (Victory over Japan) Day in 1945, the US Navy had about 1,300 ships. (These comparisons count major vessels, not individual landing craft or short-range patrol.) By the end of the Korean War, the navy was down to about 600 vessels; after the Vietnam War, to about 450. Taking office in 1981, Ronald Reagan listed among his primary goals a "600-ship navy" able to fight two all-out wars simultaneously, as the navy once did across the Pacific and Atlantic.

The 600-ship navy never quite happened, peaking at 594 in 1987, the year Reagan became an advocate of arms control. A 295-ship navy may seem small in comparison to Reagan's ambition. The battle force of 295 is large, however, compared with budget realities and firepower.

In today's dollars, the Reagan maritime buildup came in at $400 billion per year, more than twice the $170 billion the United States spent on its navy in 2020. A 2019 study conducted by Brown University found that recent American fighting in Afghanistan, Iraq, Pakistan, and Syria has cost $6.4 trillion in operations funds and future obligations to injured soldiers and aircrew.[9] Whether or not these actions were moral, or in the American national interest, it is incontestable the money was subtracted from social needs and from keeping the US military modernized—especially the navy, whose shipbuilding budgets lagged whenever Congress upped the ante in Iraq.

But that's water under the bridge, to use a wet metaphor—spending decisions involved in the occupations of Afghanistan and Iraq cannot be undone. Increasing naval expenditures to anything like the level of the Reagan buildup is out of the question. Even to sustain the navy's current spending may be a long shot. The 2020 US Navy budget worked out to $700 per American adult. That's plenty.

Debt-based transfer payments and debt-based tax cuts were already burdening the American future before the virus pandemic. All Pentagon line items are likely to diminish as the United States tries to recover from the Obama splurge of entitlement programs, then the Trump splurge of tax cuts for corporations and the rich, then the COVID-19 economic contraction, then the President Joe Biden identity-group splurge.

Via Social Security, Medicare, Medicaid, Obamacare, housing subsidies, cash assistance, food stamps, unemployment extensions, unemployment bonuses, forgiven loans, tax cuts for the middle class, and elimination of federal income taxes for the working class, the United States is more generous to average citizens than is commonly understood. Adjusting to current dollars, for population growth and for consumer prices, today's regular federal social programs generate transfer payments about four times as much, per year, per American adult, as did the programs of the New Deal.[10] Add the $5.3 trillion of debt incurred for several forms of COVID-19 assistance (cash to individuals, schools, hospitals, small businesses) during the 2020–2021 emergency—an extra $25,000 per American adult transferred.[11] During the 2020–2021 virus period, America knew many problems but was also the most generous the nation had ever been, the generosity secured by borrowing against the future.

In 2013 Senator John McCain, a former navy aviator and lifelong supporter of maritime assertiveness, called the notion that the navy would grow to more than 300 ships "a fantasy," for budget reasons. Since the late senator said those words, the United States has gone another $9 trillion into debt for average people, retirees, and immigrants, plus COVID-19 aid, plus tax cuts for Donald Trump's social set.

The United States has known for decades that retirement of the baby boomers would generate higher spending for Social Security, Medicare, and Medicaid and known for decades when the retirement wave would begin. The prudent action would have been to save. Instead American government borrowed without restraint to appease interest groups, reward political donors, cut taxes, and postpone painful choices. The result was that in 2020, trustees of the Social Security system reported $43 trillion in unfunded liabilities (genteelly called a shortfall) for pensions and health care for the ever-growing ranks of the aging.[12] These numbers suggest anything more than a 300-ship navy will be "a fantasy" indefinitely.

Philosophers long have supposed that ethical arguments might end war. In the United States and other nations, the burden of government debt has become an antiwar influence.

AT THE 2012 PRESIDENTIAL debate, Mitt Romney said the size of the navy, on that day 285 ships, was "unacceptable . . . I want to make sure we have [more] ships." Barack Obama replied that a reduced fleet was sufficient: after all, the army has "fewer horses and bayonets" than in the past. By 2016, Trump upped the ante and campaigned on wanting a 355-ship navy, a goal he repeated from the Oval Office but never made any attempt to obtain funding for.

Firepower allows today's smaller number of vessels to be more potent. Not just the awful world-ending might of the nuclear-missile submarine: conventional naval firepower has risen too. The Royal Navy shrank from eighty capital ships in 1815 to six today, and the current Royal Navy is deadlier than any of the past. A single contemporary US attack submarine, or a single US aircraft carrier, could sink the fleet Japan sailed toward Hawaii in 1941, and do so from a secure distance. A single modern US destroyer could sink every battle cruiser Germany sent to Jutland in 1916, and do so long before the dreadnoughts drew close enough to shoot back at the destroyer.

Decreased numbers packing greater firepower is a common thread across modern militaries. In the 1950s, the United States possessed thousands of heavy bombers, while Britain and the Soviet Union had hundreds. Today the Russian Federation has about 170 bombers, mostly antiquated piston-engine ugly duck-lings; the United States has about 160, all jets; the United Kingdom has none; China has about 30 jet bombers; no other nation in the world so much as flies a heavy bomber.

Though there are fewer heavy bombers, contemporary models and their ordinance are so much more effective that if you were, say, trying to defend Romanian oil refineries, which were a pri-ority aerial target for the United States in 1943, you'd face more danger from the current light force than was posed by the previous sizable force. The rule for warplanes—today's small numbers are more effective than yesterday's large numbers—obtains for fighting ships as well.

REDUCTION OF THE TOTAL of US Navy vessels equates to more time at sea per ship, since the size of the fleet may change but the size of the globe does not. More time at sea brings more risk of mistakes. In 2017 there were two terrible collisions in which US destroyers hit merchant ships, one crash near Tokyo and another in a packed sea-lane approach to the Strait of Malacca. The collisions killed seventeen American sailors.

That advanced warships fairly sagging under the weight of high-tech electronics would fail to notice gigantic merchant vessels moving along predictable courses seemed impossible. But ships collide more often than might be expected, even in an era when most have transponders and radar masts.

In 2010 a British attack submarine with the wonderful name *Astute* slammed into the Isle of Skye, home of some of the world's best whiskeys. State-of-the-art electronics aboard *Astute* failed to detect a 639-square-mile island. In 2015, another British attack submarine with an even better name, *Talent*, hit a Russian sub underneath the Arctic ice cap. Fortunately there were no casualties, but what did *Talent* think that other mammoth self-propelled object was, Nessie the sea serpent on holiday? In 2019, two immensely large cruise liners collided at a Mexican port, smashing glass and terrifying passengers (no one was harmed) after failing to notice each other—which seemed rather like walking around Colorado and failing to notice mountains.

Following the destroyer collisions, a navy report concluded the causes were "complacency, overconfidence, lack of procedural compliance . . . and lack of adherence to sound navigational practices."[13] Warships based at the US Navy facilities in Japan, closest to China, tend to be overworked and overdeployed. Both destroyers involved in the 2017 collisions were based in Japan. For the navy's shrinking force to project the same presence along the world's sea lanes, crews were spending too much time on duty while not getting enough rest; ships themselves, spending too many days steaming as opposed to refitting.

Time deployed is tiring for crews and leads to mental errors that rested crews don't make: warships need about the same maintenance as jets. In 2019, the supercarrier *Eisenhower* (the *Ike* to crews) was at sea for 161 days without a stop at port. The strike group of the supercarrier *Truman* was deployed for 295 consecutive days, stopping at port only for supplies, not for leave. At Norfolk, I watched refitting of the *Ike*. Hundreds of workers and machines were involved, in a scene reminiscent of construction of the Brooklyn Bridge. Keeping large, complicated ships utilized for long stretches far from home is an improbable feat.

Since the 2017 accidents the navy has monitored how many days each sailor has been on duty away from shore. But too much at-sea time continues, as only the United States, alone among maritime powers, attempts to be forward-deployed everywhere.

The five aircraft carriers the United States had underway as I wrote this section exceeded by five all aircraft carriers underway for other nations. This was a measure of the extraordinary sea power of the United States—but not sustainable at a time of rising national debt.

THE NEAR FUTURE MAY hold the replacement of some crewed naval vessels with autonomous ships designed to be small and stealthy. In 2018, the navy began experimenting with an autonomous little boat that hunts submarines.[14] That year, the first unmanned helicopter was deployed on a US Navy warship; because the space that would have been used for crew is given over to fuel, the unpiloted helicopter can fly farther and longer. That year the Naval Postgraduate School in California began to study "lightly manned" vessels that would have a few people aboard to make the decisions but would be small, flat, and low (for stealth), using the space other warships devote to crew for extra munitions.

Both technical research and budget numbers point toward a future fleet that has few big, expensive ships and lots of smallish boats, distributing force and risk. Small, nearly silent autonomous hunter-killer submarines seem likely to join the expensive crewed submarines built by Western navies. Many drones or remote-controlled vessels bearing missiles, torpedoes, and sea mines might be as effective as a few squadrons of traditional destroyers that cost a great deal and are crewed by more than three hundred people (that's the complement of the *McFaul*). American admirals intensely love naval aviation, which was the deciding factor against Japan in the Pacific, represents a technological and human-performance marvel, and, with jets soaring up off the carrier deck, provides a backdrop for dramatic footage. But drone fighters are likely to supplant Top Gun models.

Pilotless naval aircraft are in the development stage, including a pilotless tanker for refueling pilotless planes in flight.[15] Computer-flown planes will be cheaper and smaller, able to handle maneuvers no person could stand. Computer-flown small drone attack jets might not need a flattop-style aircraft carrier, splashing down in water to be retrieved by cranes the way biplanes were in the early years of naval aviation. Drones bearing antiship missiles could remain above contested areas for long periods, firing at the first sign of hostilities. The result might be a return to large-number navies like in the old days—but large numbers based on little ships with few if any people aboard, sailing underneath air wings without pilots.

PERHAPS YOU THINK, "I don't want the US Navy to be even more effective. I want fighting at sea to leave and never come back." Amen. More than one dream of the past has been realized; perhaps this dream will be, too.

For present generations, a world without war is too distant to represent a practical goal. Disincentives to war are more pragmatic. The strongest disincentive to war on the blue water—and, thereby, the best protection for trade that benefits nearly everyone on earth—is the strength, scope, and forward placement of American naval power.

Greg Baker, captain of the *Wasp*, summed matters this way: "Anywhere you go on the world's oceans, United States Navy ships are already there. We've been deployed since 1801, when the first *Enterprise* went to the shores of Tripoli, and we stay deployed, all the time, everywhere, come what may. Doing this is expensive for taxpayers and exhausting for crews. Because we do, there is peace and commerce, and those are"—he paused—"a lot better than the alternatives."

Until we meet again, here's wishing you a happy voyage home! (A lyric from "Anchors Aweigh.") Yet to the extent the blue age has been made possible by the invincibility of the US Navy, it's well to remember that all previous invincible navies have been overcome.

PART TWO

PEACE ON THE WATERS

5

MARLON BRANDO WOULD NOT
RECOGNIZE A MODERN PORT

THE WONDERFULLY NAMED CONTAINER SHIP *EVER LOADING* HAD a busy year in 2020. Newly built in Taiwan, at the sprawling shipyard of Kaohsiung—a city most in the West have never heard of, Kaohsiung has more influence on the global economy than Atlanta or Barcelona or Copenhagen—*Ever Loading* is owned by Evergreen Marine, a Taiwanese firm that is among the world's largest global trade consortiums.

All markings on *Ever Loading* are in English, and the vessel flies the flag of the United Kingdom. These steps reduce political tensions when the vessel calls at ports of the many nations that do not recognize Taiwan.

One month in 2020, *Ever Loading* steamed up and down the US West Coast, stopping at the California cities of Long Beach, Los Angeles, and Oakland and at Tacoma, Washington. It then crossed the vastness of the Pacific to Tokyo, continued on to Qingdao in Shandong Province of the People's Republic, a port of call where the Union Jack smoothed things over, even if the harbormaster knew the flag was of convenience.

For a century, Chinese patriots fought to regain control of Shandong from Germany and Japan and from gangster overlords. Today, Shandong is a bustling commercial jurisdiction, its Qingdao port a hub for the Maritime Silk Road initiative. A nodal hub, to be precise, in a blue-age economic sphere where nodal and intermodal carry the import that the terms iron ore and coal shovel once did.

Later, *Ever Loading* stopped at Ningbo, Xiamen, Kaohsiung, Hong Kong, and Yantian. Completing these calls the vessel headed east across the Pacific toward the Panama Canal. Reaching the Atlantic, *Ever Loading* turned north along the American coast, bound for the port of Saint John's in Newfoundland, in weeks to come, calling at Savanna, Georgia; Colón, Panama; and other places.

Through the course of 2020, *Ever Loading* transited the Pacific Ocean ten times, the equivalent of sailing the circumference of the earth four times. The ship was almost continuously in motion, docked only for quick-choreography loading and unloading of containers, fueling, and restocking the galley. Airlines make money when their planes are flying, not parked at a gate. International shipping firms make money when their ships are sailing. Broadly across the blue-age economy, to make money, it's got to be moving.

I encountered *Ever Loading* in the Port of Los Angeles, the largest trade facility of the United States. Here, the overstory of a metal forest stretches as far as the eye can see. Docked as a tourist attraction is the retired battleship *Iowa*, fastest big-gun vessel ever put to sea. Visitors pay twenty dollars a head to clamber up the corridors and ladders of the *Iowa*, squeezing through bulkhead doors with giant wheels for sealing off compartments taking water. Anyone showing an Iowa driver's license boards *Iowa* gratis.

My first impression of *Ever Loading* came as the vessel passed *Iowa* in a channel of the Los Angeles harbor. The warship disappeared from view, because the container liner is *way* bigger than the leading battleship of history's apex war. *Ever Loading* is the length of four football fields, much longer than *Iowa*, and substantially taller. As *Ever Loading* slipped by, you wouldn't know a battleship was there, which is a bit like the new Salesforce Tower in San Francisco being so enormous that from some angles the Transamerica Pyramid, which dominated the Fog City skyline for a generation, is eclipsed.

In the harbor channel *Ever Loading* barely seemed to be moving—an optical illusion created by large vessels. If you're ever out on the water near a harbor, compare the movement of pleasure boats, tugs, and ferries to gargantuan container ships, oil tankers, or ocean liners. Visual perception of speed is linked to how long an object needs to transit its own length. A cabin cruiser or shore-patrol boat passes through its own length in one or two seconds; *Ever Loading* requires thirty to forty seconds to pass through its own length. This makes the little boats appear to zoom along while the big vessels seem hardly to move, even if the big boys are making more knots.

Between *Ever Loading* and the battleship in the background, size was not the only comparison. Mobilized for war, *Iowa* had a crew of 2,900. The far larger *Ever Loading* has a crew of 23. Warship crews fulfill multiple tasks, including damage control. Modern commercial vessels, which travel along predictable paths and never go into harm's way, need people primarily to monitor systems, prepare meals, and administer first aid. Still, the distinction in size (*way* bigger) and crew (*way* smaller) was striking. Deck hands get around *Ever Loading* on bicycles, communicate with each other by radio because they often are far apart.

The punchline: *Ever Loading* carries eight thousand shipping containers, 140 times as many as *Ideal-X*, the vessel that, in 1956, became the first container liner.

FIFTY YEARS AGO, THE world's largest ports were New York City and Oakland; at number seven, Yokohama was the sole Asian harbor in the top ten. Today Los Angeles has taken over as the busiest harbor of the United States, though ranks just eighteenth globally. Arrivals and departures at the Port of Los Angeles have grown in spectacular fashion since the 1970s. But trade is growing even faster elsewhere. Today New York and Oakland are minor-league harbors while nine of the world's top ten ports are in Asia.

The mechanized overstory of the Port of Los Angeles is made up of cranes, some able to travel on mammoth rubber tires, others—ship-to-shore gantries—higher than the tallest building of a midsized town.

Cranes lining harbor quays are the distinguishing feature of coastal China, Singapore, Hong Kong, Rotterdam, Baltimore. Before the Port of Los Angeles began, in 1985, to prepare for the dawn of the blue age, Los Angeles possessed 16 harbor cranes. Today the Port of Los Angeles has 83 cranes. Before China began to liberalize, in about 1990, Shanghai possessed 6 harbor cranes. Today Shanghai is the world's busiest port, with 154 cranes.

Port Klang, near Kuala Lumpur, for many generations was a backwater. Since the World Trade Organization began pushing ocean globalization, Kuala Lumpur, on the Strait of Malacca and home of the soaring Petronas Towers, has become more important to the international economy than Dallas or Cairo. Port Klang has 60 quay cranes; 8 cranes that move on large rubber wheels; 5 that move via railroad track; and a Terex harbor crane—dockworkers call this a T-Rex—that is a status symbol, owing to futuristic appearance. In 2019 a Japanese logistics firm, Sankyu, received the contract to expand Port Klang still further—one of the few blue-age Asia ocean infrastructure projects not won by China. More cranes are on order.

In the days of wooden sailing ships, the sort of cargoes loading in a place like Port Klang were small casks of luxury items. By 2018, nearly all of Port Klang's trade was not in luxuries for aristocrats but consumer products for ordinary people in Europe and North America.

In large ports are terminals leased by trading consortiums as tenants, roughly in the way that airlines lease gates at airports. Nippon Yusen, a subsidiary of Mitsubishi, leases a terminal at the Port of Los Angeles. There Chinese-made cranes lift containers out of British-flagged ships arriving from South Korea for processing by a Japanese company that sells to California consumers. This outcome was not planned. Almost everyone is better off because it happened.

Tall harbor cranes both symbolize global trade and are themselves an aspect of globalization. A generation ago, no one in China knew how to build gantry cranes. Today the world's best come from the Middle Kingdom, which not only has perfected the efficient harbor crane but also lays down specialized vessels for transporting finished units across the world atop the waves.

All of Los Angeles's cranes were delivered, prefabricated, by ship from China. In 2019, traffic around the waterways of Seattle came to a halt as thousands watched the engineering vessel *Zhen Hua 33* deliver four towering gantries to the Port of Tacoma. Arriving were the latest thing: "super post-Panamax cranes," capable of servicing next-generation container vessels, the kind with double the displacement of an American supercarrier.

After completing the transport to Tacoma, *Zhen Hua 33* returned to China to pick up cranes ordered by the Port of Felixstowe, a busy English trading city in Suffolk. Then the vessel sailed back to China, essentially completing a circumnavigation, to take on cranes for delivery to the fast-growing Port of Melbourne. Lately Australia has been signing anti-China defensive alliances with several nations of the Pacific Rim. But business is business.

Built in Nantong, *Zhen Hua 33* is a semisubmersible, able to dip low into the water to come up underneath and recover a crippled ship. Extra-large ballast tanks allow that trick and compensate for the high center of gravity of oversized cargo such as gantry cranes or skyway components.

Following the call at Melbourne, *Zhen Hua 33* steamed to Zhongshan Shipyard near Hong Kong to load an entire metal bridge manufactured to the specifications of the Swedish company renovating Slussen, a transportation nexus at the center of Stockholm. *Zhen Hua 33* carried the bridge 12,600 miles, through the Suez Canal, up the English Channel, on a voyage that took nearly two months. Because of the top-heavy load, the semisubmersible had to anchor off Spain for a spell, waiting out rough weather that is common on the windward coast of France. Contemporary international economics are such that it was cheaper for Stockholm to order a bridge custom-built in China, then ship the product

12,600 miles through ocean squalls, than to have construction done locally by Swedish steelworkers.

High-value wages were transferred from Sweden to Hong Kong in the process, while Stockholm residents saved money. Which is better—keep the wages local, which would reduce the Stockholm standard of living via higher prices and infrastructure taxes, or keep local prices and taxes low while surrendering some paychecks to a distant factory? This question comes up regularly in globalized economics. In the United States and Europe, consumers and tax-payers always say, "Keep prices low." They don't sometimes say this; they *always* say it. Then they complain about wages going overseas.

If you would like to hire *Zhen Hua 33* to move very heavy objects a long distance in crashing waves, fax your signature to Shanghai Zhenhua Shipping at your earliest convenience, because since its launch in 2017, the dance card of this consummate blue-age vessel has been full.[1]

MORE AND TALLER CRANES, more and larger container vessels—these add up to more trade. Until about 1985 the Port of Los Angeles was a drowsy harbor, arrivals and departures few. No trains served the port, because there wasn't much to carry.

In the early 1980s Japan was expanding its presence on the global economic scene. Tom Bradley, mayor of Los Angeles and a farsighted politician, sought to make his city a destination for international waterborne commerce. Bradley wanted to add a countercyclical business to Southern California's reliance on Hollywood and aero-space, and knew California-to-Asia-and-back could be part of the American future. The mayor understood this before trade with China was a consideration—then, China was a closed society with an underperforming economy. But Japan, South Korea, Singapore, Malaysia, and Indonesia beckoned. Bradley committed the city to a major expansion of the Los Angeles harbor.

Many thought the project a boondoggle. Bradley lost his 1986 race for governor in part because Republicans mocked the port expansion as a bridge to nowhere. Construction nevertheless went ahead. Eight million tons of rock were moved to create landfill for piers, roadways, and railheads. Container commerce is measured in TEUs—(twenty-foot equivalent units), roughly the size and shape of the box in the trailer part of a tractor-trailer rig. By 1994, the Port of Los Angeles was handling 900,000 TEUs per year. This volume was viewed as extraordinary success and vindication for Bradley.

Few thought the numbers could get higher. By 2000, the Port of Los Angeles was handling 4.8 million TEUs per year—fivefold the level that had defined success a short time before. In 2018, the port was receiving or sending 9.4 million TEUs, ten times as much as in 1994. A spectacular rise, happening with little public notice. So many tractor-trailer trucks arrived at or departed from the Port of Los Angeles that a new freeway had to be paved just to accommodate them.

In progress now are initiatives to make the Port of Los Angeles significantly bigger while able to move goods faster. Satellite-relayed transponders that allow merchant ships to report location, course, and speed also allow customers to know how many hours the vessels bearing their precious cargoes are moored while loading or unloading. The harbor terminal business is highly competitive: having reached the top in the United States, the Port of Los Angeles does not intend to relinquish that crown. Staying on top requires speeding up even more.

AMONG THE DISTINCTIVE ASPECTS of modern Southern California geography is the Alameda Corridor, twenty miles of rail lines that join the Port of Los Angeles, and a companion port in nearby Long Beach, to a national rail-lines switching center. Surely distinctive when viewed from space, much of the Alameda Corridor is not seen by Angelinos, because it is below-grade, effectively underground. Opened in 2002 as a child of international trade, by 2006 the Alameda Corridor carried 13,889 trains—a train every thirty-seven minutes, round the clock. The box cars and flatbeds were laden with goods and materials arriving or departing by ocean.

Putting the Alameda Corridor below-grade was an expensive proposition. Depressing much of the rights-of-way into the ground reduces noise and risk from traffic's not stopping at grade crossings, since many roads go over the tracks via bridges that appear to drivers as just more road. The effect is jarring—"Wait, did we just pass over a ditch with a giant train in it?"

Removing the trains from easy view also was political. Surveys told managers of the Port of Los Angeles that community groups associate railroads with environment harm—though locomotives built in the last decade emit less pollution and less greenhouse gas per ton-mile than do diesel trucks. The Alameda Corridor track system lets in only the new low-emission locomotives, a clean-tech advance many people are unaware of. Notably, the first iteration of low-emission locomotives was designed and manufactured in Pennsylvania, by General Electric, under contract to a Chinese railroad.[2] That a heavy industrial product was built in the Rust Belt for sale to China at a nice markup is the kind of information that seemingly cannot cross America's cable-news shouting barrier.

Southern California has the nation's strictest emission controls, resulting in big declines of smog, yet also has a boom economy. That a highly populous region attained clean air while the local economy flourished is among indicators the world could cut greenhouse gases, an air-pollution problem, without harming GDP growth.

Controls initially placed on cars and electricity generation in Southern California are now applied to the port, which no longer allows trucks with dirty-diesel power trains. Nearly every internal combustion engine in the Port of Los Angeles is being swapped out for clean-diesel motors that use low-sulfur fuel. By 2035, the state of California will ban diesel, in favor of zero-emission trucks running on batteries. The port hopes to reach the standard of electric-only trucks before 2035, which would be great PR. Soon the port also will allow only zero-emission electric tractors for shuttling cargo around the docks, a role called drayage from the days this task fell to dray horses.

The next round of renovations will see the Port of Los Angeles become fully intermodal, meaning the big boxes that carry the world's trade can shift seamlessly among ships, trains, trucks, and short-range devices such as drayage tractors. Most of the world's big ports are going intermodal to keep pace with rising global commerce.

THE CLASSIC FLICK *On the Waterfront*, released 1954, depicts a dockside reality in which brawny workers lift shipping cases one by one while small cranes use slings to pull individual items of cargo up from deep within tramp steamers. Marlon Brando plays the strapping longshoreman Terry Malloy who, as movie buffs know, coulda been a contenda. Malloy gets sucked into mob corruption in a script based on actual waterfront racketeering at Hoboken, New Jersey.[3] In one scene, stevedores deliberately mishandle a case of scotch so the slats will crack, the case will be logged as spoiled, and each man can take home a bottle. Other sleaze is much more serious.

The harbor style the movie depicts, called break-bulk handling, was the style of cargo ports for centuries—and, in the current generation, has nearly vanished. Today's ports use the much larger gantry cranes to lift sealed containers that attained the "twenty-foot equivalent" name from their size. No longshoreman is strong enough to hoist a TEU box. Rather than come from the hold of a ship, as in Brando's movie, the boxes have been strapped to the deck. The modern container liner looks like a gigantic moving collection of shoeboxes with a bow at the front and a bridge jutting up toward the back (so the skipper and XO can see the length of the vessel). Thousands of TEU boxes strapped to the deck is efficient—less time to load and unload.

The rough-edged stevedores of *On the Waterfront* have been replaced by skilled workers, such as crane operators who make up to $300,000 per year at Los Angeles. Injured backs and knees no longer are common, nor deaths. The economist Marc Levinson notes the port of Marseilles averaged five longshoremen per year killed by fallings crates in the 1950s; today, handling greater volumes of cargo, the port is safer. The same phenomenon—more tons, fewer injuries—applies to practically all of the world's harbor terminals.

In a far corner of the Port of Los Angeles is an old frontage of antiquated slings and break-bulk dollies. No container vessels park there. Why isn't this area modernized? Because the Port of Los Angeles rents out the pier to movie and television producers wanting to shoot dockside scenes that correspond to what producers think docks are like, from the days of *On the Waterfront* or the 2003 season of *The Wire*.[4] In 2017, the Netflix series *Iron Fist* depicted a superhero battle at a present-day New York City port where there were small shipping crates in stacks, slings, break-bulk equipment, conveyor belts, and plenty of dry-ice mist. Ports like this now exist only in the imagination of screenwriters, or perhaps one should say, in the lack of imagination of screenwriters.

More representative is Pier 400 at the Port of Los Angeles, where the gantries have operators but where freight handling—the drayage—is automated. Boxes are shuttled around by robot things called automated straddle carriers. Pier 400 is the cleanest and best organized at the harbor, since the robot things never take breaks, laboring only for recharging and software updates. Mischievously they work through the night, warning lights flashing, while the rest of the port slumbers, placing each box into the ideal position for quick transfer to or from assigned truck or train.

Auto straddles are not a hit with labor organizers. On the other hand, during the 1950s there were about 400,000 port workers in the New York City area, and now there are only a few hundred, because frequent strikes in New York and New Jersey forced shippers to other ports while encouraging terminal operators to switch to machines (substitute capital for labor, in econ-theory terms). Los Angeles unions know this story and don't want the City of Angels to drive away business like New York–New Jersey did.

Because the Golden State is associated with celebrities and high tech, we forget that unions, trucks, and trains are essential to the economy of the LA basin. Labor leaders, who in California tend to be well informed and sophisticated, agreed to allow some auto straddles on the Los Angeles docks because the increase in trade associated with mechanized efficiency would keep the total number of dockworkers at the Port of Los Angeles about the same while boosting wages and benefits. So far these things have happened.

Goods arriving at the port are transshipped to nearly all congressional districts. About two-thirds of goods arriving in California end up east of the Rockies. It takes two weeks for a container liner to sail from Shanghai to Los Angeles, almost a month to sail from Shanghai to Baltimore via the Panama Canal. This difference can make it attractive to unload at the Los Angeles then put the boxes onto trains.

Much of LA's city and county government is financed by fees generated by the Los Angeles port and its sister in Long Beach. These two ports account for about 1.4 million of California's 18 million jobs and generate about $400 billion in economic activity each year, more than the GDP of Denmark. Everybody knows Denmark exists. Many Californians don't know about the big ports of Southern California.

GENE SEROKA, DIRECTOR OF the Port of Los Angeles, has lived his professional life in the blue age, working at harbors in Dubai, Jakarta, and Shanghai, where he was among the first Western executives to reside in China during the liberalization overseen by Deng Xiaoping. "Walmart is the world's largest corporation and the shelves at its stores are always stocked," Seroka says. "That's not magic; that is a leading success of international trade."

A lifelong Democrat whose father was a Teamster, Seroka says his blood boiled when Bernie Sanders came to the Port of Los Angeles and employed the quays, thick with foreign-flagged ships, as backdrop for a 2016 campaign speech in which the Vermont senator declared, "Free trade ships our jobs overseas." In other campaign appearances, Sanders said, "Free trade hurts the American worker."

Surely many voters believe free trade hurts American workers. As candidates for president in 2016 and again in 2020, Sanders and Donald Trump loudly pushed that view, which is flat-earth thinking.

Sanders's and Trump's minds seemed stuck in the 1970s, when Detroit was losing sales to Toyota, Honda, and the marque then called Datsun. On the 2020 campaign trial, Sanders complained that importation of cars from such companies was bad for American workers—without noting that today many vehicles sold in the United States by Toyota, Honda, BMW, Volkswagen, and the company now called Nissan are built in American factories by American workers. Today not only are foreign-marque cars manufactured in the United States, this occurs at factories that pay the same as or better than United Auto Workers wages: while Kia designs its autos in California, Toyota has a headquarters in Texas, and Honda has a headquarters in California.

On the campaign trail in 2016, Trump complained about cars "pouring in" from Japan—which was an economic problem for the United States in the 1970s and 1980s but no longer is.[5] The US Big Three lost market share to Japan in the 1970s not owing to mercantilist conspiracies but because their products were inferior to imports. The issue has been remedied, with Detroit cars and trucks often highly ranked for quality by consumer organizations.

Car carriers I watched dock at the Port of Los Angeles are sleek Raymond Loewy designs compared with unwieldy container vessels. But the leading imports arriving at the port are not vehicles, rather, furniture, manufacturing parts, toys, clothing, and building supplies. There are radiation detectors around the harbor to guard against terrorist plots. Sometimes they are triggered by ceramic tiles that are naturally radioactive, and imported ceramic tiles are in high demand. Would it somehow be better if Americans were barred from purchasing imported tiles?

That two important political leaders, Trump and Sanders, think it's still the 1970s in the way trade operates says a lot more about them than about the global economy.

BESIDES BEING PASSÉ, SANDERS'S "trade hurts workers" is not factually true. During the period international waterborne trade has grown, job totals and living standards have increased in nearly every nation. American and Europeans tend to think of trade as a source of low-cost electronics, but the decline of poverty in Asia, India, and parts of Africa is the signature achievement of liberalized trade.

When Bernie Sanders was a child, 60 percent of humanity lived in extreme poverty, according to the World Bank definition. By the time he stood on the Los Angeles pier to denounce free trade, only 10 percent of the human family was chronically impoverished—despite that family's trebling during Sanders's lifetime.

Marxism says free trade causes poverty: actual experience shows free trade reduces poverty. The academic extreme left and politicized far right both prefer theory to actual experience. That, on trade, from the left Sanders invoked Marxist theory while ignoring actual experience was just as bad as Trump, from the right, invoking nativist theory over actual experience. (Trump said immigrants are awful, yet the more immigrants the United States admits, the stronger the United States becomes.) Mental blocks of left and right being as they may, this actual-experience rule obtains—in the twenty-first century, every place you find a busy port, you find the lives of average people improving.

But aha, you note, Sanders wasn't talking about average people around the globe; he referred to American workers. Does free trade harm their prospects?

Numbers say no. The blue age has seen urban revivals of Buffalo, Cincinnati, Cleveland, Columbus, Detroit, Pittsburgh, and other old industrial foci, this having been accompanied by the rise of median household income and per-capita buying power. The blue age coincides with the record low unemployment that prevailed from 2014 till the virus emergency of 2020. Since the World Trade Organization was founded, the United States has consistently led the West in job creation. If trade is hurting the American worker, labor markets have a funny way of showing this.

Free trade by ocean improves the lives of large numbers of Americans by holding down consumer prices: in adjusted dollars, most retail goods now cost less than a quarter century ago. These lower prices are easily taken for granted—so use your time machine to visit the 1970s, when there was something bordering on general panic regarding the steep rise of retail prices. There is also the price-quality curve, easily overlooked. The price of the typical new American car or light truck has risen just 5 percent since 1995. This typical new car includes antilock brakes, traction control, seatbelt pretensioners (a little-known safety feature more important than airbags), improved crash resistance, more horsepower, higher MPG, far lower air emissions, better audio, brighter headlights, lengthened service intervals and longer life till replacement needed. Today's new car is a dramatically better product than the new car of a quarter century ago—yet costs just 5 percent more.[6] Safer, cleaner, affordable cars did not come about by the waving of a wand. Without competition pressure from Germany, Japan, South Korea, and Sweden, this improvement might not have happened.

While helping many via lower prices, free trade by ocean harms the lives of relatively few. Had imports been restricted, some US industries, for example, manufacturing of home appliances and farm machinery, would not have contracted.

But in most cases where high-wage hourly jobs have been lost, market forces and innovation, not trade, are the reason. For example, papermaking, dwindling in working-class areas of Ohio, Maine, West Virginia, and Wisconsin, is the victim of a customer-driven switch from newsprint to digital, not of international trade.[7] Should the smartphone edition of the *New Yorker* be banned? That would raise demand for domestic production of glossy stock. The fancy-college graduates who produce the digital *New Yorker*, and deliver themselves of outrage about the decline of manufacturing jobs, would be even more outraged if Congress prohibited their product, though their product is poison for working-class papermaking wages.

To believe free trade is a hobgoblin, one must think the United States would be better off going backward fifty years—when standards of living were lower for almost everyone, pollution was far worse, and US GDP per capita, adjusted for inflated, was less than half of today's.[8]

But politics and punditry demand boogeymen. For centuries depicted as the Oriental enigma, China fills the scapegoat role nicely. Take a gander at the Chinese Exclusion Act, passed by Congress in 1882, or its predecessor, the Page Act of 1875: both show bigotry against the Chinese is entrenched in American politics. In today's variant, Trump, Sanders, and many others speak as though the United States has become hooked on Chinese goods. Don't you mean hooked on Canadian and Mexican goods? Imports from Canada and Mexico exceed those from China. But Chinese dragons make better boogeymen than do Canadian moose.

Columnists and political campaign consultants speak as though China has stolen the international business realm from the United States. China holds 13 percent of the global trade market; America holds 11 percent; then again, China has four times as many people as the United States has. Per capita, America does better at international trade than China.

The two major areas with rising consumer costs in the United States, health care and education, are not linked to international commerce. The economics writer Jim Tankersley notes in his compelling 2020 book, *The Riches of This Land*, that trends since the outset of globalized trade gave middle-class Americans "cheaper consumer goods, more access to entertainment and communication, a better variety of seasonal products . . . [while] it got harder for them to send a kid to college." This statement is inarguable—but college, like health care, is a domestic industry not affected by international trade. Elimination of globalization would not reduce education or hospital costs, only cause other prices to rise too.

Trump, Sanders, and their like correctly say the American middle class has become smaller during the period of rising international trade; incorrectly assert this is bad. The American middle class is shrinking because most who exit are ascending toward the upper middle.[9] For two generations, many more leaving the middle class have gone upward economically than downward, suggesting the phrase "shrinking middle class" should be celebrated.*

Every US generation since the 1930s has been better off than the generation before, and this remains true today. That people *think* certain things about class warfare and economics is a political reality, but does not make what is thought true.

HAVING SEEN FIRSTHAND HOW blue-age ports and the mega-ships that ply them changed China and Indonesia for the better, Gene Seroka is firm in his belief that liberal trade is good for the Americas and Europe. He harks back to a recent alarm quickly forgotten—the 1980s fear that imports from Japan would devastate the US economy.

The bestselling nonfiction book of 1979, *Japan As Number 1*, declared the land of the Rising Sun soon would have the world's largest GDP and would dominate science and engineering. Through the presidencies of Ronald Reagan, the elder George Bush, and much of the Bill Clinton administration, pundits and economic consultancies predicted the Nipponese economic juggernaut would smash the United States. What happened? The US GDP is now four times the size of Japan's, the American job market is far more vibrant, and Japan's GDP growth has trailed America's for twenty-five years. As regards the top colleges essential to global economics, America has a profound edge over Japan. The United States continues to lead the world in important pursuits—inventions, hard science, technology, startup firms, music, art, and engineering—while dominating the Nobel Prizes for

---

* Details on the middle-class economic situation are in my book *It's Better Than It Looks* (PublicAffairs, 2018). Short version: Americans *think* the middle is losing ground, yet a 2014 Brookings Institution study found that through the current generation, middle-class economic power rose 36 percent. Americans who *think* vaccines are bad for your health don't hesitate to supersize an order of french fries.

science. In retrospect the book should have been titled *Japan As Number 3*.

"During the 1980s everybody was afraid of Japan taking over," Seroka says. "Instead we found ways to do business with Tokyo, both nations improved, and America lost no ground. We should be trying the same with China. Beijing doesn't play by the rules, and not just regarding intellectual property. But we should be working out the problems that we have with China, instead of blustering. In the end both nations will be better off."

Blustering has risen in popularity. Seroka reports that during the Obama administration, he had regular contact with top officials of the Treasury and Commerce Departments and the Office of the United States Trade Representative, a small but influential agency. During the Trump term, Seroka never reached any top trade officer in Washington—even though, as director of the Port of Los Angeles, he administers America's most important engine of international commerce.

Seroka thinks the problem ran deep: Trump and the people around him either didn't understand that trade is good for America or, more telling, didn't want to understand. A Trump confidant named Peter Navarro, from 2017 to 2021 the personal adviser to the president of the United States on China, cannot speak Chinese. Does anyone suppose Xi Jinping's personal adviser on the United States cannot speak English? Seroka, who holds Navarro in low esteem, notes, "He said China is just about to take over the world. Well, two hundred years ago Napoléon said the same thing."

But Trump liked it when the Navarro told him China was about to take over the world—that was what the forty-fifth president wanted to hear. So Trump and those around him covered their ears against evidence from the Port of Los Angeles, where China, Japan, South Korea, Taiwan, the Netherlands, Malaysia, France (whose CMA CGM is among the leading operators of container vessels), and Denmark (whose Maersk is the world's largest shipping concern) are more or less cooperating to make all nations better. In office, Trump liked to say China paid the tariffs he imposed, though in every case those tariffs were paid by American consumers, as higher prices.

Trump covered his ears against anyone who tried to tell him his statements about trade and tariffs were factually wrong, just as Sanders covered his ears against evidence his statement that free trade is "a race to the bottom" is factually wrong. Recent elections and media politics have shown that what people want to hear is significantly more powerful than what the late Swedish analyst Hans Rosling called *factfulness*.

THE DOCKS HAVE CHANGED so much since 1954 that Terry Malloy wouldn't know what he was looking at. Will they change again in ways that would baffle today's port workers?

There is a possibility waterborne trade will decline if additive manufacturing—3D printing—renders practical the generation of products near or even at the point of use. In that case there would be less need for shipping finished items, though bulk transport of raw materials still would be required. Large amounts of 3D printing in homes, schools, and offices sounds far-fetched—seriously, the gym teacher makes the soccer ball by pressing a button at her desk? But when the expensive, constantly malfunctioning Xerox 914 went on sale in 1959, the idea that cheap and reliable photocopiers would become ubiquitous was far-fetched.

Supposing manufacturing will matter for many generations, ocean trade will matter for many generations: why this is good is the subject of the next chapter. Unless we disagreeable human beings foul everything up, which will be the subject of the final chapter.

FINISHING THIS CHAPTER I checked the position of *Ever Loading*, reported by its AIS, the airliner-style transponders used by most commercial vessels. *Ever Loading* was off the Mexican state of Oaxaca, calling for permission to approach the western entrance to the Panama Canal.

Ever Loading had multinational funding, multinational paperwork and a multinational complement. As the writer Rose George has noted, aboard large commercial vessels of the blue age, a high fraction of captains are Irish, Scottish, or Dutch by birth, many XOs and engine-room officers are Filipino, many deck hands Pakistani or Ukrainian.

As *Ever Loading* asked for a slot in the Panama Canal queue, the XO and the Panamanian harbormaster conversed in English. Like air traffic control in all nations, commercial ship communication in all nations is conducted in English—though Modern Standard Mandarin increasingly is heard on the seas.

6

FROM IDEAL-X TO THE MEGAMAX

FOUNDED ABOUT TWO THOUSAND YEARS AGO BY THE BELGAE of Gaul, font of the modern word *Belgians*, Paris hosts 2.5 million people. Founded at least six centuries ago by the Lenape, New York City has 8.3 million residents. Founded by the Romans, London has 9 million residents. All these great metropolises pale before the capital of the blue-age world—Shenzhen, China.

Shenzhen did not exist until 1979 and already has 13 million residents, more than London, New York City, or Paris. The largest share of those in Shenzhen are engaged in some aspect of water-borne trade.

Within living memory, Shenzhen was a provincial village in the shadow of Hong Kong. During the late 1970s preliminary phase of Chinese liberalization, the Shenzhen area received permission to use free choice rather than dictatorship: the result was a place the size and importance of New York City raised up in a single generation. Thousands of schools and restaurants, dozens of hospitals, millions of dwellings—the seasonal population of Shenzhen can swell to 20 million—assembled with dizzying speed by a Chinese system that, when held back by central planning, could not grow rice; when set free, required just weeks to erect a skyscraper.[1]

In the offices and academic buildings of Shenzhen are small armies of engineers and coders, for their city is known as the Silicon Valley of China. The tech giant Huawei is based in Shenzhen; Ping An Finance Center, world's fourth-tallest building, towers over Shenzhen. Between city center and Hong Kong are Shenzhen's docks, which a generation ago were just cadastral maps and now are the world's third-busiest port, outpacing any harbor in Europe or North America. In 2018, the Port of Shenzhen, a jungle of cranes, roads, and rail lines, including sky-scraping post-Panamax gantries, zero-emission electric cranes, and the latest dual-hoist tandem-lift models, dispatched 28 million TEUs, which was three times the 2018 figure for the Port of Los Angeles.

Twenty-eight million large container boxes can be hard to visualize. Suffice to say this number works out to more goods than Antwerp, Hamburg, Hong Kong, Los Angeles, Rotterdam, Shanghai, Singapore, and Tokyo *combined* handled in the year 1990, just before the World Trade Organization. Ten container vessels per day departed Shenzhen in 2019, almost all of them bigger and more burdened than the largest commercial ships of 1990. There are 31 million seconds in a year. Through 2018, the Port of Shenzhen shipped a big, heavy boxful of goods *almost every second*, day and night.[2]

HISTORY SHOWS THERE HAVE been nations focused on trade, prominently the Republic of the Seven United Netherlands of the seventeenth century, when the ruthless Dutch East India Company was essentially the government of the country. Today there is an entire region focused on trade. The Pacific Rim has become a waterworld. Half of the human family lives in the water-focused society of the Indo-Pacific. The West would do well to regard this more closely.

Shanghai, Singapore, Shenzhen, Ningbo-Zhoushan, and Guangzhou of China; Busan of South Korea; Hong Kong, Qingdao, and Tianjin of China—nine of the world's top ten ports—are in the Pacific Rim waterworld, with Jebel Ali of Dubai the sole top-ten port that is not Asian. Each port in this paragraph handles at least five times the trade volume that passed through the largest port, New York City during the *On the Waterfront* period.

Trade figures have risen much faster than population growth in many nations. In 1971, as Japan completed its recovery from war, Japanese ports shipped 24,000 containers; by 2014 the figure was 5.3 million containers, or 221 times the 1971 number. Singapore's exports rose by about 75-fold in the period from 1990 to 2014. In 1971, China was shipping almost nothing to other nations and, by 2014, was exporting 36 million containers, or 1,500 times as much as Japan a single generation prior.

The trend of ever-more commerce by water has been in progress through much of modernity. Before central heating, fur was highly desired in the English and Nordic parts of Europe: intent to develop fur trade with North America, replacing fur trade with Russia became a primary element in British, Dutch, and French seventeenth-century excursions to the New World. To this day the Seal of New York City is emblazed with beavers, representing the furs sought. Paul Kennedy has noted that in the year 1615, about twenty-five tons of tobacco moved by sea worldwide; by 1715 it was 19,000 tons, approaching a thousandfold increase. Though stone and gravel roads were being built in the period, no land commerce rose at such a rate.

Flash-forward close to now, and the pace of increase in waterborne trade accelerates. In 1956, the vessel named *Ideal-X* became the first oceangoing ship to carry modern shipping containers, moving a small test batch to Houston. Flash-forward to April 2020, at a South Korean shipyard, when a bottle of champagne crashed against the bow of *HMM Algeciras*, the first megamax—the biggest freighter that, beam and draft maximized down to the meter, can transit the enlarged Suez Canal.

Algeciras is a port city in Andalusia, from which many antiquarian battles for control of the Mediterranean were staged. Globalization is symbolized by the placing of this name on a container ship built in Geoje, South Korea, owned by Hyundai, and

optimized for the ports of Europe. *Algeciras* carries 24,000 containers—more than four hundred times the cargo of *Ideal-X*. Eleven
megamax sisters of *Algeciras* were launched in 2020.

The Belt and Road Initiative, a trillion-dollar effort by China
to improve the public-works aspect of commerce in Africa, Central
Asia, and the Indian Ocean basin, is promoted as intermodal—
suitable for trucks, planes, trains. But nearly all the Belt and Road
Initiative will happen on water, putting Beijing at the helm of
modern infrastructure in much of the world.

THE NEW YORK-NEW JERSEY harbor complex that gave rise to the
agency that built the Twin Towers has dropped to twenty-third-
ranked global port, trailing Laem Chabang of Thailand. American
trading activity has not declined—it's just that other harbors are up
so much more. In 2019 the Port of Rotterdam, largest maritime facility in the European Union, handled a record 517 million tons of
cargo, which is the weight of 1,416 Empire State Buildings. Nearly
four Empire State Buildings per day moved through Rotterdam's
harbor! Yet Rotterdam still trails busier ports in the Pacific Rim
Waterworld.

Preparing for so much in motion in so many places has meant
infrastructure projects with high import but low public profile.
Dredging of harbor channels has been ongoing for hundreds of
years, as silt flowing down toward the oceans must be removed.
Today the focus of dredging is to open ports to larger ships. About
$2 billion was spent recently dredging New York harbor to oblige
deep-draft liners. The state of Virginia is spending $350 million
to dredge the port complex at Hampton Roads along Chesapeake Bay—long ago named Hampton *Roads* because natural
formations offer roadsteads to weary sailors. Dredged ports will
accommodate both large container liners and the unusual buoy-
ant-skyscraper vessels that install offshore wind turbines. The
turbine-installation vessels must be able both to jack themselves up
out of the water and to clear the seabed where the turbine shafts
will be pounded into rock.

The Bayonne Bridge connecting New Jersey and Staten Island was raised during the 2010s so new *Panamax*-class container boats could pass under. In 2017, *CMA CGM Theodore Roosevelt*—French-owned, built in South Korea, named for an American, and flying the flag of convenience of Malta—became the largest ship ever to transit the Panama Canal and largest ever to dock in New York, taking advantage of deepened channels and the raised bridge.

CMA CGM Roosevelt is longer than a supercarrier and has a crew of just twenty-seven. Deckhands enjoy large cabins and hotel-style lounges. It's fair to say most Americans and Europeans have never seen a vessel like *CMA CGM Roosevelt.* Yet these container liners are a central component of what's for sale in Walmart or Tesco.

Canals have been expanded in the Netherlands, Canada, and Panama to allow for larger ships with deeper drafts. Short channels such as the Lake Washington Canal near Seattle have been joined by mid-length waterways such as the expanded Kiel Canal in northern Germany and really long canals such as the Saint Lawrence Seaway, shared by the United States and Canada, providing regular improvements in the ability of vessels to reach destinations.

ANCIENT CANALS ARE A subject of fascination in history classes; the role of the modern canal in the arrival of industrialization is less noted. I grew up in Buffalo, New York, a water-economy city despite its inland location. Buffalo was the western terminus of the Erie Canal, dug beginning in 1817 to carry heavy loads between the Great Lakes and what was then the thriving industrial region around the classically named cities of Rome, Syracuse, and Utica. A few years ago I stood at the base of the Erie Canal's Lock 34, in the city of Lockport—both parts of the name drawn from trade—and marveled at the immense metal structure that for a century has held back the hydraulic pressure of the 128 trillion gallons of water in Lake Erie.

For generations, Buffalo was the city where lake freighters stopped to unload ore and grain from the Upper Midwest, transferring the cargo to the Erie Canal or to railcars bound east to foundries or mills, or to ocean ports from which commodities would ship overseas. In 1959 the Saint Lawrence Seaway was completed. More impressive than the Erie Canal in size and scope (though, excavated by machines, less so in construction than the older channels dug by hand), the Saint Lawrence Seaway and the associated Welland Canal carry large vessels from the Great Lakes to the Atlantic, and vice versa.

When the seaway opened, the transshipment business of my hometown disintegrated. There was no reason for freighters to unload at Buffalo: they could steam directly to the ports of the Eastern Seaboard or straight across the ocean. Today Buffalo's concrete piers are lonely for big ships; Buffalo Harbor, once an international nerve center, has become a tranquil state park; the waterfront silos are a nightclub district, pounding with the sounds of dance music rather than of industrial labor.

ALL TRUE SONS AND daughters of Buffalo consider the seaway an unspeakable calamity, changing the city from magnet of commerce to national afterthought. A rusting, derelict ore carrier I played on as a child was a floating metaphor that requires no further explication. But as long as you didn't live in Buffalo, the opening of the Saint Lawrence Seaway was good news. The trade efficiency afforded by this busy waterway is one of the reasons prosperity has risen for almost all Americans.

Other nations know they could benefit from more or better canals. Thailand hopes to build a canal that would allow container vessels to circumvent the political tensions—to say nothing of traffic jams—of the Strait of Malacca. Should the Kra Canal come into existence, some localities that today do business along the sea lanes in and out of the Strait of Malacca would be harmed, while nearly everyone else on earth would benefit. Turkey hopes to build a canal that would allow freight traffic to bypass the crowded Bosporus waters that nations have been fighting over for thousands of years. By reducing the cost of commerce, an Istanbul Canal would benefit vast numbers of people in Anatolia. Like the proposed Kra Canal, the proposed Istanbul Canal seems prohibitively expensive—yet back in the day, the Panama Canal seemed outrageously expensive and now seems a bargain.

If the Kra Canal and Istanbul Canal are built (both pose significant challenges), the world would have four great canals rather than the present two, with the earth's surface again altered for the efficacy of moving ships.

The likelihood of significant reserves of natural gas beneath the Mediterranean may increase momentum for the Istanbul Canal—or increase momentum for war. Turkey has been making bellicose gestures toward a heterogeneous coalition of Cyprus, Egypt, Greece, and Israel, each asserting overlapping claims to underwater natural gas in the eastern Mediterranean. Israel's offshore underwater gas field is named Leviathan, after the biblical sea monster, and the dispute has a monstrous aspect because some of the claims cannot be resolved through imposition of customary-law national-zoning lines at sea. As of 2020, Germany was attempting to mediate the quarrel; the thought of Germany as peacemaker goes beyond postmodern.

Considering that Cyprus, Egypt, Greece, Israel, and Turkey are US allies, it's hard to figure which side the US Navy would take. If natural-gas production from the Mediterranean can be worked out amicably, millions of people will benefit from a clean energy source, while the world's other gas producers will grimace as prices drop.

Often in international economics, what brings pain to localized areas, such as low-cost imports or the Saint Lawrence Seaway or a new gas field, brings benefits to everyone else. News coverage, and such political campaigns as those that Donald Trump conducted in Ohio in 2016 and 2020, drum relentlessly on the small-scale local pain while skipping the large-scale benefits.

THE PREDOMINANT ASPECT OF modern container ships versus old tramp steamers is that the new system cuts costs. Generally the boxes—the TEUs—are closed at the production end by the shipper and not opened till received by the customer or customs official at the delivery end, moving by cranes at every stage. The elimination of manual handling reduces prices while shortening the process. The less time spent at the port, the better.

When harbor services were expensive and unreliable, many manufacturers saw little point in trying to sell in other nations. Since about 1960, commercial vessels' time in port has dropped in stages from about a week to load or unload, to about a day currently. This cuts handling fees and improves customer service.

When containers began to replace manual cargo handling, ocean firms, railroads, and truckers squabbled over container size, with an alphabet soup of regulatory agencies confusing the picture. Around 1970, a consensus emerged on the standardized container now known as the TEU. Standardizing allows any product made anywhere to travel on any boat, truck, or train without special arrangements—to be intermodal. This further controls price while speeding delivery.

A generation ago, the expense of ocean transportation often kept a producer in one country from selling in another. "Today," says John Butler, president of the World Shipping Council, a business group, "to ship a TEU from Shanghai to Los Angeles costs less than to move the same box across Los Angeles." A TEU filled with electronics bound for a Best Buy might have a final retail value at many multiples of the cost of transferring the product from China to California.

The 1995 arrival of the World Trade Organization, an intergovernmental organization—China joined in 2001—encouraged commerce. Yet declining costs of operating container vessels, and loading and unloading them at port, likely were a greater influence on increased trade than were agreements negotiated through governments. Political speeches do matter, but business managers respond more to numbers. When the numbers began to show that containers full of goods could be moved around the world quickly and inexpensively, business managers grew enthusiastic about trade.

Among other benefits, fast, affordable global shipping promised to free many types of production from the tyranny of the inventory cycle, boosting economic growth and living standards. Developed in Japan during the early postwar period, the production concept of kanban—parts arrive just in time, rather than sitting in storage, requiring carrying charges—allowed Japanese factories to be lean and profitable. Fast, inexpensive shipping had the unintended consequence of extending kanban to most of the world. This particular benefit of ocean shipping may temper as the 2020 virus pandemic causes nations to rethink supply chains. But for the last two decades or so, an ocean-borne inventory system has been a godsend for the global economy.

DURING THOSE LAST TWO decades or so, one mystery of Western politics is why ceaseless borrowing and money printing by the Federal Reserve in the United States, the European Central Bank on the continent, and the Bank of Japan has not activated inflation.

Inflation bedeviled presidents Lyndon Johnson, Richard Nixon, Gerald Ford, Jimmy Carter, and Ronald Reagan, rising from a long-established rate of 2 percent per year in the mid-1960s to 14 percent per year by 1980, while mortgage interest rates increased from around 5 percent for a thirty-year loan to 16 percent in 1981. (With compounding—interest on the interest—a 1981 mortgage cost the borrower more than double a 1960s mortgage.) Americans who today grumble about prices have forgotten the twin sledgehammers of inflation and interest rates, which harm average people more than any monetary forces observed in the current generation.

Standard economics holds that money printing causes inflation while government borrowing raises interest rates. Yet during the most recent twenty years, prices have been stable and mortgage rates hovered at historical nadirs. According to standard economics, bruising levels of inflation should be harming the United States, the European Union, and Japan, while mortgage rates should be soaring. Neither has happened. Runaway borrowing has reached levels standard economics would call alarming—but at this writing, nothing has happened.

On the first day of the year 2000, the US government owed $8.6 trillion in public debt. (Public debt is the serious kind—contractual obligations to third parties—versus intragovernmental debt, such as Social Security promises that Congress can alter.) On the first day of 2021, public debt was $21.6 trillion.[3] That's nearly twice as much borrowed by the American federal government in the most recent 20 years as was owed for the previous 211 years of the republic. Presidents George W. Bush, Barack Obama, and Donald Trump borrowed like there was no tomorrow: to cover the payments, printed money like there was no tomorrow, hiding behind the euphemism "quantitative easing." Monetary policy has been similarly loosey-goosey in Japan and most of Europe.

Yet mortgage interest rates stay low, and by the end of 2020, inflation had not exceeded 4 percent during the lifetimes of millennials. The follow-on Generation Z is accustomed to 1.6 percent inflation, the average for the most recent decade. This is the mystery. Prices have been so restrained that in 2020, Federal Reserve governors declared they would take steps to increase inflation, Fed chair Jerome Powell saying, "Inflation that is persistently too low can pose serious risks." Through the 1970s and 1980s, the notion of policymakers calling inflation *too low* would have caused the brains of economists to explode.[4]

There are surprisingly few proposed explanations of why interest rates and most prices have not been rising—economists tend to change the subject. One proposal, popular with the left, is modern monetary theory. Funky on its best days, modern monetary theory holds that money is just strings of numbers, so any government that issues its own currency and exerts a monopoly over currency (the United States meets these tests; not all governments do) can add zeros and spend away. National debt can be ignored, borrowing doesn't matter, federal spending can rise without consequences. Drinks are on the house!

Modern monetary theory underpinned the 2016 Bernie Sanders campaign platform, which (essentially) said federal spending could nearly double without new taxes on average people and without inflation.[5] This was lampooned, to say the least. In 2020, during the COVID-19 emergency, federal spending nearly doubled without new taxes and there was no inflation—just what Sanders's advisers forecast. Yet if modern monetary theory were correct, inflation should have been mild during the 1970s; instead, inflation ran at three times the rate of the previous decade. And it's far from clear why, if national debt actually doesn't matter, none of the world's finance ministers has ever mentioned this.

A more commonsensical possible explanation for twenty years of stable retail prices and low interest rates is that inflation pumped by government borrowing is offset by the price cuts and competition generated by international trade. For years inflation was the chief domestic policy concern in Washington, D.C., and many European capitals. Inflation came under control, dropping off the political radar. What else happened around the same time? Global waterborne trade rose, creating downward pressure on prices.

An ocean-related possibility is that newfound prosperity in Asia—which coincides almost exactly with newfound lack of inflation—is benefiting the West via restraining the price of money. N. Gregory Mankiw, a Harvard economist and former chair of the Council of Economic Advisers, notes Chinese consumers have a much higher savings rate than their Western counterparts. (Whether Chinese savings is voluntary or government enforced is a separate issue.) Suddenly hefty Chinese cash reserves cause a "vast pool of savings flows into capital markets, and interest rates around the world fall," Mankiw wrote in 2020. Money responds to supply and demand like other commodities. When there's ample money (Chinese savings) the price goes down (low interest rates), which equates to less inflation.

These factors suggest we are, indeed, living beyond our means— but the blue age is bailing us out. If the blue age ends, the waiter will present the bill.

REDUCED LABOR COSTS FROM replacing break-bulk cargo with crane-based container handling is only one of several reasons shipping expense continues to decline. Another is the speed associated with improved harbors and container vessels.

Ships like *Ever Loading* sustain about twenty miles per hour at sea, allowing the vessels to complete more trips per year than older versions. The latest container liners can make close to thirty miles per hour, similar to the speed of warships, though usually stick to around twenty miles per hour to control fuel consumption. (Friction with the sea imposes an upper limit; only a few warships and specialty craft are capable of making more than about forty miles per hour.) Shipping companies earn revenue when their vessels are sailing: the faster on the waters, the better the company spreadsheet.

Marc Levinson has written that as lading fees per TEU fell and ocean delivery pace increased, "shipping costs no longer offered shelter to high-cost producers whose great advantage was physical proximity to their customers. Even after paying customs duties, factories in Malaysia could deliver blouses to Macy's in Herald Square more cheaply than could manufacturers in nearby lofts of New York City's garment district."

Container companies have simplified operations with flat-rate pricing that hastens the movement of boxes through terminals. International rules taking effect in 2020 required container ships to reduce the amount of pollution they emit. This created an incentive for shippers to retire old vessels with dirty engines and replace them with newer, cleaner, and improved designs. Container liners powered by natural gas, the low-carbon fuel, are beginning to appear at ports. The latest vessels, like *CMA CGM Roosevelt*, tend to be better equipped for swift loading and unloading than are the liners being taken out of service.

New container ships also incorporate antiboarding features that impede scaling their hulls. The result is a decline in the modern piracy that was an issue roughly from 1990 to 2010.

By 2020, piracy was a concern primarily in the Bay of Campeche, source of most Mexican oil, where low-slung drilling platforms and support vessels have sides that can be surmounted, and along Africa's Gulf of Guinea. Just after Christmas 2019, pirates boarded a Greek-flagged oil tanker, *Happy Lady*, at anchor off Cameroon and held the crew—Greek officers, Filipino and Ukrainian deck hands—hostage. After three harrowing weeks, they were released unharmed.

The US Navy's fast corvette was designed for conditions of the African coast, anticipating a regular navy presence there as America became dependent on African oil.[6] Instead, US domestic output increased so much the United States is today the world's number one petroleum producer, outpacing Saudi Arabia. When the corvette program was cut back, that undermined patrols off West Africa, allowing bandit assaults on oil tankers in the region.

Though piracy against tankers and small merchantmen continues, piracy against container liners is singular to some extent. The new ships are so big, they ride on hulls too high for a pirate to scale. Helicopters would be required to put a boarding party on one of the new container vessels.

HOLY CATS AND LITTLE fishes, are the ships bigger. *Ever Loading*, discussed in the previous chapter, is gigantic in comparison to 1940s battleships. Yet *HMM Algeciras*, newly crowned king of the megamax class, carries three times what *Ever Loading* can handle. *Algeciras* is so tall—waterline to deck greater than the height of the Cinderella Castle at Disney World—that for a pirate to clamber aboard would be like scaling a moving skyscraper.

It has long been possible to build extremely large vessels. But shippers and their insurers wanted to spread the risks of sinking or military capture. As vessel design improved such that accidental sinkings became less likely; as radar and sonar fell in price while GPS arrived, reducing the chance of hitting sand bars and marine rocks; and as the risk went down of warships opening fire, the size of container vessels and oil tankers went up, further cutting costs.

The design parameters for *Ever Loading* were the ability to take a sizable amount of cargo anywhere in the world. The parameters for *Algeciras* were the maximum freight on one specific route— Pacific Rim to Europe and back.

In 2020, *Algeciras* made its first docking in Britain, at London Gateway, a new "fully integrated, semi-automated" port down the Thames River from the English capital. London Gateway aims to move the goods consumed by an ever-more-prosperous region even faster, and at lower cost, than ports that are merely modern. "Fully integrated" means customs and warehouse facilities are amalgamated with the terminals. The grocery chain Lidl, which has an ambitious management style, built its United Kingdom warehouse complex in London Gateway. It's an Amazon-like distribution center that features creepy robotics and fast throughput. Lower costs aided by globalized design allow Lidl to offer upmarket products at discount.

The arrival of *Algeciras*, a vessel so massive it must cause a disturbance in the time-space continuum, was a hit with maritime-minded Brits, who queued on roads along the route to observe. This one ship carried more Asian goods than England would have received in a full year not long ago.

Whether megamax-style container vessels will last remains to be seen. Boeing and Airbus are ending production of their outsized 747 and A380, because medium-large jetliners are proving more popular with airlines. The container ship market might shift toward medium-large, such as *Ever Loading*, as well.

Whatever happens in trends for nautical architecture, that *Algeciras*, the biggest free-trade vessel ever, was built at a dry dock in South Korea, to sail halfway round the globe to the nation that convinced the world to trade by sea, is the kind of thing that happens in the blue age.

BEGINNING ABOUT 2010, INTERNATIONAL trade slowed—an effect some wag dubbed "slowbalization"—while the World Trade Organization was perceived as losing momentum. The slowing of trade was only in rate of growth. Water transportation, sometimes by river or lake but mainly by ocean, keeps rising in political and economic importance. The apparent natural constant—that at every stage in history, 95 percent of goods in commerce travel via water—is grounded (excuse the pun) in the fact that weight moves more easily on river or sea than on land, and much more cheaply atop water than through air.

Simply the weights involved in contemporary business—finished goods, agricultural products, bulk commodities such as bauxite—make the cost advantages of water transit necessary. Those 1,416 Empire State Buildings that passed through Rotterdam: imagine trying to move them on trucks or trains or aircraft, let alone on camels, as with the ancient Silk Road.

Ocean transit has another appealing feature: no roadblocks. Roads can be closed by soldiers, or barriers emplaced. Rail lines can be obstructed or torn up by governments, by rebels, or, in some parts of the world, by organized crime. Even when all is well, each border may require a stop for document inspection and, in much of the world, bribes.

The troll—can't cross the bridge without paying the troll!—was not just a children's story. One reason the fifteenth century saw such an increase in sailing between Europe and the Malaccan lands, despite the severe difficulty of this voyage, was that the Persians (now Iran) and Ottomans (now Turkey) were in a near-constant state of war along the Silk Road, making land passage more treacherous than confronting Neptune.

In olden days, once reaching the Indian Ocean, a trading vessel feared only nature and its own limitations. Today, once on the open seas, a container ship sails wherever it would, a vital feature of the blue age.

A few water choke points cannot be avoided. Britain sought control of Gibraltar and Singapore because they guard the world's most important ocean narrows. In the main, sea lanes, many with romantic names—the waypoints along Sandettie Bank near Dover are known to many mariners—offer open highways without trolls or tolls.

THAT IS TRUE AS long as warships do not challenge merchant ships, and in the period of US Navy hegemony, this almost never occurs, because the USN is the police force of nearly all blue water. The result is that nations too poor or small to have navies, or that should not divert money from higher priorities to a fleet, enjoy the freedom of navigation the United States generates. In December 2020, the guided-missile destroyers *McCain* and *Mustin* sailed around the Spratly Islands, the Côn Đảo Islands, and in the Taiwan Strait, using sea lanes that are claimed by China, Taiwan, and Vietnam, though most nations regard the waters in question as international. Freedom-of-navigation challenges to such disputed water jurisdiction benefit the many nations that wish to sail but lack the naval muscle or political clout to enforce their maritime rights. In such cases, the United States is either giving away freedom of navigation graciously or imposing it for self-interest, depending on one's perspective.

The *Mayaguez*, a cargo vessel seized by Cambodia warships, precipitating an international incident, was a rare post–World War II instance of the armed vessel that dragoons an unarmed merchantman. The *Mayaguez* affair was quite serious—and happened in 1975. Except for the Persian Gulf, where conflicts involving oil tankers continue, the *Mayaguez* seizure was among the last blue-water instances of an event once customary: military interference in commerce.

One would look long and hard for any other forty-five-year period since the Phoenicians when no merchantman was taken by a warship. No major battles at sea, almost no seizing of commercial vessels at sea—these are without precedent from a centuries-long perspective, and put us into the blue age.

Less war on the waters translates to more trade. More trade benefits almost everyone because . . .

7

WHY SEA TRADE IMPROVES LIVES

OUR PALE BLUE DOT MUST LOOK GORGEOUS FROM SPACE. MOST of us never will behold that view, but anyone can contemplate the outer-space perspective using Google Earth or NASA's Earth Observatory utility.

I examined orbital images from twenty-five years ago of night-time coastal China, the most populous region of the most populous nation, and compared them, in the same reference year, with night-time images of the Eastern Seaboard, the most populous region of the United States.

Many if not most ancient civilizations were built around rivers. The two greatest nations of human history—contemporary America and contemporary China—both chose ocean-facing coastal regions as their centers of population, economics, research, academia, and government. This is the blue age in a nutshell.

Back to the space pictures. Twenty-five years ago, from orbit the night lights of the eastern United States looked like the Sagittarius Arm—the river of stars, stupendously bright, that for centuries has dazzled astronomers gazing at the central Milky Way. That same twenty-five years ago, the coastal portion of China was alight but dim—not as vivid as the cities of Kansas or Nebraska of the time, to say nothing of the Eastern Seaboard. The relative dimness of China as seen from orbit some twenty-five years ago meant most Chinese citizens lacked access to electricity. In 1995, North America was the world's leading region for primary energy consumption, by a whopping margin, far ahead of the Pacific Rim.

Next I pulled up space-taken views of the present day, just before the COVID-19 pandemic. The Eastern Seaboard remained sparkly bright—but coastal China had become the new Milky-Way-on-Earth, almost solid white at night, à la galactic center. Since 1995 primary energy generation per capita in China is up 160 percent, with most new energy produced as electricity. Today the Pacific Rim consumes twice as much power as North America does.

Perhaps you are thinking, "Using energy is bad. China shouldn't use more energy." Rising curves for energy consumption closely correlate with reduction of poverty. "The vast disparity between the global rich and poor is . . . defined by the disparity between those who have ready access to electricity and those who do not," energy analyst Robert Bryce wrote in 2020 in a book subtitled *Electricity and the Wealth of Nations*.[1] Since the electrification of Wabash, Indiana, in 1880, everywhere in the world where energy use has risen, poverty has fallen, while in no nation has poverty gone down without energy use going up.

Better life need not go hand in hand with environmental harm—once national income reaches a middle-class standard, people can afford energy-efficient technology. This transition has occurred in the United States. Since 1995, American per-capita energy use is down 12 percent, and greenhouse emissions per capita are down 17 percent (the number for 2019, before the COVID-19 lockdowns reduced emissions further), while all metrics of living standards remain positive. Rising national income has been accompanied by higher energy efficiency and stable or declining greenhouse emissions in most of Europe, Japan, and other Western economies.[2]

China, India, and other developing lands first must reach the stage of solid material standards to have enough income for clean forms of energy production (coal-fired electricity is dirty but cheap, renewable electricity clean but capital-intensive) and efficient systems of energy use. The view from space shows that the initial steps toward general prosperity have arrived in China. Next China must control its greenhouse emissions, the worst in the world.

How did China overtake the United States in the view-from-space sweepstakes so rapidly? Two primary forces: free-market economics and waterborne trade. Perhaps you are thinking, "Government should control the economy." This chapter will consider that. For the moment let's focus on trade.

A GENERATION AGO—JUST A generation ago!—China engaged in almost no commerce with the United States and Europe, while Chinese (and Indian) businesses were under the boot of state central planning that failed to use market signals to allocate resources. Someday humanity may achieve a post-scarcity economy, in which resource allocation ceases to matter. To this juncture, market-based allocation of resources, for all its many flaws, has served average people better than any form of central planning. And a generation ago—just a generation ago!—China and India did not benefit from free economics.

During the 1980s, China and India dipped their toes into market reforms. Whether Deng Xiaoping actually said "To get rich is glorious" is disputed. But the basic shift in philosophy spread throughout China. Making money replaced the previous goal, which was losing money.

Around the time of membership in the World Trade Organization, China had so many in poverty, and thereby so little domestic demand, that if the country were to sell the goods it began producing, the customers had to be North America, Japan, and Europe. The Middle Kingdom readied to export on a scale no nation had ever attempted, a scale that made the Manhattan Project seem a leisurely undertaking.

Here are the results, stated as GDP per capita, which is the measure the World Bank deems the best way of understanding economic circumstances for average people.* A reminder: the numbers are converted to 2020 currency, so comparisons are apples to apples.

United States. In 1995, GDP per capita was $49,000. By 2020, US GDP per capita expanded to $63,000. Both numbers are similar to median household income in those years and reflect net economic growth, from 1995 to 2020, of 29 percent.[3]

China. In 1995, per-capita GDP was $1,000. By 2020 China's per-capita GDP was $9,900, reflecting twenty-five-year economic growth of *890 percent*.

This growth rate is extreme in part because China started from such a low level. Nevertheless the growth is stunning. In 1995 the US economy was forty-nine times more productive than the Chinese economy. By 2020, the United States was down to six times more productive than China. Through the period, the pace of Chinese economic expansion was thirty-one times faster than American economic expansion.

Economic growth of 890 percent in twenty-five years. Life expectancy at birth raised to seventy-seven years, almost catching up with the United States. Low education levels yield to twice as many new college graduates as in the United States. Starvation and flooding across the countryside supplanted by plenty of food and big gains in personal safety. Life is stressful in China, corruption permeates government, elections are rigged, and there is no freedom of speech or religion. These said, China's living-standards improvements and poverty reduction from 1995 to 2020 rank high in any accounting of the human family's great accomplishments.[4]

Ships, cranes, and the oceans made it happen.

---

* These comparisons are in nominal output. Purchasing power parity is preferred by some economists. Whichever metric is employed, the acceleration of the Chinese economy is vibrant.

THERE ARE REASONS OF geography, economics, and psychology that ocean trade is almost always good for nations.

Forty percent of Americans live in coastal counties, among the highest coastal-dwelling ratios in the world. Once upon the waters, the ocean "exclusive economic zone" of America, at 3.4 million square nautical miles, slightly exceeds the land area of the fifty states.[5] Via the 12-mile and exclusive economic zone rules, the United States has legal jurisdiction over more of the oceans than does any other nation: another of the geographic blessings behind America's position. When the Chinese analyze US success, they notice what so many Americans overlook—sea power—and seek the same.

Little England for several centuries controlled much of the globe. English imperialism was morally offensive—and not just in the dim past. As recently as the early 1940s, London decision making led to starvation in parts of India, even as Indian soldiers were dying against the Japanese to defend their own subjugation. Morals aside, British dominion over so much territory starting from such a small foundation raises the question—how did they do it?

The British Isles are islands, a culture focused since antiquity on the seas. No spot in England, the main British nation, is more than seventy miles from blue water. Many dozens of English generations were raised viewing the oceans as the key to conquest, to national defense (in the age of sail, the Royal Navy was known as the Wooden Wall because no invader could reach English soil), to commerce, and to culture. England has an unusually high fraction of coastline relative to interior and large numbers of port cities and harbors—including Bristol, where a distant ancestor of mine, a sea captain, would head down the Severn Estuary for the Atlantic.

The China of yore was a relatively advanced society at a time when Europe was mired in the Dark Ages. China beat Europe to productive agriculture, to a school system, to a civil service, to public-works engineering, including what is still the world's longest artificial canal. Then China fell behind as Europe surged. Historians long have puzzled over why.

There are many theories: one turns on the sea ban (*haijin*), which, beginning around 1400, outlawed most construction of oceangoing vessels. Until around 1400, Chinese ships were ubiquitous in the Pacific Rim, many twice the size and crew of the sailing vessels Europe could build. China's fantastical Treasure Fleet of the 1400s may be part legend, but after the anathema on oceangoing ships, Louise Levathes has written, "the Chinese began to lose their technological edge over the West." The kingdom turned inward, giving ground in science and culture, unable to protect itself when the masts of European warships were sighted. Eventually China grew so weak and fragmented, the "century of humiliation," 1839 to 1949, could not be prevented.

During the same period of China's humiliation, the nations that invested ever more in ships—America, England, Spain, France, Denmark, the Netherlands, Germany, Japan—gained in engineering skills, in (sadly) weaponry, and in exposure to new ideas. Trade helped them raise living standards. Harbor cities became notably different, sociologically, from inland towns. Harbor and river cities long had been cosmopolitan compared to upcountry locations. As ships grew better and more numerous, the harbor–inland distinction rose in significance, and favored the ocean-focused lands.

Harbor cities tend to take an outward, international view. This was true in the far past and remains true in the present day. Dubai, Los Angeles, Singapore—their psyches are attuned to the larger world. Harbor cities and, in some places, river cities can adjust to change: they expect a regular influx of new products, different ideas, and discoveries made in other places. Heartland cities by contrast tend to be inward-focused and fretful. In 2016, in the US presidential campaign and UK vote on European Union affiliation, Donald Trump and Brexit proponents tailored appeals to heartland areas, with their fear of outsiders and assumption that change is automatically bad. Whatever might be true in a perfect world, in the actual world, opposition to change is a formula for being left behind.

This book is hard on Alfred Thayer Mahan; to give due, Mahan believed a nation's coastline has more value than any other natural resource, and the last century upheld him in this. Adding to his books on naval power, Mahan is remembered for a treatise, *The*

United States Looking Outward, published 1890 in *The Atlantic* (then *Atlantic Monthly*). Today's reader would approach *The United States Looking Outward* with horror, for the treatise argues America should seize power over developing nations—if we don't, Captain Mahan contended, Germany will. Mahan in 1890 foresaw that Germany would become history's worst malefactor, that waterborne trade would be essential to the coming century, and that national success emanates from coastlines: from awareness of "outward."

Coastline helps Great Britain more than coal and tin deposits ever did. Canada, Greenland (Denmark), and Russia lead the world for coastline (as opposed to sea area controlled). Australia, Indonesia, Japan, New Zealand, Norway, the Philippines, and the United States are the other nations in the top ten for coastline. Only one of them, the Philippines, has a faltering economy. The rest of the coastline-rich nations are doing well, thank you, in the blue age.

BRITAIN BECAME PROSPEROUS BY embracing authoritarian trade, then liberal trade. England's old Navigation Acts, which were authoritarian laws, led to years of conflict with other polities, especially the colonizers of New Amsterdam. In 1849, Britain repealed the Navigation Acts, opening British ports to all flags. As Paul Kennedy has written, this action showed that "liberal free trade mentality was gaining strength in English political thought."

Today, *liberal* is a political dog-whistle that sets many breeds to barking. In the eighteenth and nineteenth centuries, a liberal was someone who believed in natural-law rights to speech, religion, individuality, and property.

The right to property is deceptively important, as it has been contested by many social systems, including fascist, aristocratic, and communist. If at root your property is yours, just as your thoughts are yours, you have an incentive to build, create, and trade, profiting while helping others. If at root your property belongs to the commissar, prince, or gauleiter, why work hard? That far-left and far-right nations are economically sluggish compared with the for-profit nations is explained in this way.

THOSE WHO, A COUPLE decades ago, had high-paying factory jobs in the American Midwest or British Midlands and now do not may blame international commerce for their change of fortunes. Since China's membership in the World Trade Organization became effective in December 2001, till just before the COVID-19 lockdown of 2020, US factory employment declined by about 3 million.[6] This drop has been taken by Donald Trump, Bernie Sanders, and others as proof that free trade is bad for the United States. Yet a trend of reduction in American manufacturing employment was long-standing before the first container vessel departed from China.

US manufacturing employment peaked in 1979 and had already fallen by 5 million in 2001, the year Chinese imports became material. The transition in the United States to fewer blue-collar jobs and more white-collar employment—in itself, a desirable outcome for most workers—was in progress well before Chinese production could have been the explanation. Claiming manufacturing jobs went to China makes for nice, simplistic slogans. Contemporary society rewards simplistic slogans, so we get more of them, which is textbook economics.

Research conducted by economists at Ball State University in Indiana and at the Massachusetts Institute of Technology shows net impact of trade with China: the United States lost about 1.5 million manufacturing jobs—hardly inconsequential, but well less than the minus 5 million manufacturing employment that happened entirely for American domestic reasons.[7]

Economic research indicates that several factors in US manufacturing employment hold more sway than does globalization: among them factory automation, shifting consumer tastes, white-collar job growth especially in health care, and improved reliability that causes new products to last longer than old ones, reducing the need to replace home appliances and cars. Should higher product reliability have been banned? Such a move would have preserved manufacturing jobs in some places while harming almost everyone else.

In 2020, a two-year research project at the Massachusetts Institute of Technology concluded that at least until about 2040, industrial nations "will have more job openings than workers to fill them."[8] The dissatisfaction about employment in the United States may not have to do so much with the jobs themselves as with the decline of social mobility associated with work. The political power of wage labor has declined in the United States while adults who lack college degrees have less social mobility than do similar adults in Western Europe, where the sociological power of organized labor remains solid despite the rise in globalization.

Less social mobility and the erosion of blue-collar influence are disturbing problems in American society, but ones caused by political forces, not by ocean trade. About 80 percent of Chinese exports go to nations other than the United States—so most of what China produces has no direct impact on American employment. The manufacturing jobs that moved to other nations are offset in many cases by the trade-based jobs that arrived in the United States and the growth of white-collar opportunity. Politically, this leaves workers in California and New England happy, workers in the Ohio Valley unhappy—which predicts their votes in the 2016 and 2020 elections.

In turn, US factory output is not down anywhere near as much as popularly imagined. Campaigning in 2020, Donald Trump said Barack Obama's tenure "destroyed American manufacturing." Mainstream commentary supported this claim; the *New York Times* fact-checker feature decreed Trump's statement "mostly true." On the day the *Times* said this, US manufacturing output was down 5 percent from its all-time peak.[9] If 95 percent of a thing remains, the thing is not "destroyed."

In turn, the peak for American manufacturing was not in some idealized misty past but in 2007.[10] The 2007 peak came after the "China shock" of globalized trade reached the American system and mainly reflected the knowledge-economy transition that leaves most Americans better off while reducing pollution and increasing life spans.

But voters, pundits, politicians, and fundraisers want to believe trade is bad and manufacturing is destroyed, perceiving that such pessimistic beliefs bring them benefits—donations, subscription payments, ratings, government subsidies. What people *want* to believe is so much more powerful than factfulness.

SUPPOSE WE WERE TO conclude that free trade should be reined in. Marxists would be over the moon. Literary figures and academics would cheer, at least until prices rose, which literary figures and academics would become incensed about.

The majority of those in the United States, Europe, and Japan live better lives owing to trade—because of lower prices and because competition improves products and services. Reining in free trade would harm millions of people—average Americans whose living standards would fall, the powerless in Asia and Africa who would stay mired in the poverty that globalization has begun to cure. One can't just assume away these complications.

Were there higher barriers to trade, some who lost manufacturing jobs in the United States and Europe still would have those jobs. Most who lost manufacturing jobs would have lost them regardless, because technology and market forces were the drivers of their situations.

The night dread that kept Thomas Malthus awake was population's rising faster than output. Instead economic growth has run far ahead of population growth, with the gap widening as trade increases. From 1700 to 1900, global population doubled, while global GDP rose fivefold: more trade was one of the reasons economic growth ran ahead of population growth, rather than trailing, as Malthus feared. In the most recent century-length period, 1920 to 2020, global population trebled, while global GDP rose twentyfold.[11]

The acceleration of economic growth compared to population growth occurred as liberal international trade intermediated by the seas was expanding fast. No one can prove one was necessary for the other. Yet many other fortunate tendencies accompanied more ships and bigger harbors. During the same period that ocean trade has flourished, longevity has risen sharply. Global life expectancy at birth was fifty years in 1960. Today, it's seventy-two years, by far the largest half-century improvement in life expectancy ever.

Since 1960, global literacy has risen from 40 percent to 90 percent. Through the ocean-trade period, global malnutrition has declined in almost every year, even as population rises.[12] Secondary schooling for girls and women has progressed from rare to common almost everywhere in the world. And even during the COVID-19 pandemic, many measures of global public health improved.

Given that international trade produces consistently favorable results—higher living standards for the West, less immiseration for Asia—do we really want to hurl a giant monkey wrench into the gears of globalization, as Senator Sanders and other commentators propose? [13]

What might be called the cornucopia viewpoint has taken command of many Western institutions. This viewpoint holds that production, a principal social goal for centuries, is no longer particularly noteworthy: distributing, not making, should now be society's primary concern.

It would be nice to think that production has become a cinch, but this is at best generations off. In a world of mostly urban life— 2008 was the first year at least 50 percent of humanity lived in cities; the share continues to grow—sustaining production and supply chains so that goods, food, and medicine increase faster than population, while empty shelves do not cause famines or panics, is elemental to human well-being. Producing and shipping may not be as engaging to think tanks and editorial boards as grievances, but if there is insufficient production, little else will matter. Factories must hum and ships must cast off.

Peace on the waters led to prosperity. Of course when events are concurrent, it may not be that one causes the other. But sometimes two plus two equals four. Trade rises faster than expected; poverty declines faster than expected; two plus two equals four.

SINCE DAVID RICARDO, BORN 1772, students of economics have been taught that comparative advantage underscores free trade. If, in Ricardo's example, one nation can make a product cheaper or better than another (in his day English cloth offered the best value) and another nation can make a different product better or cheaper (in his day Portuguese wine was prized), both nations will be served by trading with each other.

Workers of Ricardo's era might have felt differently; conditions in the textile facilities of England were appalling. But if you could have tailoring from Saville Row and port from the Douro Valley, you'd be happier than with just one, especially if you save on both transactions. The logic of this proposition is close to bulletproof.

Ricardo and later followers found comparative advantage mostly in labor rates, labor quality, and management skill and somewhat in local conditions such as climate and natural resources. Ricardo assumed shipping costs need not be considered, because they would be about the same for every producer. English and Dutch merchants of the nineteenth century, with their sleek sailing vessels and elaborate keiretsu of interlocking trade houses and admiralty insurers, had, Ricardo thought, already driven shipping prices about as low as possible.

Adjusting for the value of money, it cost far more, when Ricardo was alive and thought trade could get no cheaper, to ship a pound of goods across an ocean than it costs today.

As recently as the early postwar period, the high price of Marlon Brando–style ports meant that inefficient industries or overrated goods did not face international competition. When ocean trade became inexpensive and dependable, competitive pressure compelled industries to improve or shut down.

In the 1950s and 1960s, for example, brands such as RCA and Magnavox dominated the US supply of television sets: there was no competition from imports such as Panasonic. Once shipping prices fell and Panasonic could afford to offer consoles in US stores, marketing of TVs was shaken up. The same process later would hit Panasonic, which lost out to agile blue-age competitors such as LG.

Economic research is clear that pressure to improve products was a more telling impetus than were hourly wage rates in China for the industrial restructurings of the Ohio Valley, Midlands England, and other regions. Such pressure is not confined to the West. Already, Chinese factory managers are crying into their baijiu about competition from Malaysia and Vietnam.

Pressure to improve may be bad for individuals who lose jobs in specific places, but is good for society overall, including by resulting in more jobs overall. Pressure to improve always existed locally, at least in the free-market countries. The blue age took that pressure global.

Extensive trade-based competitive tension has only existed for two generations, the generations of container shipping. Those are generations of economic turbulence, in which most things have gotten better for most people—but anxiety is up too.

ONE OF THE AMENDERS of comparative-advantage thinking is former Princeton economist Paul Krugman, who has won the Nobel for economics and, more prestigious from the perspective of economists, the John Clark Bates Medal. Krugman's academic research concerned whether comparative advantage of nations still mattered.

Two hundred years ago, when David Ricardo was publishing, England and Portugal were very different societies; it stood to reason each would have strengths and weaknesses compared with the other. Through recent generations, many nations converged in development levels and social structures. Some economists conjectured that if the free-market countries are just not that different, comparative advantage will fade.

Krugman replied with "new trade theory." First, he supposed, because prosperity is rising, consumers want lots of options, not merely whatever is made nearby. In the 1970s and 1980s, for example, American consumers sought small sporty cars with high MPG, which domestic factories did not produce; cars imported from Japan and Germany filled the gap. (Today American consumers want bulk and horsepower, a preference that harms the environment but helps domestic marques.) Second, Krugman showed, using econometric models, that even with industrial output becoming more efficient, economics of scale continue to matter. One large factory that makes, say, office chairs may be able to price them low enough that they are the best buy even after adding the expense of international shipping. Thus there remains comparative advantage of nations, just as in centuries before.

New trade theory was amended by other economists, but Krugman's basic reasoning was not. Since container shipping became practical, much of the world has benefited from having products made by whoever does the best, then shipping those products over the blue water quickly and cheaply. There is a similar effect with the rising proficiency of FedEx-style air freight: it's just that ships carry so much more than planes carry.

Krugman used his findings to argue in favor of unrestricted trade and low tariffs, against industrial policy, which was a modish 1980s idea to have governments select winner and loser industries. Free trade, low tariffs, and letting consumer preferences (that is, the market) decide have hands-down aided vastly more people than alternative approaches. For instance, there's no way there would be in your pocket or purse a 128 GB smart phone if industrial policy, once advocated by many politicians and pundits, ruled the roost: only government officials and billionaires would have such devices, if they existed at all. Since becoming a newspaper columnist, Krugman has joined the journalism reality show where the brass ring is grabbed by whoever shouts loudest. Today he may come across as an enraged Jacobin. As an academic, he proved the worth of the blue age.

ANOTHER WAY TO THINK about the rise of ocean trade is through the work of Jane Jacobs, who died in 2006. Jacobs was a founder of the field of urban studies. Her superb book *The Death and Life of Great American Cities*, published 1961, fricasseed urban-planning standards of the early postwar period. During the 1950s, freeways were cut through neighborhoods of big cities, isolating low-income areas and ruining parks. The freeways created a path to the 'burbs, but only for those with money—exacerbating racial tensions at a time when other forces seemed to point toward harmony. Divided neighborhoods without parks went downhill.

Jacobs was particularly riled up that banks and corporate offices were taking over the best streets of New York City, Boston, and San Francisco, stifling urban diversity. A bank could always outbid an Italian family restaurant or a bodega for desirable property.

This gobbling up of the little folks made city streets corporate and sterile. To Jacobs it was the Greek lunch counters, the South Side–influenced blues clubs, the dive bars run by retired Irish cops that gave cities their appeal. To preserve them, Jacobs memorably proposed that banks and Wall Street be forbidden to lease or own ground-floor space. Walk-in square footage would be preserved for mom-and-pop businesses; the corporate lobby could be on the second floor.

Establishing herself as an urban social critic, Jacobs spent the second half of her estimable life trying to refute the idea that trade is good for nations. Rather than buy from distant lands, Jacobs contended, cities or regions should make whatever they need, practicing import replacement. In today's argot, everything should be locally sourced.

Over the centuries there have been many instances of nations buying products that arrive by sea, figuring out how the item is produced, then switching to domestic manufacture. Alexander Hamilton, everyone's favorite framer, advocated import substitution for the young United States so America wouldn't need to purchase from English foundries and mills. Several Latin American nations adopted import replacement as a national goal. Jacobs extended the notion to cities: Miami shouldn't purchase beer from Milwaukee; Miami should brew its own beer.

Import replacement, Jacobs thought, not only would boost local economies but eliminate a category she viewed as pure waste—the use of resources for transportation. She wanted a world with no big ships battling ocean waves, no quay cranes, no hundred-car trains chugging through Rocky Mountain passes. In books, articles, and monographs, Jacobs pushed the notion that most long-distance commerce should end.

Few well-considered intellectual notions flamed out more spectacularly than Jacobs's import replacement. Real-world tests showed that cities with globally focused economies, such as Boston, Houston, and Seattle, consistently grew faster and created more and better jobs than did inward-focused cities such as Chicago and Kansas City. On the larger canvas, landlocked nations struggled compared to sea-power nations. Modern, liberal Germany booms; nearby Austria, with similar people, culture, and resources, stagnates, with less than half the GDP growth. Perhaps the difference is that Austria is landlocked. Development of Africa has been slow in part because the continent has the world's highest fraction of landlocked nations.

Nations that deliberately cut themselves off from intercourse with other nations show the effect most clearly. North Korea and South Korea have the same resources, people, and geography; both enjoy ample access to the seas. But the North Korean dictatorship runs a closed society without trade, except for luxuries for its inbred ruling family. South Korea, an open society whose shipyards rival the production of Britain's at its nautical summit, when *Olympic*, *Titanic*, and *Britannic* were sliding down the ramp at Belfast, is spectacularly more prosperous than North Korea.

China's change from closed to open economic organization, from no trade to an almost-spooky obsession with maximizing trade, has been accompanied by rapid increases, for average people, in living standards, education levels, and life span. Is there any chance these improvements could have been realized so fast without the container ships and bulk carriers? Switching from the closed import-replacement view to free trade caused China to become visible from space. If any idea in economics is self-evident today, it is that free trade benefits almost everyone.

NOT ONLY DOES GLOBAL commerce raise living standards for most people in most nations, but its political impact, particularly reduced poverty in China, is a case study of market economics versus central planning.

Market economics has all manner of defects; anyone who uses the phrase "the magic of the market" hasn't been paying attention. Trade-based market economies have drawbacks that include unending stress for workers who cannot be sure how long their jobs will last. However flawed, in actual use market-based systems produce better outcomes for average people than do feudal, communist, fascist, militarist, or monarchist systems.

That China under Maoism had more immiserated human beings than any society in history, then a generation later got most of them out of poverty by switching to market forces, ought to settle the issue. Yet many in America and Europe continue to speak of market forces as a horror, calling for government economic controls and barriers against trade. Some who say this—Bernie Sanders, for example, close to winning the presidency in 2016 and 2020—are wealthy and confident they themselves never will be subjected to the conditions that socialized economies impose on the powerless.

The proof of the pudding is in the tasting: market systems create desirable goods; centrally planned systems do not. Giant vessels low in the water from the weight of products that buyers actually want depart the docks of free-market nations. Venezuela can't even sell oil!

Persuasive though the statistics and examples may appear, significant numbers of people simply don't like globalized commerce. We live at a moment in history when we're supposed to be mad all the time. International trade via the oceans, involving faraway forces with hard-to-pronounce names, is a handy target of ire, and set aside that globalization supplies many of the goods and resources necessary to keep millions of people alive to be mad about globalization.

The first section of this book considered how peace came to the blue water. This second section considered how trade blossomed and improved society. Do these two reinforce each other?

Nirmal Verma, the retired Indian admiral, thinks so. "The arrival of true transnationals has more impact than most people realize," Verma says. "There have been large corporations for centuries, but always tied to a specific nation, gaining or losing as that nation gains or loses. Only during this generation have there been true transnationals. They want profit—definitely they want profit!—but do not want war, which is very bad for profit. During the same period that war per se grew unattractive to the great powers, true transnationals have come into existence, and what they seek is to trade. So we have less fighting at sea, more trade. Each amplifies the other."

True transnationals inveigle governments with graft, roll over indigenous groups, lie to the public. But suppose the question is, Which is better, warships sinking civilian ships, the condition for nearly all of human history, or peaceful seas busy with money-seeking corporate commerce? The answer is obvious.

Which leads to the third section of this book: is there a way to have both trade on the seas and improved protection for workers and the environment? Else the blue age will end.

PART THREE

OUR FUTURE ON THE WATERS

8

HEY LOOK, A NEW OCEAN!

JOHN STEINBECK, WHO SPENT A LOT OF TIME ON THE WATER, wrote in his *Log from the Sea of Cortez* that boats "above all other inanimate things [are] personified in man's mind." Sailboats personify adventure, submarines personify menace, tramp steamers personify the itinerant life. There are hundreds of types of boats, personifying a wide range of emotions and roles. Let's look at some of the outliers.

Xiang Rui Kou, a semisubmersible, designed for extremely heavy loads, by appearances an ultra-gigantic oceangoing flatbed truck. At this writing *Xiang Rui Kou* had cast off from the Bulgarian city of Burgas, on the Black Sea, bound for Shanghai. Able to transport an entire damaged cruise ship or an oil platform as a single unit, *Xiang Rui Kou* has a few elegant staterooms should corporate officials who don't mind rough seas wish to stay close to a valuable cargo during its journey.

USS *Lewis B. Puller*, a bizarre-looking expeditionary-force support ship—mysterious towers rise below the decks—so large the ship is based on the *Alaska*-class supertanker. In 2020, *Lewis B. Puller* was anchored at a US-owned dock in Bahrain, on the southern side of the Persian Gulf, and loaded for bear.

There is *Castoro Sei*, a column-stabilized vessel designed for laying energy pipe. *Castoro* means "beaver" in Italian, and the ship is industrious, having spent forty years lowering sealed tubes to the bottom of the Black Sea, North Sea, and Mediterranean. Increasingly the floors of these water bodies resemble an interstate highway system, albeit one that cannot be seen. The blue age is providing ample oil and natural gas to places that were predicted to experience horrible fuel shortages. But a few well-placed torpedoes could change that, and submarine commanders of several navies know where the weaknesses are.

There is USNS *Impeccable*—the prefix signifies US Navy, unarmed—a 5,000-ton catamaran that deploys towed arrays to conduct surveillance of ocean installations. *Impeccable* makes detailed records of the pitch of engines, the radio frequencies dialed around military towers, and similar information. In 2009, when *Impeccable* was recording sounds of Chinese submarines departing their home port on Hainan Island, Beijing sent boats from its opera buffa "maritime militia"—which the Chinese government claims with a straight face not to control—to try to cut the lines of the towed array. The US Navy responded by ordering a guided-missile destroyer to escort *Impeccable*.

The destroyer that answered the call was USS *Chung-Hoon*, named for Admiral Gordon Chung-Hoon, the first Asian American flag officer of the US military. Later, in 2016, *Chung-Hoon* was assigned to screen the Great Green Fleet, a squadron of US Navy vessels converted to run on biodiesel.[1] Every warship has a motto: the motto of the supercarrier *Abraham Lincoln* is "Shall Not Perish." *Chung-Hoon*'s motto is "Imua e Na Koa Kai" (Forward Sea Warriors!), the Hawaiian words chosen because Gordon Chung-Hoon grew up in Honolulu. During boyhood the future admiral attended the Punahou School, as did, later, the young Barack Obama. The United States has a major fighting ship named for a man of Asian appearance whose lineage was Chinese. Can anyone imagine China naming a warship for a person of Anglo-Saxon appearance whose lineage is American?

There was HMS *Furious*, a side-wheels-plus-sails vessel modeled on *Mississippi*, the boat Commodore Perry took to Japan. Commissioned 1853, *Furious* was sent directly to the Crimean War as a flagship, because it had the newest mortars in the Royal Navy. Off Odessa, *Furious* sank the Russian corvette *Andromache* in a duel that if nothing else paired ship names with prosody. After the pointless conflict of the Crimean War, *Furious* churned through the Mediterranean, down the coast of Africa, and turned east toward the Pacific Rim, leading a group of gunboats to reinforce Britain's China Squadron at Singapore.

By 1867, side-wheelers were obsolete. *Furious* churned across the Pacific, around the tip of South America, and over the Atlantic to Portsmouth, where the vessel became a "coal hulk"—no longer seaworthy, employed for storing fuel. Just fourteen years from gleaming flagship to metallic carcass.

There was *Ocean Odyssey*, a self-propelled space launch pad from which, in 1999, the first large private rocket roared skyward, carrying a satellite broadcast tower for XM Radio. Before each launch, *Ocean Odyssey* sailed from Long Beach, California, to the equator near Hawaii, to fire rockets eastbound over open ocean. Because the earth rotates west to east, and because a point on the equator rotates faster than a point at any other latitude, and because over-water launches protect cities against rocket failures, an equatorial eastbound blastoff above the sea is ideal for placing satellites in orbit. *Ocean Odyssey* launched thirty-two successful spaceflights and, in 2007, did not sink following the explosion of a powerful unmanned rocket.

Sea Launch, the independent company that built *Ocean Odyssey* and the rockets, went out of business when Elon Musk's SpaceX entered the picture, backed by federal subsidies. After Sea Launch folded, the idea of ocean-based access to space was taken up by China, which on a single day in 2020 sent nine military satellites into orbit from the newly built engineering vessel *De Bo 3*, anchored in the Yellow Sea.[2] *De Bo 3* looks like an extra-length salvage barge—with a spaceport at the center.

There was *Brent Charlie*, a drilling platform that sailed to the North Sea in the 1970s after the Brent basin was discovered. *Brent Charlie* could produce about 150,000 barrels of oil per day; for the crew, it had a full gymnasium, a movie theater, and menu dining with table service.

There was the *Glomar Explorer*, which appeared to be a deep-sea drill rig but actually was purpose-built for a Cold War attempt by the CIA to recover a sunken Russian submarine. In 2015 the *Glomar* was scrapped at a Chinese dry dock that specializes in ship-breaking, disassembling old boats for recyclable metals.

There is *MSC Grandiosa*, among the largest of the new-wave mega cruise ships. *Grandiosa* has bars, spas, and restaurants, a full-sized bowling alley, a resident Cirque de Soleil company, several LEGO parks in gradations by age, and an enclosed causeway that suggests a futuristic urban street of shopping and discos, complete with a dome of stars or bright sun depending on the time of day. This vessel pales before the current largest cruise ship, *Symphony of the Seas*, which is longer than the *Ford*-class supercarrier and weighs about twice as much. *Symphony of the Seas* offers staterooms with children's playgrounds (that is, playgrounds inside the stateroom) and a lounge where cocktails are mixed by automatons inspired by the bartending robot of the Jennifer Lawrence movie *Passengers*.

In 2019, the year before COVID-19, an estimated 20 million people climbed a gangplank for a cruise. Why so many pay premium prices to be aboard a moving object whose attractions simulate not being aboard a moving object is anyone's guess. *Grandiosa* takes the prize for best name.

Whatever boats personify in the mind, none of these top HMCS/NCSM *Margaret Brooke*, expected to be commissioned in 2021. Named for a Canadian military hero, the *Brooke* is a combat icebreaker, an extraordinary category.

The vessel has a cannon, deck guns, and an antisubmarine helicopter that launches NATO homing torpedoes. *Brooke* bears a range of rescue equipment intended for frigid weather; the gear includes snowmobiles and a snow-customized off-road truck—perhaps one should say, off-continent. *Brooke*'s hull is narrow, for a cutting-knife approach to ice floes. Its fin stabilizers, employed by modern ships to reduce roll, can be retracted during icebreaking. HMCS means Her Majesty's Canadian Ship, while NCSM stands for Navire Canadien de Sa Majesté. If all goes according to plan, *Brooke* will be joined by five sisters, a fleet built to carry the fight to enemies of Canada all the way to the North Pole, to perform rescues in subzero conditions, and to smash ice that impedes sea lanes.

The part about sea lanes matters because the world is about to get a new ocean.

FAR IN THE PAST, silhouettes of the seas were different. As recently as 200 million years ago (supposing *recently* is the proper adverb), dry land was joined into a single continent known as Pangaea, while the waters were a single planet-wide structure called Panthalassa. By the emergence of *Homo sapiens*, the alignment of oceans—the "seven" seas because tradition considers the North and South Pacific, and North and South Atlantic, to be distinct—was as today's. The arrival of the Arctic Ocean as a navigable very large water body thus will be an unprecedented event in human history. Since before the hand-carved outrigger, before cave paintings, before the wheel, we've never received a new ocean.

Boreal ice began thinning—starting the process of an ice cap becoming an ocean—around 12,000 years ago, which was the onset of the Holocene, our geologic epoch.[3] That the conclusion of an ice age accorded with the beginning of controlled agriculture and written records is unlikely to be happenstance. Because frozen sea and land glaciers have been melting for millennia, the thinning of ice was an established natural condition when the industrial period commenced. But the pace has quickened owing to artificially induced global warming.* Satellite readings in 2020 showed that the thickness of Arctic sea ice has declined noticeably over the last decade.

---

*That clunky wording is needed because most global warming occurs naturally.

In the current generation, artificially induced global warming has itself accelerated. Studies by the National Oceanic and Atmospheric Administration find that the rate of boreal air temperature increase hastened beginning roughly around 1990.[4] In the summer of 2020, there were a surprising number of wildfires across the taiga, as more snow melted than usual, allowing fuel (trees) to dry. In 2014, the National Academy of Sciences called human influence on climate proven.[5] Unless you know more about science than do all members of the National Academy of Sciences—apparently what some Fox News hosts believe about themselves—you should accept that artificial climate change is in progress.

In coming decades the impact of artificial global warming may be gravest in the boreal latitudes, where melting engages a feedback loop. Pale-colored snow and ice have high albedo, reflecting the sun's warmth into space. Dark color gives seawater one of the lowest albedos of substances naturally found across large areas. The result is that as boreal snow or ice melt, replacing whitish frozen water with darkish liquid, more solar heat is trapped.[6]

God must have a sense of humor, since the shrinking of the North Pole ice cap will allow more extraction of fossil fuels, whose use will speed up the shrinking of the ice cap. The Maker's sense of humor practically went into comedy-club standup mode in 2020, when the Norwegian mining company Store Norske Spitsbergen reported that melting of a glacial ice dam flooded a large coal mine on Svalbard, an archipelago midway between the North Pole and the northernmost territory of Europe. The flooding interrupted the digging of coal, a primary source of greenhouse gases that cause melting and flooding. Don't worry, Store Norske Spitsbergen used fossil fuels to pump the water out.

The world learned of these events from an article in the *Barents Observer*, a newspaper produced, in English and Russian, in Kirkenes, Norway. Much of its coverage concerns the Barents Regional Council, a project of Finland, Norway, Russia, Sweden, and several indigenous organizations. Little known, the Barents Regional Council governs an area larger than most of the world's nations.

A LESS ICY ARCTIC Circle will have winners and losers. Changes in sea temperatures and currents may harm the walrus, while the bowhead whale may prosper as never before. Other animals and plants will be helped or hurt. As the Arctic Circle warms, indigenous groups of the high north, such as the Sakha and the Dene, will gain money but lose their customary ways of life. (Whether their customary ways of life always would have ended anyway is unknowable.) High-latitude nations with Arctic sovereignty—Canada, Denmark (which essentially owns Greenland), Finland, Iceland, Norway, Russia, Sweden, and the United States (via Alaska)—will obtain usable coastline, along with significant fisheries and access to undersea fossil fuels and mineral resources.

These eight countries might be called the Narnia Nations. In C. S. Lewis's Chronicles of Narnia series, "To the north!" was the battle cry of Narnia, a snowbound realm protected by the lion-god Aslan. The Narnia Nations will come out ahead as the polar ice cap melts. Low-latitude countries, which is to say, most countries, may be losers as the North Pole changes and only the Narnia Nations, already among the best-off, add territory and treasure.

There are almost certainly basins of natural gas under the boreal ice: the low greenhouse content of natural gas suggests this fuel will be valuable well into the future. Indications are North Pole undersea oil is "sweet," a wildcatter term for the most desired category of petroleum. Brent crude, an international benchmark for oil, takes its name from the Brent Field in the sea between the North Pole and Scotland. Brent crude is high north and practically honeyed. Venezuelan oil is equatorial and "sour," the less valuable kind. The Narnia Nations are likely to get more of the type of oil the world fancies. Southern nations are likely to get nothing.

AS FOR SHIPS—THEY LOVE liquid and hate frozen. Northern icebergs are turning liquid. Because the South Pole is mostly rocks and soil to begin with, ocean changes will not be pronounced there. In the high north, a lot more blue water is coming.

Already parts of the Arctic Ocean are navigable in the summer. Soon a parade of container vessels, warships, trawlers, and tourist cruises may sail to latitudes that skippers of previous centuries considered certain death. Already the luxo cruise liner *Crystal Serenity* has been sidling as far north as possible for tours that cost up to $150,000 per person.

This is why Canada decided to build a fleet of militarized icebreakers, ready for combat, for rescue missions and to smash a path. Probably there will be an evolutionary period during which the Arctic Ocean is unpredictably frozen or liquid; later, all water. During the interregnum, icebreakers will rule.

Russia has the world's only nuclear-powered icebreakers. They are much larger than *Brooke*, though not militarized. One is named *Yamal*, an indigenous word from the Nenets language, meaning "end of the land"—the Yamal peninsula extends to the point where Arctic ice once began. *Yamal* has a bow brightly adorned with sharks' teeth, since the bow chews the ice. Russian icebreakers cannot steam too far south, because their reactors are moderated with cold water from intakes: the vessels are mechanically allergic to warmth. By ingesting cold seawater then expelling reactor-warmed water, Russian icebreakers add tiny amounts to the rise of boreal sea temperatures. Fish that like warm water follow them.

Finland and Sweden sail modern icebreakers, though nothing with the bulk of *Yamal* or firepower of *Brooke*. Beijing has no plausible Arctic Circle jurisdiction, yet in 2018 launched a heavy icebreaker, *Xue Long (Snow Dragon)*. The US Coast Guard has one icebreaker, and the US Navy none, despite USN submarines often cruising beneath Arctic ice pack. The Coast Guard has been seeking funding for heavy icebreakers.

Given Arctic ice is melting, icebreaker crews may someday be out of jobs, their ships converted to museums. For the moment, on the waters of the high north, icebreakers express power—and there are many temptations to misuse power. In 2007, *The Atlantic* warned, "Today it seems absurd to imagine governments of the world fighting over the North Pole seas, but in the past many causes of battle seemed absurd till explosions began."[7]

There's a new ocean coming—will we spoil it, share it, or go to war over it?

AS LONG AGO AS the days of Flemish cartographer Gerardus Mercator, born 1512, sailors understood the North Pole region was frozen water rather than land, that during the season of midnight sun the ice softened and perhaps became passable. Navigators began seeking the Northwest Passage, a shortcut to Asia. The name Northwest was chosen because a ship departing England or Ireland would take that compass heading.

If there were a Northwest Passage, skirting the topmost terrain of what's now Canada, the fact that the high latitudes of earth are not as long as the equatorial latitudes—the crown of the basketball instead of the middle—might allow weeks or months to be shaved off voyages to and from Asia. A Northeast Passage, departing Russia or Scandinavia with compass heading northeast, possessed similar appeal. Then as now, trade with Asia was the ultimate objective.

Many explorers died trying to find a polar passage. USS *Jeannette*, seeking the Northwest Passage, was immobilized in ice from 1879 to 1881 with loss of twenty souls.* Sponsors of that expedition believed a warm current flowed toward the pole; the plan was to map what was expected to be a navigable flux. (Salt water has a lower freezing point than freshwater.) From 1903 to 1906 the Norwegian explorer Roald Amundsen became first to transit the Arctic Circle above Canada. That it took him three years indicated the Northwest Passage of a mostly iced-in Arctic Ocean was not the hoped-for shortcut.

During the postwar period, the combination of thinning ice and better ships—double hulls, stronger engines, heated quarters—renewed interest in northern routes between the hemispheres. Research began to reveal that as well as fishing grounds, the northern polar seas held deposits of oil, gas, and polymetallic nodules, little spheres rich in precious minerals. Mining of the nodules is only somewhat regulated by the International Seabed Authority, which as everyone knows is headquartered in Kingston, Jamaica.

---

* The harrowing tale of the *Jeannette* is well told in Hampton Sides, *In the Kingdom of Ice* (Doubleday, 2014).

When container-trade mania intensified, shippers looked northward for the next competitive edge. Even if prices are falling, as shipping costs have been for a generation, further reductions are good business—an effect shown by cell-phone plans. Each time ocean shipping costs fall, global standards of living rise a little.

In 2013, the Danish-owned coal carrier *Nordic Orion* became the first large merchantman to transit the Northwest Passage. *Nordic Orion* departed the Port of Vancouver and sailed via the Arctic to the Port of Pori along the Gulf of Bothnia in Finland, accomplishing a voyage of which mariners dreamt for centuries. Using the northern route shaved about eleven hundred miles off the distance traveled, reducing fuel costs and greenhouse gas emissions. On the other hand an icebreaker had to accompany *Nordic Orion*, at the Canadian government's expense.

In 2020, the tanker *Christophe de Margerie*, purpose-built in 2017 to carry natural gas in a liquid state of minus 260 degrees Fahrenheit—trading by sea in liquefied natural gas is a growth market—departed a high-north Russian facility along the wonderfully named Gulf of Ob, crossed near the North Pole and sailed to China, an enthusiastic customer for clean fuels. The journey of *Christophe de Margerie* was the first time a tanker employed the polar route to change hemispheres. *Margerie* is one of an innovative class of polar tankers with "double-acting" design that enables the ship to crack through thin ice alone. For this voyage, an escort was present, the mammoth *Yamal*.

Requiring icebreakers, the voyages of *Nordic Orion* and *Christophe de Margerie* were too expensive to represent a viable business model. But these trips staged a proof-of-concept demonstration that the Arctic Ocean can be used by commercial vessels to shorten the distance between sides of the world. Now it's a matter of ironing out details. And with each passing year, there will be less ice.

ONE REASON THE NATIONS have been able to maintain the uneasy Long Peace to be discussed in the final chapter is that for all their foibles, organizations such as the United Nations and World Bank reduce international strains, while their less-known siblings have constructive impacts. The International Maritime Organization, based in London, keeps shipping companies in reasonable harmony. The Amazon Cooperation Treaty Organization helps balance development and preservation in the Amazon basin; the Association of Southeast Asian Nations does welcome work in the lower Pacific Rim; the United Nations Office at Geneva, an offshoot of the primary body, convinced big militaries to destroy stockpiles of land mines and cluster munitions, which are more dangerous to civilians than soldiers. The International Federation of Red Cross and Red Crescent exhibits heroism in making fighting less brutal.

There are other unfamiliar offices that prevent nations from going rogue. Among them is the Arctic Council. Expect to hear more about it.

When founded a quarter century ago, the Arctic Council was a backbencher agency with a base of operations in remote Tromsø, Norway, charged to serve indigenous peoples and coordinate rescue preparations for subzero weather. Then governments began to realize the Arctic Ocean would become navigable.

The original Arctic Council members were the Narnia Nations adjacent to the pole—Canada, Denmark, Finland, Iceland, Norway, Russia, Sweden, and the United States. In early years, representatives attended meetings grudgingly. Today the Arctic Council is among diplomacy's hot tickets. Near-north countries, including Germany and the Netherlands, are honorary members. China, Japan, Singapore, and South Korea, concerned their waterborne trade soon may sail toward Santa Claus, have signed on as observer states that send nonvoting delegates.

At international organizations, observers lack clout but get their feet in the door. Turkey, a hot-climate nation, has petitioned for an Arctic Council observer seat. Over the top? Istanbul is a popular destination for cruise liners. Someday, towering pleasure ships with in-room waterslides and twenty-four-hour martini bars and traveling casts of Broadway shows may depart Istanbul, cross the Sea of Marmara, motor through the Mediterranean past Gibraltar, take a sighting of Polaris, and set course for the North Pole.

During the first two years of the Trump administration, the secretary of state was Rex Tillerson, former CEO of ExxonMobil. In Washington, Tillerson is viewed as having botched almost everything he touched, including going to Moscow for negotiations but refusing to bring Department of State Russian-speaking analysts or security-cleared notetakers. No worries, comrade, FSB most happy to provide American guest with special interpreter! Have another vodka! Tillerson performed so poorly at the Department of State some wondered whether it must be really easy to run ExxonMobil.

There was one matter Tillerson did not botch—the Arctic Council. He attended council meetings, knew the issues, vigorously pressed the American position. Tillerson's successor, Mike Pompeo, like Tillerson hopelessly in over his head, also like Tillerson at least did well by the Arctic Council. Speaking at a council session in 2019, Pompeo called the far north "a land of opportunity and abundance."

Commentators get easy laffs by mocking United Nations and World Bank excess. Yet bureaucracy and boring speeches are a small price to pay for fewer artillery bombardments. The Arctic Council so far has been effective in the peacekeeping role, another indicator that less war coincides with the proliferation of international organizations.

BOTH RUSSIA AND CHINA are expanding the ability of their warships to operate on the boreal waves, and their submarines to linger below. The US Navy runs high-profile fleet exercises such as RIMPAC. Two can play at that game—in 2019, Moscow staged Ocean Shield, a seventy-ship drill along the Northern Sea Route, Russia's preferred Arctic waterway. The Northern Sea Route shadows the roof of Asia rather than the roof of Canada; Beijing is more or less cooperating with Moscow in establishing this passage.

At one level, Ocean Shield was about showing off some flashy new ships. Disguising fleet movements today is frustrated by coverage from space sensors using optical, radar, heat-plume, chemical-plume, and other detectors. Knowing they will be seen, navies have pivoted to a *look at me* approach. At another level, Ocean Shield was practice for operating in the bad conditions of polar waters.

Paula Dobriansky, a former American diplomat and Naval Academy instructor, says the pace of military activity in the Arctic has been increasing: "Denmark and Norway have been showing concern about Russian submarines in the high north. In recent years Chinese warships were observed in the Arctic." Though much of the Arctic Ocean is international water where anyone can sail, movement of Chinese naval power so far from home was striking. Laid-back Sweden in 2017 imposed conscription, citing a need to prepare to defend the Arctic Circle.

In 2019, Donald Trump gave comedians a gift of material by suggesting the United States would purchase Greenland. Denmark did not post the world's largest island on Craigslist under FOR SALE BY OWNER. Not without virtues of its own, Greenland's value in great-power politics is a claim on the Arctic Circle. Whether Denmark would ever sell Greenland, and whether if so the United States could outbid China, remains to be seen.

In 2020, the Senate Armed Services Committee held confirmation hearings for the incoming secretary of the navy. There were more questions about the Arctic than any other topic, including whether Moscow and Beijing will form an alliance to outgun the United States at the top of the world.

FAR SOUTH, THERE IS international consensus that no one owns Antarctica. During the 1950s, as the Cold War and nuclear apocalypse loomed, the great powers had to identify something they wouldn't fight over. The something was the South Pole. Antarctica cannot offer a path to warships or commercial vessels; submarines cannot hide under it; settlers don't want to live there. The South Pole holds scant allure. Capping a forgotten event, the 1958 International Geophysical Year, the great powers agreed to reserve Antarctica for science.

Like northern polar air temperatures, southern polar air temperatures are rising faster than air temperatures in other parts of the world. But though threats to the austral ice shelves have environmental significance, this does not shake politics in the way melting boreal ice does, since there's no prospect of a new ocean. There are research stations on Antarctica and a few national contentions—Chile claims Vinson Massif, a landmark taller than Pike's Peak. But the combination of mean winter temperature of minus forty degrees Fahrenheit and mountainous terrain makes Antarctica unappealing. Political conditions in Antarctica are not likely to change much in the coming generation, as opposed to conditions in the Arctic Circle, where change is rapid.

If no one owns the South Pole, does anyone own the North Pole?

Generally, nations assert sovereignty up to twelve miles off their shorelines and exclusive economic rights—to fish, drill oil, build windmills—up to two hundred miles. In some places the boundaries are undisputed. Cape Hatteras, say—from there you'll sail a long time before you encounter another nation's land. But in places where distinctions are not clear, nations have bickered for centuries. The Kuril Islands, roughly equidistant between Japan and Russia, are claimed by both and were issues in two Russo-Japanese wars. At the Yalta Conference in 1945, with the world in flames and thousands dying each day, Stalin interrupted the agenda to ask FDR for the Kurils.[8] Then, land territory was a measure of national wealth. Today, sea territory may be foremost, and whoever wins jurisdiction over each big rock of the Kurils gets to draw an exclusive-rights circle.

Where national boundaries interlace, disputes become complex. Such is the situation in the Arctic Circle. "Ottawa thinks the Northwest Passage is internal Canadian waters, so you need Canadian permission to navigate there," says David Balton, a retired US diplomat who once ran the Arctic Council. Canada makes this claim by considering every solid object, even if minuscule, within its twelve-mile boundary to be territorial, then describing a twelve-mile perimeter around said object. Enough of these, and presto, areas that look like open ocean become restricted. Using similar reasoning, Russia claims most of the

Northern Sea Route as national territory. Moscow wants to require vessels on this route to hire a Russian icebreaker escort. For their own safety, comrade!

The United States maintains that neither the Northwest Passage nor the Northern Sea Route are national territory; anyone may enjoy freedom of navigation in these lanes. Once I read Paul Gewirtz, a professor at Yale Law School, going into learned detail on "rocks which cannot support human habitation," a phrase used in classifying ocean outcroppings as part of national polities. This concept is at issue in the South China Sea and Arctic Circle and other places, for example the Liancourt Rocks, islets claimed by Japan and by South Korea.

The asterisk is that sometimes nations can assert that their zones begin not at the shoreline but, rather, at the end of their continental shelf. Because the continental shelf is an undersea structure that cannot be observed directly, claims may be shrouded in jiggery-pokery, as the late Justice Antonin Scalia liked to say.

IN 2019, IN CONCERT with Greenland (that is, with Denmark), the United States began mapping the Arctic seafloor, including undersea shelves. Much of the seafloor is a mystery. More is known about the terrain of Mars than the terrain of the benthic depths.

Attaining reasonable knowledge of the surface of the sea took centuries, and the surface is a small fraction of the whole. Around the time the many German city-states were coalescing into a modern nation, German explorers wondered what they might do that others had not already done. They choose mapping surface currents of the Pacific Ocean, familiar to Polynesian travelers for millennia but little known to Europeans. In the late 1880s the barque *Paula*, built near Bremerhaven, crossed the Pacific, tossing overboard thousands of bottles containing letters asking the finder to post an enclosed document to the German Naval Observatory in Hamburg. A surprising number were sent. By comparing file numbers on each document to where that bottle was put overboard, and where found, researchers compiled a rough sketch of Pacific Ocean currents. The project entered the realm of trivia-contest winning answer when one of the original items washed up on a beach in Australia in 2018—a message in a bottle received 130 years later.

America has proposed resolving the continental shelf question via creation of a complete map of the global seafloor. China opposes a multinational seafloor charting project, presumably because Beijing fears such a map would diminish its claims around the Pacific Rim while placing boreal sovereignty more firmly into the hands of the Narnia Nations. As a warm-up, Chinese vessels have been mapping the continental shelf near Malaysia. Beijing has been mum about the results, perhaps because the maps do not uphold Chinese assertions regarding the South China Sea. The Chinese Academy of Sciences has been installing underwater sensors in the Arctic Circle while *Snow Dragon*, packed with instruments, is believed to be imaging the polar seafloor.

Russia devoted considerable effort to surveying the Lomonosov Ridge of the undersea Arctic, named for the brilliant eighteenth-century chemist. Moscow was delighted when the Lomonosov Ridge was labeled Russian, rather than Danish, on the General Bathymetric Chart maintained by the International Hydrographic Organization, which as everyone knows is headquartered in Monaco.

In 2019 a Russian nuclear submarine customized for deep diving had some kind of awful malfunction in Arctic waters off the far-northern city of Vidyayevo. Fourteen were killed, including two recipients of the title Hero of the Russian Federation, the equivalent of America's Medal of Honor.

Rumors about the mission abounded. Was the vessel seeking undersea passageways? Parts of the seafloor resemble the Grand Canyon; maps of undersea canyons would have military value. Was the vessel testing ways to cut US Navy cables during war? Had the Russians obtained a technology to eavesdrop on the overwhelming share of internet traffic that travels along the seafloor? (Your data isn't in the cloud—it's in the oceans.) Some intelligence analysts speculated the submarine was tasked to document the precise extent of the Russian continental shelf to bolster sovereignty claims in the Arctic.

China is thought to be trying to build a submarine similar to the one in the 2019 Russian mission. The United States already has three heavily armed submarines that are equipped for intelligence work at extreme depths. Named the *Seawolf* class, they are the most advanced attack subs ever; at $4 billion each, they'd better be.

In 2017 a *Seawolf*-class submarine, the *Jimmy Carter*, returned to base in Washington State on the surface, flying the Jolly Roger from its sail (the part of a submarine that movies call the conning tower). By tradition, showing the Jolly Roger when bound into home port signals that a voyage was a tremendous success. The Pentagon has never explained what *Jimmy Carter* did in 2017. There's a theory it found something very deep under the sea that the Russians and the Chinese have been trying to find since.

THE SOUTH POLE CANNOT be a hiding place for submarines and sits a long distance from the capitals of the great powers. Because there is water under the North Pole ice, and a relatively short ballistic flight time to those capitals, sailing strategic-missile submarines beneath the northern polar cap was an early Cold War objective for Washington and Moscow. The result is that great powers have been eyeing each other warily in the high north since today's leaders were born.

In 2019 an Air Force B-2 stealth bomber took off from Missouri, refueled at a Royal Air Force base in England, headed straight at Polaris, and flew around the Arctic Circle for a day, accompanied by two aerial tankers. The bomber was simulating a loiter mission, in which a jet seems innocuous, then suddenly launches the navy's much-feared homing torpedoes. This was a way of letting the Russians and Chinese know that anywhere in the Arctic Circle, there could be hellfire from the sky without warning.

Exercises such as the bomber's flight assume Russia and China are not just competitors but enemies. Is the United States misreading the situation? Though Russia is building military infrastructure in the Arctic Circle, Moscow does not necessarily want war in the region. Russia has the most fossil-dependent major economy, David Balton notes, and "sees the Arctic Circle has a place for development of oil and gas. The Russians want to show the world they can be reliable business partners. Nobody's going to lend Moscow money if it's engaged in cowboy adventurism at the North Pole." In 2017, Beijing advanced Moscow an estimated $1 billion to enlarge the Russian port at Arkhangelsk ("Archangel" to GIs) along the boundary of the Arctic Circle. Tidy sums like this may be contingent on good-boy behavior.

China's Belt and Road Initiative, aiming to build highways, railroads, and harbors around the Indian Ocean basin, is so expensive and ambitious that adding some kind of polar Silk Road seems beyond China's financial reserves, at least for the moment. Nevertheless, since 2015, in diplomacy China has asserted "near-Arctic status," which is an ingenious interpretation of the surface of the earth.

But then America asserts possession of Guam, more than six thousand miles off the coast of California. In 2020, the navy's new Indo-Pacific Command asked funding for a "360-degree persistent and integrated air defense capability" on Guam. If Washington thinks Guam belongs to the United States, why can't Beijing think some corner of the North Pole belongs to China?

Reasoning this way, China bid to acquire a gold mining complex at Hope Bay in Nunavut, the northernmost part of Canada. In early 2021, the deal fell through as the Ottawa government put its foot down. The Hope Bay camps, part of a "greenstone belt" geologically, have produced little of the shiny metal but include a sizable frontage on the Northwest Passage. Beijing may have thought that owning some of the greenstone would improve China's "near-Arctic" contention.

With Canada arming its icebreakers and US Air Force stealth bombers overhead, the odds of the Middle Kingdom's invading the Arctic seem low. Gray eminences, including Henry Kissinger, have been saying China takes the long view and simply wants to be involved in whatever's happening, hoping some future turn of events will redound to China's favor. On the blue water, what's happening is a new ocean up north.

PART OF THE "OPPORTUNITY and abundance" of the Arctic Circle swims.

For millennia, fish have been a staple. Old Mediterranean society revolved around fishing; the Bible reports that after Jesus was resurrected, his first request was a breakfast of roast fish.[9] As prosperity increases, more of the world's citizens opt for protein-rich diets. Providing beef or pork to the world's ever-larger consumer class would, at the least, mean more acres tilled and more greenhouse gases. Ocean fisheries generate protein with fewer environmental consequences than raising cows, pigs, and fowl. (Whether plant-based diets are the future is a separate issue.) The population of the earth will continue to increase for at least a few more generations, and almost surely will demand more fish.

Many fisheries in warm parts of the oceans already are stressed by modern trawlers that take whole schools. Some fish species evolved for cold water. These points cause fisherfolk to look north, to untapped areas.

In general, managed fisheries can sustain themselves if there are catch limits and regulations against bycatch, or unintended killing of species people don't eat. Overfished areas may deplete quickly. By the same token, fish schools may recover quickly: reproductive crescendos of ocean life are among the many poorly understood aspects of the oceans. In 2020 China, which has the largest fishing fleet, self-imposed a moratorium on taking squid. If schools of squid restock, that will be a hopeful sign about ocean population cycles. If squid don't rebound, that will be another argument for a strict regime against overfishing.

So far, the Barents Sea, to the north of Scandinavia and managed jointly by Norway and Russia, appears to have good levels of fish. The Gulf Stream brings warm water to the Barents Sea—or does now; global warming could alter the Gulf Stream—rendering the Barents Sea more similar to the lower oceans than to the rest of the north polar region. But annual months of darkness make fishing there dangerous as well as a trial for trawler crews' nerves.

The Bering Sea, near Alaska and managed jointly by Russia and the United States, also seems in good condition. The Bering Sea is not fished as much as it might be, owing to stormy weather.

The Central Arctic Ocean that begins around Svalbard—from Oslo, fly a thousand miles due north—is iced over most of the year. As defreezing continues, fishing may become attractive. Not much is known about what sorts of fish dwell in the Central Arctic Ocean or how climate change may affect their numbers. In 2018, an international agreement banned fishing of the Central Arctic Ocean until 2033, giving researchers time to study the region. What may happen after 2033, or whether the convention will last that long, is anybody's guess.

In many aspects of the blue age, *Homo sapiens* do okay. Modern navies have improved their treatment of sailors; working on container liners and bulk carriers is monotonous but pays well; the combination of less fighting and more trade at sea has improved billions of lives.

In fishing, people often don't do okay. Ocean fishing is among the riskiest occupations, about thirty times more deadly than any form of work on the continental United States. When accidents happen, the injured are far from a hospital. Most fishing fleets lack the high safety standards or well-staffed medical facilities found on vessels of Western navies; some individual fishing boats carry little more than a first aid kit. Deckhands struggle with masses of slimy fish on slippery surfaces as boats heel from side to side. Forced labor—human trafficking—is an ongoing scandal for trawler fleets.

AUTHORS WHO CONDUCT INTERVIEWS may artfully reword to make the subject appear silver-tongued. Rare is the person, however accomplished, who speaks in finished thoughts. An exception is the North Pole expert Fran Ulmer, who from 2011 to 2020 was chair of the US Arctic Research Commission.

Ulmer has lived most of her life in Alaska, where she was, at various times, lieutenant governor, a city official, and chancellor of the University of Alaska at Anchorage. Ulmer speaks in finished thoughts, so let's just listen:

> The idea that the Arctic Ocean will become crowded with container vessels has been oversold. The Arctic Ocean has limited appeal to container lines because it is only accessible in summer months, the weather is terrible, and the cycle of perpetual midnight or perpetual noon is very hard on crews. Even if crossing the Arctic allows your cargo to skip the Suez Canal or Panama Canal, conditions of the high north may not be appealing to shippers.
>
> That said, the ice is retreating faster than projections. Regular access to the Northwest Passage and Northern Sea Route may happen as soon as about 2030. Shipping lines, navies, tourist firms will be interested. The Transpolar Route—the shortest, directly across the pole—may be navigable around 2050.
>
> Antarctica has a very restrictive treaty signed by almost everyone. This treaty holds because there are no permanent residents and no contiguous nations. The Arctic Circle has several million residents and eight nearby nations. The enviros want a total ban on development, but to expect some Arctic Circle ban on development is totally unrealistic. Development is coming. The question is, what development? It's important we don't screw this up, as the poles are the last pure virgin large territory on earth.
>
> It's not clear the Central Arctic Ocean will ever have economic value since even in a warming world, the weather there will remain terrible. It's good that fishing in this area is prohibited until 2033, so we can figure out what's happening in that ocean with nature, which we really don't know.
>
> Iceland is happy that mackerel and cod, which Icelanders like, are heading north as the mid-latitudes warm. Pollack and salmon too—both have been observed recently in the Bering Sea, well north of their traditional habitats. Traditional to us, at least.

People assume fish movements are driven by temperature, but ocean currents and nutrient streams may be as significant, and we know very little about nutrient cycling in the oceans. We do know artificial greenhouse gases are turning the oceans acidic, which is bad for many marine species, and this is occurring at a time more people need fish for dietary protein.

Probably there is some oil in the Arctic Circle, and might be a tremendous amount of natural gas. The Russians, particularly, want high-north oil and gas to work. They have been good citizens on the Arctic Council, cooperative about science and search-and-rescue. Russia's high-north mineral resources are close enough to its land mass to be within the Russian Federation exclusive economic zone, so no disputes there. But polar oil and gas locations are disputed, and a lot of the Russian economic future depends on this coming through.

Oil and gas drilling at the top of the world is going to prove easier said than done. In 2015, Shell withdrew from prospecting the Chukchi Sea, writing off a $7 billion investment. Shell led development of the Brent Field in the North Sea. So as a company, Shell knew more about cold-weather ocean drilling than anyone else. Yet Shell couldn't operate in the Chukchi, because of the rough conditions. At some point, technology will solve the problems of drilling in Arctic waters, but it could be later rather than sooner.

Norway and Demark join Russia in wanting polar oil and gas developed. Canada and the European Union are opposed; they say they won't buy polar fossil fuels. That's a desirable political position now with oil and gas markets flooded. We'll see what tune they sing if there's a shortage and the Arctic Circle is the solution.

Greenland has tremendous offshore mineral resources, and because Greenland has so much coastline, development is practical. The crews could work at sea during the day then go home in the evening to live on land.

Bunker fuel, the dregs of oil production and used by many commercial ships because it's cheap, has been banned in the high north. Bunker fuel turns gelatinous in cold and, when the stuff spills on ice, becomes like glue. The farther north you go, the less biological activity there is to break down spills. Bunker fuel really should be prohibited everywhere on the oceans because it's such a pollutant. Banning it in the high north sets a good example. Let's ban it everywhere.

No matter what, we need America to ratify the Convention on the Law of the Sea. The US position on this treaty is irrational. Irrational has been doing quite well in Washington, D.C., lately. But there must be international consensus on how to govern the seas. The sooner the world acts on this, the better.

9

THE NEXT STAGE
IS TO GOVERN THE SEAS

IN THE 1980S, I WAS A STAFF WRITER FOR *THE ATLANTIC*, WHICH
was then at the peak of an illustrious existence stretching from
founding in 1857 as the journal of learned abolitionism, continuing today and, one hopes, for generations to come. [1]

When writers and editors of *The Atlantic* of that decade went
out for drinks, often there would be mention that our article topics
could be a tad arid: electric utility regulation, farm price support
formulas, what is the role of the art museum? (Actual examples.)
If the dullness of *Atlantic* subjects was raised, the standing joke was,
"At least we're not writing about the Law of the Sea!"

Life, the poet Conrad Aiken said, is a great circle. Here I write
about the Law of the Sea.

Three-quarters of the earth's surface is water. A visitor arriving
from a faraway star system might describe our home as an ocean
planet that also has some land. Most likely there are multitudes of
distant spheres, but water worlds like ours may prove rare. Because
we live on the minor part of earth that is dry, we think of land as
what it's all about. Arguably, sea is the defining aspect of our earth.

The centuries have shown that of the possible conditions—ungoverned, poorly governed, and well governed—well governed must be the goal. The sea is still at the first stage, ungoverned.

FOR MILLENNIA, FORCE OF arms and whims of nature have been the edicts of the sea. Neil deGrasse Tyson and Avis Lang contend acceptance of lawless risk on the oceans might have begun as far back as forty thousand years ago, in migrations without maps or compass from eastern Africa to what the ancients called Sahul and we call Australia. Those who ventured upon the blue water knew they had no chance of rescue if imperiled, no hope of assistance if attacked, no judge to plead to if wronged.

Many who rowed, sailed, or rode currents beyond the horizon were never heard from again. Evidence of their voyages sank beneath the waves. Just as land battles scatter dropped weapons and broken bodies of men and horses while sea battles leave no trace, land migrations and trading by land bequeath evidence for archeologists to sift, while attempts to migrate or trade by sea leave behind only legends.

Roughly five centuries ago, jurists and scholars in Europe and Asia began to assert that warships could not seize unarmed vessels willy-nilly, that sailors should not be executed by captain's fiat, that naval batteries must not bombard towns that refused to pay tribute, that marines coming ashore should not seize whatever they desired. This led to "prize rules," imposing at least some structure on whether treasures could or could not be taken by ships with carronade and boarding parties.

When sails and cutlasses were supplanted by engine rooms and torpedoes, a set of marginally civilized "cruise rules" arose to give a measure of protection to noncombatants during sea fighting. Elaborate customs regarding treatment of those on civilian ships sometimes were observed, often ignored, German butchery against unarmed vessels being the cause of the American declaration of war in 1917. Rules were observed sporadically through the next generation. In 1939, the German raider *Graf Spee*, before sinking a British merchantman off Pernambuco, gave fair warning so the crew could abandon ship, then radioed Brazilian authorities to report that men in lifeboats required assistance. British intelligence intercepted the message, and not long after, off Montevideo, *Graf Spee* was on the bottom. Chivalrous rules of naval engagement soon were to end.

Early in the seventeenth century the Delft-born humanist Hugo Grotius became the European known for arguing the sea is the common property of humanity, in the same way as the air, an idea already widely accepted in the Indian Ocean region. At that time the Dutch Republic had a strong navy and a vested interest in the Dutch East India Company, whose primary business competition came from Portugal. For their part, Portuguese jurists contended sea lanes to the East Indies could be closed by property claims. Grotius averred that if the sea, like the atmosphere, belongs to all, Dutch ships have as much right off Singapore as do those of the Iberian Union.

History is written by the winners. Dutch and Portuguese vessels fought near Singapore. The Dutch won; Amsterdam got to compose the rules for three hundred years of exploitation of the East Indies. The legal framework expounded by Holland's Grotius also would win—travel upon the blue water would come to be viewed as a right held by every member of the human family.

There were some exceptions. Common law of the sea, sometimes called "customary law," would more or less wrestle with those exceptions—how far into an ocean a nation's border extended, what responsibility ships engaged in combat had relative to neutrals, universalizing a duty to assist those in peril on the seas.

Reflecting customary law—obviously this account is simplified—for many generations every harbor had an official similar to a sheriff, whose role was to declare vessels impounded for reasons of unpaid debts; or interned under rules of war, forbidden to return to battle; or obliged to quit neutral waters. From the 1907 version of the Hague Convention: if a neutral power "which has been informed of the outbreak of hostilities learns that a belligerent warship is in one of its ports or roadsteads, it must notify the said ship to depart within twenty-four hours."

By the early postwar period, fighting ships had acquired so much firepower, and commercial ships so much scope, while environmental concerns were rising—human action was sufficient to *alter the sea*—there was consensus that customary law needed to be revamped. Especially there was felt a requirement for standard water boundaries, as some nations were restricting three miles, others twelve miles, still others publishing extravagant claims.

Enter the Law of the Sea, initialed by many nations at Montego Bay in 1982, taking effect in 1994, when Guyana put the treaty over a threshold for ratification. Quaffing beer in Boston, my younger self saw the agreement as so much verbiage. My younger self was on the wrong side of history. The delegates who signed the Law of the Sea accord were on the right side of Montego Bay.

THE LAW OF THE Sea is more or less a United Nations product and, to backers, known by an imposing moniker, UNCLOS, for United Nations Convention on the Law of the Sea. Opponents call the agreement LOST, for Law of the Sea Treaty, emphasizing the negative.

In the main, the Law of the Sea codifies Hugo Grotius, representing a late touchdown for seventeenth-century Dutch merchants. Under the agreement, undisputed national boundaries at sea are made standard; overlapping boundaries, such as in the South China Sea, are made even more confusing; environmental goals are established but not mandated; most of the waters, and whatever turns out to be underneath, become common property of humanity; sometimes sorta kinda what's beneath the waters can be claimed; the continental shelf may extend a nation's territory; the United Nations is granted another reason to expand.

Law of the Sea negotiations began not long after the United States, under President Jimmy Carter, agreed to hand over the Panama Canal to Panama. Those who viewed that accord as a giveaway saw the Law of the Sea as its sequel—first the United States surrenders the historic Path Between the Seas, then America surrenders open-ocean control only the US Navy has sufficient power to seize by force.

As the hard right went into a fury regarding the Law of the Sea, the hard left did, too, realizing the agreement grants color of law to the freedom-of-navigation exercises of which the navy is so fond. The hard right wanted the United States to have nothing to do with international order on the oceans. The hard left wanted the Law of the Sea to restrict the US Navy to home waters, while granting the developing world a cut of whatever value the Narnia Nations may discover by drilling or prospecting.

Many found impenetrable the Law of the Sea's 1,752 pages—longer than the Bible—with 436 articles in the main text plus nine annexes. You thought the Bay of Fundy was foggy!

Most of the world's nations, including landlocked Bolivia and Mongolia, signed, along with umbrella organizations such as the European Union. Since 1994 nearly every member of the Joints Chiefs of Staff, the leadership committee for the US military, has expressed support for the Law of the Sea.

But the United States has never inked the pact. The retired admiral John Richardson, once a member of the Joint Chiefs, notes, "The United States has not signed the Law of the Sea, but observes it. China has signed the Law of the Sea, but does not observe it. Which is better?"

THE PEN STROKE MATTERS, as the US Navy has always been a stickler for international tenets.

In 1916, when America had yet to enter the Great War, a German U-boat pulled into Newport, Rhode Island. The captain went ashore to buy newspapers and mail some letters, proving he'd had the nerve to cross an ocean—early submarines were reliant on currents—then declare himself in public. The next morning the U-boat took up position near the Nantucket lightship that was passed by merchantmen bound toward open sea. The German submarine sank several, giving warning so their crews could abandon ship. US Navy destroyers watched and did not intervene, because in that year the United States was neutral: to sink a merchantman outside US waters, if first giving warning, was lawful by customary rules of the time. Editorialists were incensed that US destroyers allowed a belligerent to fire on friendly vessels leaving an American harbor. But the US Navy followed the rules to the letter, and the same remains today.

China hears a different drummer. Though Beijing ratified the Law of the Sea and often praises the convention for public consumption, when China was placed in the dock (legally, not nautically), Beijing was livid. In 2013, the Philippines activated an arbitration clause of the Law of the Sea to protest China's nine dashed lines, some of which bisect what are obviously Philippine waters. The case went to the Hague, heard at the wonderfully named Permanent Court of Arbitration in the wonderfully named Palace of Peace. Human beings can only hope our institutions will be permanent and that someday the peacemakers will reside in a palace!

Alternatively, the Philippines might have chosen to have the case heard by the International Tribunal for the Law of the Sea, where twenty-one judges from a diverse selection of the world's nations occupy a glistening complex on a hill above the Elbe in Germany. Or Manila might have taken its legal briefs to the International Court of Justice—Court of Justice is a wonderful name, too—in the Hague, which manages some Law of the Sea disagreements and investor-versus-government disputes that arise from globalized trade.*

Jurists at the Hague found China had no legal basis for claiming historical rights in waters belonging to Manila and that building landfills around the Spratly Islands does not generate new national territory at sea. China thumbed its national nose, defying the court.

LEGAL DISPUTES REGARDING BLUE-WATER areas preceded the Law of the Sea. For instance, though any vessel may transit between the Pacific and Atlantic oceans by rounding Cape Horn, that name strikes fear into mariners owing to the strong currents, tall waves,

---

* On the mashup of magistrates for international trade, I commend to readers the fine book by Haley Sweetland Edwards, *Shadow Courts: The Tribunals That Rule Global Trade* (Columbia Global Reports, 2016).

and icebergs common at the southernmost headland of Tierra del Fuego. Two natural straits a little north of Cape Horn allow ships to make the passage between the oceans by riding mostly atop sheltered water. One of these straits, the Beagle Channel, named for Charles Darwin's brig-sloop, had since the early nineteenth century been the subject of jurisdictional disputes between Chile and Argentina. Each claimed islands in the channel, and thereby waters around the islands.

During the 1970s, there not yet being a Law of the Sea, the two nations submitted to arbitration by—this sounds like a Monty Python sketch—Queen Elizabeth II and Pope John Paul II. When queen and pope ruled for Chile, Argentina attempted a military strike. Chastened by failure in naval war, Buenos Aires later acquiesced to a papal award favoring Santiago.

Having lost the South China Sea ruling, Beijing did what Argentina did—ignored the decision. Landfilling around the Spratlys continues. Doublespeak is no stranger to politics. Today China demands impartial enforcement of international norms above the Arctic Circle but special privileges that trample others in the South China Sea.

Zheng Wang, a professor at Seton Hall University, has written that the Hague ruling made Beijing consider withdrawing from the Law of the Sea accord. By contrast, the Russian Federation, which ratified the Law of the Sea grudgingly, has begun to like the agreement because the convention makes clear that great-power navies can, with few restrictions, steam where they please. Lynn Kuok, a fellow at University of Cambridge, has written that since roughly 2010, "as the Soviet navy transitioned from a 'reactive coastal fleet' to a 'proactive, expansionist, blue-water navy,' the Soviet attitude toward the Law of the Sea became favorable."[2] Russian ambitions in the Arctic Circle and Mediterranean are for the most part sanctioned by wording of the Law of the Sea—as are US Navy ambitions worldwide.

Regarding Admiral Richardson's question—"Which is better?"—the United States constantly emphasizes that all nations active on the seas, whether militarily or for commerce, must observe the protocols of international order. John Butler, president of the World Shipping Council, says, "Everyone assumes business is opposed to regulation, but not necessarily. The shipping industry favors global regulation. We want the same norms for every nation and company. Standardized labor protection. Nondiscriminatory freedom of contract. Strong emissions controls. Regulating the sulfur emitted by container vessels is a great idea for human health and ocean protection, but must be enforced globally to prevent important actors from cheating." In this context, "important actors" means China.

This said, it is infuriating the United States does not simply ratify the Law of the Sea. The convention accepts the United States position on major questions. Refusing to ratify surrenders high ground—in return for what, exactly?

BEYOND WHETHER THE UNITED States should ratify the Law of the Sea is what to do regarding maritime issues such as labor abuse and environment harm.

To shanghai long has meant to trick someone into becoming a crew member of a vessel or to kidnap for that purpose. Shanghaiing still exists in the contemporary world. China catches more fish than does any other nation; crews of its trawlers are often mistreated, in some cases shanghaied. Fishing boats throughout Asia and sometimes in other parts of the world are crewed by men held against their wills and paid little. Ian Urbina, a writer and a fellow of the Safina Center, which studies ocean conservation, has called it "fantasy" that "any firm could pay workers well, fish in a sustainable fashion and deliver a can of skipjack tuna at $2.50."

Over the course of generations, the human family may shift of its own accord toward a plant-based diet, even toward cultured substances that taste as good as cheeseburgers but don't involve animals. For the moment, the world's growing population needs fish for protein. As ever-bigger and ever-more-efficient trawlers put to sea, labor abuse intensifies. The great nations, the United Nations, and the mechanisms of the Law of the Sea have yet to deal with this problem.

One possible solution to Wild West circumstances at sea is private property rights. Private property can result in extremes of wealth but also in job growth, economic activity, and higher living standards.

In the two most recent centuries, countries that enforce private property rights—the United States, most of Europe, a few others—have been *much* better places for average people than have societies without such rights, including the Soviet Union, Maoist China, parts of Africa, and parts of South America. Owners of property have incentives to maintain and conserve. Areas with neither good governance nor property rights may become polluted, overexploited, or both. And at present, "areas with neither good governance nor property rights" describes, via the oceans, most of the earth's surface.

Traditionally, once a fishing boat went to sea, what happened was the skipper's prerogative. With many ocean fisheries near depletion and demand for protein rising, free-for-all no longer works. Studies at the University of California, Davis, show that privatizing fishing rights usually makes fish populations less prone to collapse. The holder of the permit acquires a stake in preventing depletion, which would erase the permit's value.

A few American states, and provinces of other nations, have established in effect ocean property rights in their 200-mile zone. In the 1980s, Australia, Iceland, and New Zealand pioneered tradable catch permits. Their fish stocks have for the most part recovered nicely.

In other places, including lower parts of the Arctic Circle, nations have established what are in effect ocean property rights by issuing a range of tradable permits for catch. On the day I wrote this paragraph, I checked AlaskaBroker.com, a market for fishing rights in waters off the forty-ninth state. Catch permits were on sale for sea cucumber, Dungeness crab, herring, and other species. Some offerings were impressively specific—"northern southeast Chatham sablefish, longline." Nine categories of salmon permits were out for bid, specific to type of trawler. Prices were rising and falling almost continuously, which is how markets operate.

Around Alaska, these systems work well, though the fishing community grumbles. A few years ago at the Double Musky Inn, a Cajun restaurant in Girdwood, Alaska—only in the twenty-first century can there be fine New Orleans cuisine in a remote part of a wilderness state—I had creole-style crab-stuffed halibut that was so delicious, I can still taste that dinner. The chef knew what she was doing, but fisheries management was essential to the meal.

Until the 1990s, Alaska approached the halibut catch as a short season in which anyone could do anything. The result was a few chaotic days marred by colliding boats and tangled lines, followed by freezing of the fish and a price bust as everything hit the market at once. Now halibut season does not happen over a brief period. Instead, owners of a fishing business holding an assured right, won by bid, spread their work over months. This system obviates cutthroat competition among boats and allows halibut to come to the market fresh, not frozen. (One must have fresh halibut in Alaska to savor the difference.) Prices don't soar or plunge. Spared a concentrated onslaught, halibut stocks are sustainable.

Tradable fishing permits require the public to accept there's nothing wrong with running a business that makes a profit—increasingly a controversial notion, especially among academics and politicians who live on donations from people who made a profit. Within the exclusive economic zones, nations can enforce rules for sustainable or tradable-permit fishing.

FOR THE CONCEPT TO be effective, economic zones must be respected. China has been dispatching fishing fleets to the edges of the zones around Ecuador and the Galapagos Islands, seeking hammerhead shark, an endangered species that is a delicacy on menus of the opulent halls where Chinese Communist Party officials dine at the people's expense. In theory hammerheads cannot be sold, owing to the Convention on International Trade in Endangered Species, an agreement that in theory binds most countries. China is a signatory but ignores CITES restrictions. Chinese trawlers "accidentally" cross into Ecuadorian waters.

Off Indonesia, the Natuna Islands lie mostly within the Jakarta exclusive economic zone. Chinese fishing fleets, accompanied by light gunboats the Beijing government preposterously claims not to know about, have been taking fish around the Natunas, knowing there is scant chance Indonesia will open fire.

Problems such as these plague areas close to national territory. Once beyond the 200-mile limit, no fishing rules govern open ocean—and most of the surface of the earth is open ocean. Large and sophisticated factory trawlers, the majority Asian, can take from the open ocean without concern for maintaining a healthy fish population. Asia must be fed. But overfishing open ocean epitomizes the "tragedy of the commons," in which exploitation leads to breakdown because no one has a property interest in safeguarding the resource.

The Law of the Sea convention, written when there was little experience using tradable fish quotas, provides no enforcement mechanism for violations such as those being staged by China against Indonesia, or beyond the 200-mile mark. Tradable fishing permits may sound like cap-and-trade proposals for greenhouse gases, but they have nothing to do with taking on climate change. In that category almost all the needed reforms (regarding fuel use, agriculture, and livestock management) would happen on land.

Some oppose converting fish schools into tradable property, but on a practical basis, the alternative is overfishing. An international system of tradable open-seas fishing permits would not be easy, but as a high school teacher surely told you, there is no shortcut to any place worth going. The carrot at the end of the seine is that because fish lay prodigious quantities of eggs, when overfishing stops, marine populations recover more quickly than land mammal populations do when hunting is regulated.

Bouncing back from its initial Law of the Sea misjudgment, in 2009 *The Atlantic* said, "Property rights are the most promising solution to overfishing of the open seas."[3] And most promising in diplomatic terms—if nations accept that some parts of the ocean are the property of other nations, there's less to fight about.

WHALES AND DOLPHINS, OCEAN dwellers that are not fish, are sources of fascination and are almost certainly more intelligent than most animals. Many people believe whaling and dolphin hunting have been outlawed or rendered moot by synthetic replacements for whale oil. Neither is true.

In 1986 the International Whaling Commission—based, everyone knows, in Impington, England—announced what seemed to be strong action against whaling and dolphin hunting. Nations had representatives theatrically sign the prohibition, patting each other's backs. Soon many signatories ignored what they had initialed.

Among the leading contemporary acts of environmental hypocrisy—there has been spirited competition—came one from Gro Harlem Brundtland, former three-term prime minister of Norway. She ran an international conference that in 1987 produced the Brundtland Report, warning of impending ecological ruin (which should have happened by now) and recommending, among other actions, emphasis on species protection, such as strict adherence to the previous year's whaling ban.[4] Norwegian popular sentiment favored whaling. Returning to Oslo from the conference, Brundtland ordered Norway to resume hunting whales. She wanted to ensure her reelection.

Today, nations that continue whaling include Canada, Denmark, Iceland, Japan, and South Korea. The worst offender is the Faroe Islands, which appear on paper to be independent; Denmark holds the deed to this real estate and benefits from the continuing slaughter of whales. A decade after the Brundtland conference came the 1997 Kyoto Protocol, signed by most nations amid greener-than-thou speechifying. At Kyoto, picturesque ancient imperial capital of the Yamato, Japan made a national commitment to environmental leadership, among other things agreeing to stop hunting whales. In 2019 Japan said, "Never mind." Once again, whale meat is a delicacy on Tokyo menus.

From 1960 to 2019, total whaling was well down, from a peak of 89,861 animals caught to 1,134.[5] But with whales no longer needed for oil or nutrition, each whale taken is an outrage, as is each dolphin hunted.

WHALING WAS INTEGRAL TO arrival of the blue age. One reason New England developed in the colonial period was that by 1775, the city of Nantucket led the world in whaling. Nantucket whalers of the eighteenth century ventured as far as the Falkland Islands for catch. It's useful to examine a desktop globe to appreciate just how remote the Falklands are. Yet sailing ships went that distance *centuries ago* looking for ocean commerce.

After the United States became a nation, London began to subsidize English and Irish whaling—ostensibly so England would not rely for an important product on those ornery rebels, actually to harm the young United States by undercutting a profitable industry. By this juncture, the mid-nineteenth century, New England whaling ships had to go past the Falklands, all the way around Cape Horn, reaching the Pacific, to find catch. Melville's *Moby Dick or the Whale*, published 1851, reflected not only the author's personal angst but New England's communal angst that whaling, once local, had become trans-Pacific and very dangerous because of the need to round the bottom of the world twice (going, returning) for decent pay at the end of the voyage.

The International Union for Conservation of Nature, the best source of data on species, says humpback whale populations are in recovery but gray whales are endangered.[6] The IUCN recognizes eighty-seven species of cetaceans, finding thirty-six in good condition, twelve in moderate peril from human action, thirteen in dire peril, and the rest—unknown. There's a lot about the oceans that is unknown.

SURELY YOU'VE GUESSED THE Law of the Sea does not resolve whaling or dolphin-hunting questions. Nor does this convention resolve the disposal of plastics in the seas. Mainly a godsend, rising global prosperity has downsides, among them more garbage. Ocean dumping of plastics is estimated to have increased tenfold in the last two generations, with most of the fifty million tons in the oceans having come from China, Indonesia, and the Philippines. Some nations discourage the use of the oceans for disposal; the United States, Japan, Canada, and the European Union restrict the practice but are not setting any records for enforcement.[7] There is no international consensus.

Nor does the Law of the Sea resolve issues invisible, more to the point inaudible, to genus *Homo*. Vast slow-moving wooden fleets, such as the 317 ships that cast off from Suzhou in 1405 under the mariner Zheng He, no longer exist. But the total number of powered ships at sea has never been higher—50,000 commercial vessels; hundreds of warships, police, and coastal patrol vessels; tens of thousands of pleasure craft from cuddies to *Azzam*, the 590-foot moving-city yacht owned by the president of the United Arab Emirates. Unlike wooden ships of the past, today's vessels are fast because they have motors—loud motors—and propellers that roil the waters with noisy wakes.

Nautical lore holds that dolphins and porpoises were curious about the old sailing ships and often accompanied them. Perhaps dolphins and porpoises realized that passage of a man-made object would help them locate food; perhaps chasing ships was a form of play. (Several marine creatures, prominently the otter, clearly enjoy play.) Ten miles per hour was flank speed for wooden ships, slow enough that marine mammals could get out of the way. Today even lumbering supertankers and bulk carriers move at fifteen miles per hour. Most ocean vessels can make twenty miles per hour; *Azzam* hits thirty-five at firewall throttles. Dolphins, porpoises, manatees, and whales can't react quickly enough. Not only do sea mammals breath air like us, but also like us, they are vertebrates. When a whale is struck by a fast vessel, the animal's backbone may break.

The effect of man-made noise on the seas is not well understood. Sounds carry long distances in water, propagating differently than in the air: what seems to us a rumble may seem to fish a roar. Vacuum cleaners, the suburban leaf-blower—chances are that's what propellers sound like to fish. Many sea creatures have sensitive hearing, perceiving the world via sound waves and echolocation. The sudden arrival of thousands of loud engines cannot be good from the marine-life standpoint. Engines could be muffled and propellers redesigned to limit marine noise; so far no nation requires this.

Contemporary ships use powerful sonar, radar, and other electronics. Microwaves that move through the atmosphere rarely strike an organism; moving through the oceans, artificially generated energy strikes living things continuously. Wide-scale electronic emissions to the oceans have occurred only for a few generations. It is not clear what the impact may be; research is needed. A 2020 antisubmarine training exercise by the US Navy and NATO involved saturating coastal areas off Iceland with very strong sonar signals: this is believed to have killed marine mammals.

At depth, submarines cannot receive radio transmission. The same water columns that prevent submarines from being found prevent them from being contacted. The US Navy uses low-frequency bands to send brief codes that instruct a submarine to rise to communication depth and deploy an antenna. China, India, Russia, and the United States have built sci-fi-style facilities (one was in Wisconsin) that simulate transmitters thousands of miles apart, to transmit extremely low-frequency codes to submarines. Navies may also use what's essentially rock-concert sonar to alert submarines to rise to communication depth. Imperceptible to people, such signals almost surely are bad for marine life.

BEYOND NOISE AND ELECTROMAGNETIC pollution in the oceans is physical pollution. All those centuries of sailing ships threw trash—and sometime mutineers—overboard. But lacking engines, sailing ships emitted no soot, smog-forming compounds, sulfur (the precursor of acid rain and ocean acidification), or waste oil. Plumes of dark coal smoke are no more: soot continues, particularly from the low-grade fuels many oceangoing vessels burn. The reason that today's four-star cruise liners have what appears to be a towering letter T amidships is that the T is a pair of sideways smokestacks to push exhaust gases away from the paying customers. Waste oil discharge can be so bad that satellites locate ships at sea via oil wakes, which from space appear shiny—and are poisonous to marine life.

Pollutants can be removed from fuel chemically at the refinery stage. The advent of reformulated gasoline, with most impurities removed, is a reason smog has been declining, rather than increasing as expected. Reformulated ship fuels, similar to reformulated gasoline, are needed on the seas.

Another possibility is commercial vessels powered by liquefied natural gas. Low in smog and greenhouse content, LNG may always be impractical for small vehicles such as cars: for large vehicles like ships, LNG is just what the doctor ordered.

In 2019, CMA CGM christened *Jacques Saade*, an ultra-large transport—twenty-three thousand TEUs, four hundred times the capacity of the first container liner—powered by liquefied natural gas. The *Saade* emits only 1 percent as much sulfur as do container ships running on bunker fuel, only 15 percent as much smog-forming chemicals, and somewhat less greenhouse gas. *Saade* is now CMA CGM's flagship and represents market-driven environmental technology, since no government mandate requires natural gas power for ocean travel.[8]

A 2020 International Maritime Organization rule that container vessels use low-sulfur fuel is a good start, as is an IMO standard that container ships reduce greenhouse gases by a third by 2050. Will such rules have teeth? Flag-of-convenience shippers select convenient flag states partly by shopping for nations that do not enforce environmental standards. An estimated 60 percent of commercial oceangoing vessels fly a flag of convenience. The Law of the Sea creates no antidote to this obvious subterfuge.

Some shipping companies are complying with the sulfur rule by installing exhaust scrubbers similar to those at coal-fired generating stations; others by paying extra for cleaner fuels. Either alternative raises costs, and international commerce has become habituated to cheap shipping.

Many wish-list items—environmental protection, higher wages for ship crews, noise abatement—boost the price or result in lost jobs. In 2018, Stena Lines, Europe's largest operator of passenger ferryboats and *Ro-Ros*—vessels with snouts that allow cars and trucks to roll on, roll off—announced it would add air-pollution scrubbers to ships and order the design (in China) of a new generation of ferries with low air emissions. This was good news for the ecological health of the North Sea. But Stena Lines laid off hundreds of workers to finance the capital improvements. Environmental protection at sea engages the same conundrum as on land—the money must come from somewhere.

What degree of damage is being done to oceans by the noise, electromagnetic signals, and fossil-fuel by-products of humanity's many ships is not known in any comprehensive sense. The statement that we are better informed about conditions on Mars than the seas below our pelagic level is not hyperbole.

Sea chemistry and ocean currents, which mean to marine plants and animals what weather and seasons mean to life on land, are invisible to people, but not inconsequential to us. Marine plants generate more oxygen than trees. The Amazon rainforest commonly is called "the lungs of the world." It's more like the nostrils: ocean organisms account for about 70 percent of the oxygen of the atmosphere.

If ocean currents change, disruption to society may be extreme. Most of Europe lies north of most of Maine. Yet much of Europe's climate is temperate because the continent benefits from a primary current, the North Atlantic Gyre, which moves warm water in unimaginable volumes toward the north, then submerges the warm water in a rolling motion that pushes cold water south. The speed, temperature, and salinity bands of ocean currents are another blue-water aspect poorly understood. Should the primary Atlantic current lose energy or vacillate, Europe could experience pronounced weather swings, including icebound winters, even as the world mainly warms.

Many cities and agricultural regions are where they are because of prevailing currents and the wind patterns associated with those currents. Suppose the currents change. Over decades, new currents could be adjusted to. But no one wants to go through that exercise—or pay the invoice.

Whether sea currents and ocean chemistry are changing because of artificial or natural factors or both is unknown. Since industrial production began in earnest about two hundred years ago, the average pH of the oceans has dropped from about 8.2 to 8.1. Not much? A pH of 8.1 is ten times more acidic than 8.2.

One villain is acid rain, settling into the sea and altering its chemistry. Acid rain has begun declining globally. But even if artificial acid rain is brought to heel, ocean acidification is likely to increase, because carbon dioxide, the main greenhouse gas, also lowers the pH of seawater.

Acidification will impede shell formation in marine lifeforms. Worrisome from the human perspective is that acidic oceans hold less oxygen. Anoxic seas could release hydrogen sulfide, the gas with rotten-egg smell. There is a maverick theory that mass extinctions of the past were associated with phases of naturally occurring anoxic oceans that generated hydrogen sulfide, rendering much of earth's lower atmosphere noxious. Many oceanographers don't buy this theory. Do we really want to find out who's right?

ABOVE ALL OCEAN ENVIRONMENTAL issues is artificially triggered climate change. There is uncertainty regarding the impact, which could be anywhere from beneficial (small chance) to harmful (likelihood) to disastrous (small chance). There is no uncertainty that artificial climate change has begun.

Sea level is certain to continue rising. High tide at Naval Station Norfolk is up eight inches since 1970. Eight inches may sound insignificant—unless you've ever owned littoral property. The commercial port facility at Hampton Roads, Virginia, near the navy base, spent $375 million to prepare itself for more sea level rise. Now the port's emergency generators are up on stilts, like Mississippi homes along the Gulf Coast. Current research suggests seas are rising by about 1.9 inches per year, a stark rate of increase.[9]

A combination of higher ocean temperatures (warm water expands more than cool water) and melting ice (especially at Greenland) may lead to six feet of additional sea level by the end of the century. In 2019, Princeton University researchers estimated that such a rise would place 630 million people in coastal regions below the likely tide level of the year 2100.[10] Cities, harbors, and coastal communities around the world would be inundated: Karachi, today home to 15 million, would disappear like the new Atlantis. Cities could be moved inland, but the expense would be orders of magnitude higher than the cost of moderating green-house gas emissions.

In itself, sea level rise won't affect seagoing. Ocean storms might get worse in a warming world: evidence to date is inconclusive. Hollywood envisions preposterously large future cyclones. Some models suggest a warmer world instead will have ocean storms that are not as powerful as hurricanes, but happen year-round rather than seasonally. This would be unwelcome news to ships.

Probably there is a substantial quantity of methane in the seas or on the seafloor. Methane is a more potent climate agent than car-bon dioxide. As seawater warms, dissolved gases may be released to the air. The result may be more methane in the atmosphere, which would make climate change worse.

Higher air temperatures could bring misery to the hot-climate nations, where average people already suffer in summertime. More use of air-conditioning could increase demand for fossil fuels, add-ing to warming. Changes in weather patterns—seasonal rains are influenced by the oceans, though the mechanisms are far from certain—could make productive breadbasket regions arid while bringing plenty of rain to areas not suitable for farming. Warming could further accelerate the melting of boreal ice, strengthening the feedback loop by altering earth's albedo. The whole thing could get way too biblical.

Greenhouse gases are an air-pollution problem, and previous air-pollution problems—smog, acid rain, soot, airborne lead, air-borne mercury, chlorofluorocarbons (CFCs)—have been addressed faster and cheaper than expected. There is a strong possibility green-house gases can be addressed faster and cheaper than expected too, should society act.

American greenhouse emissions per capita have already peaked and entered what is likely to be a long phase of decline. In this con-text, "long phase of decline" is a good thing. Wise policy decisions could hasten that process, with no sacrifice of living standards. My

2018 book *It's Better Than It Looks* details how artificial climate change can be confronted without harm to the global economy.

Because decisions about greenhouse gases must come from the level of heads of state and CEOs, climate change is a separate special case that transcends other issues in this chapter. Which leads us back to—who shall govern the seas?

ONLY ABOUT 2 PERCENT of the oceans' surface is "governed" in the sense of being national jurisdiction where a coast guard cutter might challenge a fishing vessel to ensure workers are not being held incommunicado or check that cargo ships are not dumping trash overboard. The International Maritime Organization hosts panel discussions about environmental protection and labor law but has little enforcement power. That leaves 98 percent of the oceans ungoverned. If the blue age is to continue, the work of adding safety, labor, and environmental rules to this expanse must begin.

The history of diplomacy shows that initial attempts at agreements often falter but later are replaced by success. The initial Geneva Convention, signed in 1864, generally was ignored. Improved conventions signed in 1929 set the stage for the Geneva Conventions of 1949, endorsed by most nations and having constructive influence on the behavior of armies. The Hague Conventions on national conduct, first signed 1899, initially lacked power. A dozen Hague updates through the twentieth century have been highly beneficial, making rules enforceable and extending into such areas as enforcement of cross-border child-support writs.

The Washington Naval Treaty of 1922, intended to reduce military stockpiles, was a bust. Lessons learned from that failed convention helped the highly successful nuclear disarmament treaties of the 1980s and 1990s, which created broad benefits for humanity.

Through the nineteenth century, most trade compacts were nation to nation, sufficiently prone to favoritism that *most favored nation* became a term of art. After the world wars, regional agreements came into use, notionally neutral, often undercut by politics. (A 1948 deal called the General Agreement on Trade and Tariffs proved, in actual use, barely an agreement and anything but general.) The 1995 arrival of the World Trade Organization imposed standards that are reasonably resistant to monkey business, helping set in motion the greatest global prosperity boom in human history.

The Law of the Sea falls into this progression. Its initial iteration raised expectations in an arena where previous attempts, such as the 1958 Convention on the High Seas, had been scattershot. Now the flaws of the Law of the Sea have caught up to the accord. The time has come for a successor that produces true governance for the nearly three-quarters of the earth that is ocean.

A NEW SYSTEM, SAY, THE creation of a World Oceans Organization—could centralize and simplify a plethora of current rule-makers, many barely known, such as the International Seabed Authority, others with irregular histories, such as the Montreux Convention on Marmara, which sort-of governs use of the Turkish Straits. Current writers of rule books have overlapping or conflicting portfolios and often no prosecutorial power. They can be played off against each other or simply ignored. A World Oceans Organization could change that.

A true global governance system for the blue water would eliminate flag-of-convenience loopholes, protect workers in fishing and shipping, impose strict antipollution rules, and create clear agreements about the mining of minerals on the seafloor. Prototype vessels that vacuum up nodules from the seabed discharge effluent that can pollute the towering deepwater columns essential to marine life, including the marine plants that release oxygen. If sea mining is to become common, a much better system, with close supervision, is required.

When the coronavirus began spreading in early 2020, around two hundred thousand deckhands and engine operators for container vessels, oil tankers, and bulkers were stranded aboard, according to an estimate from the International Transport Workers' Federation, unable to obtain legal permission to come ashore at any port. No international organization had agreed-upon jurisdiction to assist the stranded ship laborers. The sudden COVID-19 lock-down was an event that could not reasonably have been anticipated. But it happened, and as more of human action moves to the seas, other surprises will be waiting. There needs to be a plan.

ESTABLISHMENT OF A WORLD Oceans Organization or some similar generally agreed-upon body might prepare society for the water world of future generations. For example, if the continents become crowded, nations may realize there is in effect infinite open space at sea—and the sea is far more practical and affordable for potential habitation than the Mars settlements about which Silicon Valley hipsters rhapsodize. Not long into the future, humanity may look to the oceans for expansion. Whether this is done well or poorly may turn on how the process is governed.

A World Oceans Organization would entail the inevitable fancy buildings staffed by garrulous bureaucrats. Is that so bad? Down the centuries, starting with the Chinese competitive civil service examinations of a millennia ago, successful nations have professional bureaucracies. Successful ocean governance would require this as well.

A World Oceans Organization might impose some regulation of weapons at sea. Currently there are no controls.

The United States and Russian Federation bilaterally removed nuclear warheads from surface ships and torpedo tubes. This auspicious decision can be revoked by either capital. International precepts are not involved. As for conventional weapons on the waters, heaven knows—anything goes. Most worrisome are anti-ship missiles, which in recent decades have become lethal in accuracy, range, and ability to punch through hulls and decks.

In the skies, four times since lethal long-range homing anti-aircraft missiles became common, such weapons have accidentally destroyed civilian airliners, killing a total of 842 people. Using long-range homing missiles, the United States accidentally shot down an Iranian airliner in 1988; Ukraine accidentally shot down a Russian airliner in 2001; Russia accidentally shot down a Malaysia airliner in 2014; Iran accidentally shot down a Ukrainian airliner in

2020. In every case, missile gunners confused a military target with a civilian plane—because their screens did not distinguish between the two types of aircraft.

Screens for most antiship missiles have the same fault. They don't tell the gunner if the target is broadcasting a transponder signal using the automatic identification system now standard for nearly all civilian vessels. It seems only a matter of time until some nation's frigate, in the fog of war, or a fog of weather, accidentally launches an antiship missile at a Carnival Cruise expedition of tourists. The result may be a modern-day *Lusitania*.

An improved system of ocean governance could impose on the militaries of the world technical upgrades that make accidental firings of antiship missiles less likely. [11] Of course, militaries would resist such governance. But over the last two generations, most of the world's armed forces have accepted limits on land mines, nerve gas, and battlefield rockets. The little-known but significant Missile Technology Control Regime, endorsed in 1987 by every major nation other than China, has reduced the proliferation of projectiles that strike civilians on the ground. There is no reason this agreement could not be expanded to include long-range missiles designed to sink ships. Restrictions on long-range antiship missiles—the kind launched at a blip too far away for the gunner to see whether the target is military or civilian—would be in every nation's interest.

A WORLD OCEANS ORGANIZATION could create level-playing-field standards for offshore energy projects, such as the largest maritime object ever built, *Prelude* FLNG.

This $10 billion combination ship/gas drilling rig/industrial facility, five American football fields long and constructed by Samsung at the Geoje shipyard in South Korea, was anchored about a hundred miles off Australia in 2020. *Prelude* FLNG explores for natural gas, converting this fuel on-site into a liquid suitable for transportation around the world. In principle, platforms like *Prelude* could be positioned almost anywhere there is water above a gas field. Such offshore energy infrastructure may become essential to a low-carbon future. Better to write the rules now than go into battle over them later.

Treaty-strength standards also are needed for building, and protecting, submarine internet and telephone cables. Google is known for its search box, but college kids typing "Tex-Mex takeout" does not add up to the $162 billion of revenue that parent firm Alphabet enjoyed in 2019. Among Google's sources of money is its role in infrastructure. Many of the world's undersea communication cables, the electronic pipes that carry most internet and phone traffic, were laid by the company, which receives leasing fees. In 2020, Google began planning a 5,000-mile sea floor fiber-optic cable linking offices and computers from Europe to India, and including a first-ever direct connection between Israel and Saudi Arabia. Real-time global communication at almost no incremental cost is an aspect of human progress. But the unseen, undersea part of the system is vulnerable, and submarine captains know where the weak links are.

Global standards should be established for building and protecting energy conduits, too. The Nord Stream natural-gas pipeline, running along the bottom of the Baltic Sea about 750 miles from Russia to Germany, was in early 2021 nearly complete as the world's longest underwater construction project. The United States opposed Nord Stream, owned by the Russian energy firm Gazprom, on the grounds that it gives Moscow bargaining leverage over the European Union. Then again the pipeline will supply much of the continent with clean-burning natural gas and give Moscow a stake in good relations with European capitals. In great-power commerce, each side runs a risk and must please the other. Europe risks Moscow shutting off the gas; strapped for hard currency, Moscow risks Europe canceling the checks.

That Nord Stream is invisible to the public, lying beneath up to seven hundred feet of wine-dark cold water, does not diminish the significance of a $11 billion investment involving Russia and Germany and crossing the ocean boundaries of Denmark, Finland, and Sweden. Environmental and safety regulations for Nord Stream and similar natural-gas submarine pipelines under construction are a jumble of agencies and acronyms. No accountable organization has uncontested jurisdiction—and a few torpedoes could render a continent-width energy system worthless.

DEEPLY SUBMERGED POWER CABLES also are coming. North Sea Link, expected to be completed in 2022, will carry electricity along the seafloor about 450 miles from Norway, which has excess capacity, to England, which needs power. North Sea Link will be a win-win for both nations, while reducing greenhouse emissions throughout the region.

Australia and Singapore are in negotiations for a subsea electricity cable. The sunny Outback can produce far more solar electricity than needed locally; Singapore is hungry for power and has a reputation for paying bills on time. If the cable between these nations is built, it will stretch twenty-eight hundred miles—quite an extension cord.

Far longer seafloor cables are a promising idea for balancing the world's electricity supply while reducing utility baseload fuel consumption. Energy use will spike during business hours and early evening, drop as people unwind and hit the sack. In principle, a global grid could transfer electricity production from the dark side of the world, where power drain is low, to the sunny side, where amperage is needed, every twelve hours reversing the process.

Such a grid would make a range of clean-energy ideas more practical. Nuclear generators (zero-emission, safe), wind electricity, geothermal, and tidal power are better capital investments if their outputs can sell as steady baseload twenty-four hours a day. Many thousands of miles of subsea cables would be needed for a global grid, as would international agreements on laying the cables while defending them against military attack. Perhaps fifty years from now, something like the World Oceans Organization might serve as an all-planet utility agency.

A WORLD OCEANS ORGANIZATION also could mount a sea peacekeeping force. One reason the tenuous Long Peace is in progress is that land peacekeeping forces—soldiers called Blue Helmets for their distinctive appearance, both blue tactical gear and fashionable bright blue dress berets—have in the main been successful. At sea a white ship means coast guard or other law enforcement, a gray vessel is a warship. There could be blue hulls on the blue water, peacekeeping forces ready to interpose themselves against naval assaults, such as the one Russia staged in 2014 at Crimea.

In 2019, an ad hoc assemblage—the United States, the United Kingdom, several Gulf states, Australia, Lithuania, and Albania (Tirana takes pride in its patrol-boat presence on the Ionian Sea)— came together to protect freedom of navigation through the Strait of Hormuz. These nations formed an alliance with a weird name, the International Maritime Security Construct. The members placed themselves on the right side of history with their Persian Gulf peacekeeping idea. A true international sea security alliance would be an even better idea.

On a practical basis, a blue-age ocean peace force would be composed mainly of US and Chinese contingents, since Washington and Beijing have the most ships and the most money. Joint peacekeeping actions involving the US Navy and the People's Liberation Army Navy inevitably would entail tension. But the two navies would learn how to live with each other—which they need to learn, in any case.

10

END OF THE BLUE AGE?

THE CENTURIES IN WHICH THE OCEANS BECAME BUSY WITH SHIPS coincided with industrialization, nearly all the population growth that has ever occurred, nearly all the rise in literacy that has ever occurred, nearly all the increase in longevity that has ever occurred, mass distribution of newspapers and books, mass media starting with radio, leaps in science—and world-scale war. Much about the web of connections among these developments remains vexing. Better comprehension might help us avoid wars to come.

Many questions are daunting, others basic. For example, of the basic questions—when did World War II begin?

Many Americans might say on December 7, 1941, as Japanese carrier-based planes bombed American battleships in a navy-on-navy attack. Many Europeans might say the appalling conflict commenced on September 1, 1939, as German soldiers invaded Poland. Many Asians might say on July 7, 1937, at the Marco Polo Bridge in China.

When did World War II end? Many would say on May 8, 1945, in Berlin, as the Soviet Union, America, and Britain accepted the Nazi capitulation. Others would say the worst of all wars ended September 2, 1945, when Japan surrendered to the United States aboard the battleship *Missouri*, anchored in Tokyo Bay just in case anyone was unclear about what had happened. A third view is this awful struggle transformed into the Cold War and continued until September 12, 1990, the day, in Moscow, the Allies signed an accord resolving a range of Cold War disputes and releasing each other and Germany from claims.

A great deal changed in affirmative ways after the 1990 Moscow ceremony. The Germanys reunited, with East free rather than West enslaved; most proxy wars in Africa and South America stopped; negotiations for nuclear arms reduction picked up steam (the first agreement became final shortly afterward); Soviet internal tyranny crumbled; Soviet border tyranny collapsed (the "autonomous republics" were neither); China began to liberalize when the country's leaders realized it was no longer possible to believe communism would vanquish democracy.

The big 1990 global win for liberality also had impacts in India, which in that year shifted from a controlled economy to market forces. As in China, India's embrace of economic freedom began a movement from general misery to moderate living standards and higher education levels.

The collapse of Soviet tyranny, the return of Germany to the family of nations, poverty-reducing market economics helping two billion people in China and India—these made 1990 a kind of year zero for optimism about the human prospect. Obviously, multiple emergencies continue, from climate change to the United States–Russian Federation mistrust that Michael McFaul,* former US ambassador to Moscow, calls a "hot peace." But for the most part, events of 1990 created a propitious momentum. This momentum is ongoing, even considering the 2020 phase of virus pandemic and political anger. In our world today are more positive influences than negative ones. It's just that Western institutions resist hopeful information, while politicians of nearly all nations advance a narrative of anxiety and fear for their own benefit.

---

* No relation to Donald McFaul, for whom the US destroyer mentioned earlier is named.

Should war return, this book's optimistic worldview will shatter. The sea is where war seems the greatest risk. This brings us back to the questions of when wars begin and end.

WORLD WAR II WAS a series of interwoven destructive events—police-state crackdowns, combat, genocide, repressive economies designed to keep average people powerless. Thinking about those awful events as a sequence that began at the Marco Polo Bridge in 1937 and ended in 1990 in Moscow can be a helpful way of anticipating the twenty-first century.

An even broader view is the Long War hypothesis, advanced by the scholar Philip Bobbitt, among others. Bobbitt is a nephew of Lyndon Johnson—during summers when he was a college kid, he worked in the White House. Bobbitt proposes that the span from 1912, the start of the first Balkan War, to the 1990 treaty ceremony should be known as the Long War.

Immediately after signing the September 1990 accord, delegates began negotiating what became the Paris Charter of November 1990. The Paris Charter is a second little-known agreement essential to our lives, a second aspect of 1990 as a year zero. Through the Paris Charter, the European powers mutually renounced the goal of political dominance, committing themselves instead to free trade and free elections. One could argue the Paris Charter was the crowning moment of the Enlightenment. Whether or not this is so, 1990 concluded what should be understood as a single Long War that commenced with the Guns of October in 1912 and ended in 1990.

HERE I PROPOSE ANOTHER way to think about the question of when wars start and stop—a way that sheds light on how the blue age came about and whether that age will continue or falter. I propose there have been five world wars, all linked to the oceans as much as land, and that events on the blue waters are essential to our current situation, namely, the Long Peace.

During this Long Peace, there has been no direct great-power conflict, while international trade has flourished as never before.

Capital, human energy, and brainpower previously focused on war have been redirected to economic competition. The result is improved living standards, higher education levels, and extended lifespans almost everywhere.

Framing recent centuries as a series of lengthy global wars, at last stilled, can help us chart out how to keep the current, mainly good situation in place, especially on the three-quarters of the earth's surface that is wet.

What follows contains subjective distinctions that can neither be proved nor disproved, but this can be said about most concepts in political science. The five world wars:

World War I, 1702–1781. This book began by noting that long-distance combat using ships goes further back into history than may be appreciated. In this book's view, World War I started in 1702 with the War of the Spanish Succession, entailing land combat and many-nation naval fighting around Europe, Florida (then part of Spain), the European colonies in North America, Newfoundland, the Caribbean, India, the Strait of Malacca, Indonesia, and the west coast of Africa. The thirteen-year conflict drew in (to use modern names) France, the United Kingdom, Austria, Russia, Spain, Germany, the Netherlands, Hungary, Belgium, and Portugal.

The War of the Spanish Succession is little taught in today's history classes because the whole affair seems incorrigibly inane— soldiers hacking each other with swords and pikes, warships burning thousands of leagues from home, over who would get to sit on a golden commode in Madrid. Whatever its senselessness, the War of the Spanish Succession was fought on a global canvas, mainly by ship, and thereby constitutes the first world war.

World War I, commencing in 1702, lasted through the War of the Austrian Succession; the Silesian Wars; the encounter pitting Scottish nationalism and France against England; war between Russia and Sweden with most of Europe taking sides; extensive naval fighting between England and France in the Carnatic Wars off India; the Seven Years' War, with nautical fighting off Africa,

South America, the Philippines, and on the Great Lakes of the New World; through the American Revolutionary War, with naval fighting off England; concluded in 1781 with a water confrontation at Yorktown that opened the door to creation of the United States, destined to be first among nations.

From 1702 to 1781 the great powers were in a near-continuous state of hostilities. The struggle from 1914 to 1918 is perceived as World War I because most of this horror occurred near cities and involved citizen armies, leaving battlefields, shrines, novels, poems, monuments in civic squares. Most of World War I by this book's reckoning occurred far from cities—among mercenaries' armies, or at sea, unseen and leaving no trace.

World War II, 1792–1815. Once more there was global conflict across Europe and Russia, upon the Atlantic waves, in Guyana, in the Caribbean, as far as the River Platte in Uruguay. The Coalition Wars, becoming the Napoleonic Wars, involved nearly all Western powers, adding Scandinavia, Switzerland, Italy, and Turkey to belligerents listed above, with naval blockades attempted in many places by a web of alliances. The 1803 Battle of Trafalgar is a storied naval confrontation, remembered perhaps because it occurred within view of the Spanish coast. During this period the War of 1812 was fought primarily on the Atlantic, in the East Indies, and on the Great Lakes. By its end at Waterloo, the Napoleonic Wars phase had drawn in much of the world.

World War III, 1854–1905. The great-power ceasefire established by the Congress of Vienna was broken by the Crimean War, staged chiefly for control of the eastern Mediterranean and access to the Black Sea. Decades that followed saw four-way conflict between France, Denmark, Austria, and Prussia; the Spanish-American War, fought simultaneously in the Pacific and Atlantic; several Balkan and Russo-Turkic wars, some involving access to the Aegean (events known collectively to European historians as the Eastern Crisis); the War of the Pacific; the Russo-Japanese War on land and sea, including the first confrontation between steel ships with really big guns. Most of the world's great powers took sides in at least some of the sequence of global conflicts that could be known as World War III.

After this carnage stopped, the sea-power advocate Theodore Roosevelt, sworn in as president in 1901, awarded the Nobel Peace Prize in 1906 for brokering the conclusion of the Russo-Japanese War, in 1907 ordered a fleet of American battleships to circumnavigate the globe, calling at numerous ports to show Old Glory. Teddy's battleship demonstration alerted the world the United States was preparing to claim the blue water.

World War IV, 1911–1922. Respites between world wars grow short. In World War IV, a shifting Rorschach of fighting between Italy, Turkey, Serbia, Greece, Macedonia, and Montenegro drew most of the great powers into combat alliances that were activated by the 1914 Austrian ultimatum to Belgrade. Trench horrors of what was contemporaneously called the Great War were joined by more fighting for access to the Black Sea, combat in Africa, ocean clashes in many places, including areas near the Arctic Circle and near Antarctica, plus hundreds of warships, submarines, and armed merchant vessels (*Q-ships*) sinking each other in the Atlantic.

By 1917 much of humanity, from the United States to Thailand, had joined this malevolence. Hunger and poor public health occasioned by World War IV set the stage for the Spanish flu pandemic, which killed as many as fifty million people; probably the death toll would have been lower if not for global war.

The November 1918 armistice that ended the primary phase of the conflict was followed by three-way and sometimes four-way combat in Russia and the Middle East; the weird Polish-Soviet War; the even weirder reality of German armor units invited to train in the Soviet Union, which those same units soon would invade. World War IV was capped by the forgotten Greco-Turkish War, beginning with amphibious landings at Smyrna, where techniques were devised for the many amphibious landings of the 1940s and 1950s.

World War V, 1937–1991. Again a short interval before global struggle resumes, with nihilistic ideology added to the aristocratic cruelty and nationalistic frenzies of prior struggles. Most nations became involved in a clash covering most of the world, and you are reading this because in most theaters, liberal democracy won.

Conflicts of the apex period raged from a dizzying number of well-known battles in Europe, Russia, China, the Pacific Rim; on the Atlantic and Pacific; in the sky at many places; to small, tragic moments such as the German raider *Kormoran* and Australian cruiser *Sydney* destroying each other in the Indian Ocean, with hundreds of lives lost. Sixty-seven years would pass before the wrecks were located.

After V-E (Victory in Europe) Day and V-J Day, there were wars involving the great powers across long distances in the Koreas and Vietnam; proxy wars in Africa and the Americas; wars forgotten in the West but influenced by it, such as the Sino-Vietnam War and the nine-year Iran-Iraq War; many wars in the Middle East, a region whose borders were plucked out of the air by the great powers in 1916, ensuring an ongoing century of conflict; the 1991 Gulf War, authorized by the United Nations Security Council, which drew in the United States, Canada, United Kingdom, Kuwait, France, Egypt, Pakistan, Denmark, Poland, Niger, South Korea, and Malaysia with aircraft, soldiers, and tanks of these many nations converging in the same sad place.

After the Gulf War, armed conflict did not stop. But since 1991 there has been nothing in which great nations fight each other over vast distance. Let us hope this statement always remains true.

BY THE END OF World War V, for two and a half centuries there had been more years with general global combat than without. Since the end of World War V, the globe has enjoyed a Long Peace, with the frequency and intensity of war in decline, per-capita military spending in decline, and odds of death because of war at a historic low.

The Long Peace may not last—indeed, could end on whatever day you pick up this book. Yet as I write, the world is in the thirtieth year of the Long Peace. The global median age is thirty years. About half the human population has lived only during the Long Peace, viewing it as the normative condition.

CHAPTER 3 ASKED WHY naval battle has changed from common to rare. That chapter took a practice swing at the larger question: why has the fitful Long Peace replaced bloodshed on almost all fronts? Now let's swing for the fence and declare the themes that bear on whether great-power battle will return in the twenty-first century:

1. Nations have always feared other nations; nuclear munitions make nations fear war itself. In 1985, Ronald Reagan and Mikhail Gorbachev jointly declared, "A nuclear war cannot be won." So far, all nuclear-armed nations concur.

2. Satellites allow the great powers to see each other's moves. In 1914, 1939, and 1941, Germany and Japan plunged the world into darkness using surprise attacks. The great-power surprise attack has become improbable—and satellites keep improving.

3. However much they can try our patience, the arrival of the United Nations, World Bank, World Health Organization, World Trade Organization, and other multinational institutions mitigates against war. There were no similar organizations during the endless-conflict phases of the past. Advocating creation of the United Nations, Franklin Roosevelt said it was naive to expect eradication of violence, but eradication of world war is a feasible goal. FDR was right then, and he's right today.

4. Economies of the great powers rely more on trade than in the past. The many wars between England and France, or France and the Hapsburgs, or Japan and China, could be staged with little sacrifice of profit, as there was less

trade to lose. Today Beijing and Washington, if harming the other, would harm themselves. There has never been a great-power relationship like today's between China and the United States.

5. Large numbers now can be nourished from relatively small acreage of land, so it is no longer necessary to confiscate territory to feed mouths. This situation also is unique in history.

6. There are no more colonial empires. Millions of people are mistreated in multifarious ways, but strong societies no longer methodically seize labor and value-added from weak societies.

7. Rising profitability of intellectual property creates wealth that is hoarded by the rich but not based on exploitation of the poor.

8. Improved communication has reduced misunderstandings and out-and-out blunders. Misunderstandings and out-and-out blunders have had a larger influence on great-power relations than we care to think about.

9. There are no shortages of primary resources.

Since this book is about the blue water, let's highlight a tenth reason for the observed trend of less fighting:

10. For two generations the US Navy has held hegemony over the oceans, precluding the maritime battles, invasion fleets, and colonization movements that were among the leading factors in centuries of conflict. The navy has made the oceans impassable to those bent on war, while safer for commerce. This outcome leads nations to channel their energies into trade, benefiting almost everyone.

HEGEMONY OF AMERICA AT sea could change. Sometime in the current generation, China's navy will become a peer to the US Navy, the first peer the US Navy has had since 1940s Japan.

From around 1980 to around 2010, only the United States christened a consequential number of surface warships. Today China is building such vessels with gusto, while the United Kingdom, the Russian Federation, India, Australia, Italy, Japan, Vietnam, South Korea, and even Singapore have joined the new naval arms race. This kind of expansion of naval power has not occurred in seventy-five years. The world may not be ready.

In 2008, Italy commissioned a light aircraft carrier that carries a wing of attack jets. The carrier is Italy's largest warship since the 1940s. In 2019 the National Assembly of South Korea funded construction of a light aircraft carrier. South Korea already has a helicopter carrier, ROKS *Dokdo* for islands claimed by both Seoul and Tokyo; Japan got angry about that name, but Japan has no moral capital regarding the Korean Peninsula. South Korea's planned aircraft carrier will be the nation's first vessel able to launch what analysts call fifth-generation fighters. Rome and Seoul are buying the best: the US-built F-35.

About a decade ago, Singapore built wharf frontage able to accommodate a supercarrier. US Navy flagships have stopped by to visit, causing a sensation with the public. Political enthusiasm has grown for Singapore to construct an aircraft carrier, probably a light carrier similar to the one newly funded in South Korea. It may seem ridiculous for a place as small as Singapore to possess capital ships; it's as if Toronto had an aircraft carrier. The politics of the blue age, with water trade and naval power ever-more important to the expanding Pacific Rim, push Singapore in this direction.

Even poor nations are pushed. In 2020, Myanmar accepted from India the first attack submarine ever possessed by the former Burma. India's hope was to bring Myanmar into its sphere of influence before Naypyidaw might align with Beijing. India promised to help Myanmar build public infrastructure. Let's hope this happens: till then, a challenge coin in the new naval arms race was the tender of this diplomatic transaction.

In 2020 the National Diet authorized construction of two light aircraft carriers, each to carry the F-35. They will be the first flat-tops Japan has sailed since 1945. Probably the true purpose of the vessels is, as stated by the Diet, regional defense. (Japan avoids the word *navy*, which is associated with shame; its nautical military arm is called the Maritime Self-Defense Force.) Nevertheless the symbolism of Tokyo's rearming with aircraft carriers capable of global reach cannot be discounted.

CONTEMPLATE WHAT THE OCEANS may be like a generation from now.

Perhaps the United States, China, or a few other nations will wrap their hands around each other's throats with naval combat or a protracted tariff feud. If not, the number of container vessels, oil tankers, bulk carriers, cruise ships, and large pleasure boats should continue increasing. The cruise industry will probably recover and, like other blue-water businesses, expand. The bevy of cruise ships joyriding the seas just before COVID-19 hit would have dazed the luxury-liner builders of the nineteenth century, such as Blohm & Voss. Ocean liners of the past were bound for destinations, along routes including Hamburg to New York City; cruise ships of the present are just tootling around.

Harbors of the past were chock with the wooden masts of sailing ships. Today's harbors are chock with the gigantic container ships and cruise liners, plus radar masts of excursion ships, cabin cruisers, and privately owned yachts. Despite the expense and impracticality of pleasure boats, marinas in the United States, Australia, the Adriatic, and parts of the Gulf states are running out of mooring space. Should the seas remain peaceful, the marina shortage could go global. Looking for a business to get in on the ground floor? Trading in marina-dockage futures.

The next generation of oceangoing vessels will be different. For one, they will be computer controlled.

Tech companies attempting to perfect the self-driving car are finding that gizmos for this purpose work better on highways than in cities. Highways have long sightlines and restricted access;

vehicles move at similar speeds. Cities are crowded, objects jump out, the speed of traffic changes constantly.

In this analogy, oceans are the highways and harbors the cities. The open ocean is not crowded, sightlines are long except in bad weather, speeds are steady, and electronics have good SA (situation awareness, essential to being an aircraft pilot or a conn officer). But to computers, harbors are Times Square in the dark.

Already, very large container ships and bulk carriers, which mainly travel from A to B on predictable courses at steady speed, need few crew members. *OOCL Hong Kong*, christened 2017 as the third ship to break the 20,000-TEU barrier, is a quarter of a mile long and heavier than an American nuclear supercarrier. Customized for the Asia-to-Europe route—in 2020 its frequent journey was Singapore to Felixstowe, England—*OOCL Hong Kong* has a complement of twenty-two.

Future vessels of enormity may sail with even smaller crews, augmented by harbor pilots in congested waters. Perhaps soon, container liners will have a crew of five: a cook, a medic, an IT specialist, a mechanic, and someone to say "granted" when the harbor pilot asks permission to come aboard.

It won't just be large capital-intensive commercial ships driving themselves. Some research vessels may be uncrewed, like space probes. Fishing trawlers are trending toward automation. Pulling lobster pots, and the shanty-singing Fisherman's Friends of Cornwall, are celebrated in lore. But for many, fishing is a dismal job—dangerous, low-paying, bad conditions, with some workers held as indentured servants. In an ideal world, conditions and pay would improve. In the actual world, fisherfolk will be replaced by machines.

Warships may mount more armaments that are partly or wholly automated. The close-in, fast-firing electric cannon designed to prevent what happened to the Royal Navy at the Falklands in 1982 already operate without a gunner. They can be switched off, but when armed, don't depend on the womp-rat marksmanship of Luke Skywalker looking through the crosshairs, as happened in the first Star Wars movie. Software chooses what to shoot and when to open fire. A missile flying in a straight line just above the waves at a thousand miles per hour or more would appear, to a gunner, to change from tiny dot to imminent menace in a single second. Only machines could react in time. There are more high-speed antiship projectiles in the works: they must be countered by automated point defenses.

Warships themselves may become autonomous, or semiautonomous. The Chinese navy joins the US Navy in toying with small uncrewed vessels—distributed platforms, in the lingo—whose space is dedicated to missiles and torpedoes. Rather than having to locate and sink a few very capable but large and visible fighting ships, an enemy would need to deal with dozens of little platforms that could swarm or scatter according to algorithms and whose tactical behavior could be suicidal (we're avoiding the word *kamikaze* here) because there is no life aboard to be protected.

The romance of wooden ship versus raging sea is ingrained in novels, paintings, and epic poetry. Not far into the future, the oceans may be a realm of automated zero-emission commercial vessels using sensors to steer clear of inconclusive tech battles between drone submarines and remote-controlled swarm ships. Whether fish and marine mammals will notice, one can but wonder. Since most of humanity pays no mind to the blue water—will people notice?

IN THE BRITISH ISLES, across the Pacific Rim, there is a keen sense of connection to the sea. For the British, this is because their empire was built upon the waves: even today, nearly all of England's and Scotland's residents live near a harbor. For the Pacific Rim, this is because their region was, within living memory, engulfed by a cataclysmic war borne along on waters: now is raised up, perhaps soon glorified, by the sea.

There is no similar keen sense in the United States. America has the strongest maritime position any nation ever achieved, yet for many Americans the blue water engages scant interest.

A small but perhaps telling sketch: Some of my ancestors are from Devon County, situated between the English Channel and

Bristol Channel, interwoven with rivers, canals, and graceful foot-bridges that invite lovers' strolls. If you visit Devon, tour Exeter Cathedral with its 500-year-old astronomical clock; walk to pubs by the River Exe; take the train to Dartmouth harbor, where fleets for fishing and fighting have assembled for a thousand years, and which the London government wonderfully deems, in caps, an Area of Outstanding Natural Beauty. In these places, I find local conversation preoccupied with current events on the ocean—from the Narrow Sea, what Brits were calling the English Channel long before Westeros, to the Strait of Malacca.

In Devon one encounters a quotation from Joshua Slocum, first to circumnavigate the world alone by sail.[1] Slocum is the blue wa-ter's Charles Lindbergh. Born 1844 in Mount Hanley when Nova Scotia still was part of Britain, later a naturalized American, Slocum is little known in his adopted country but adored in the Isles.

His historic solo circumnavigation took from 1895 to 1898. A decade later, seeking fresh adventure, Slocum departed Martha's Vineyard steering *Spray*, a custom one-person gaff-rigged sloop, and was never seen again. To British culture, his death was inex-pressibly heroic. Once, at Inverness, I bowed before a churchyard headstone from the eighteenth century that read FATE KNOWN ONLY TO THE SEA. British culture would hold this a life well lived.

The Slocum quotation: "To the young person contemplating a voyage I would say this—go." In almost every case that spirit has benefited society and will be needed anew whenever crossing the oceans yields to crossing the stars.

Then I return to my home near Washington, D.C.—a city situ-ated along the Potomac River, hard upon the mighty Chesapeake Bay, close to the most important maritime institution of our world, the US Naval Academy. Maybe this is confirmation bias, but I per-ceive that my well-informed, well-educated American peers in this place rarely if ever speak of the sea.

AMERICAN POLITICIANS AND MEDIA figures don't seem to have much interest, either, not in naval power or in upbeat develop-ments like the Port of Los Angeles handling ever-more cargo while emitting ever-less pollution. Perhaps this is because most Americans never lay eyes on a container liner—a vessel designed, after all, to approach the shore as little as possible—or on a warship.

Deployed, US Navy vessels are far from home. Returning, most park in places such as Naval Base Kitsap, in Washington State, that do not register in the American psyche the way Portsmouth registers in the English psyche or Shanghai in the Chinese psyche. Capital ships cannot appear at Fourth of July parades as army and national guard units do; submarines can't perform synchronized diving shows. When the Blue Angels roar through a flyover before football games or cavort above Lake Michigan near Chicago each summer, audience members may not know the orange accents mean navy as opposed to air force.

Politicians only seem interested in naval affairs when money for contractors is distributed or when contractors offer the kickbacks politicians crave. The mainstream media care mainly if there's a scandal, such as the COVID-19 outbreak on the supercarrier *Roosevelt* in 2020. The story was the banner on *CBS Evening News* three nights running, highlighted by the network because the information was downbeat. The controversy produced, at least, via the *Navy Times*, one of the best headlines ever: PENTAGON LEADER RESIGNS, CAPPING BIZARRE FIASCO.

Regarding seaborne trade, Americans seem cognizant exclusively of the downside. One reason for Donald Trump's 2016 election was his ability to convince millions that international trade was stealing their jobs and harming their well-being—pay no mind that American middle-class well-being had never been better than on the 2016 day voters went to the polls, with median household income at a record high and unemployment only 4.6 percent.[2]

Seaborne trade engenders many problems, including emboldening China to steal intellectual property and bribe its way to influence with the World Health Organization and governments of developing nations. Change caused by globalization for the most part helps but also can harm. The COVID-19 outbreak showed that the United States needs to bring home production of medical supplies.

Yet in the main, American public opinion seems to hold a distorted view of trade—supersensitive to the negatives and oblivious to the positives. If any US or British administration cut off trade with China or other nations of the Pacific Rim, the standard of living would fall for the US Midwestern middle class and the UK Midlands middle class—the English-speaking groups most unhappy about globalization.

International trade needs reform, just as nearly every aspect of human society would benefit from reform. Those now alive, the blue-age generation, have lived better than any generation before, sacrificed less, known more—knowledge is an essential of a well-lived life—been safer, and received better care than any other generation, in part because the seas are tranquil and affordable goods arrive on time.

BARACK OBAMA SAID IN 2014, "The United States must always lead on the world stage."

During the Trump administration, the United States abrogated its leadership positions in democracy and in human rights. The forty-fifth president had bromances with the tyrants of North Korea and Russia; tried to ruin flawed but important international institutions, including the United Nations and World Health Organization; and in a low point of American history, encouraged fanatics to storm the Capitol to destroy evidence of the people's votes. The world found out what it's like when the United States does not lead.

In 2014, Obama further said that although the United States often makes mistakes—Uncle Sam's track record leaves much to be desired—America is and must remain the human family's best hope.

That is the moment in which today's generations live, and whether that moment will endure or prove ephemeral has much to do with events of the blue age.

ONE FORMLESS THREAT TO the blue age will be hard to counter, absent advances of the human spirit, because this formless threat arises from the habits of nations.

For as far back as records reach, national leaders have been restive. They grow jealous of what others possess. They fear hidden agendas. They nurse grievances rather than build from within. They try to divert attention from their own shortcomings by lashing out.

Habituations of nations are seen today in ways that include antagonism against globalized trade combined with demands for tariff walls. Donald Trump was far from the only expression of this antagonism. Globalized trade has benefited almost everyone, yet generates resentment and misunderstandings. The faults in the globalization system must be ironed out. If instead the resentments get their way and the system is broken, not only will living standards decline, war could return.

Beyond the formless threat to the blue age are two highly specific dangers. One is the worst-case outcome for climate change. Probably the worst-case won't happen; intermediate outcomes are more likely. But should the worst case come to pass, with dramatic variations in regional climates, ocean currents, and agricultural production and with stronger or more frequent cyclones, all bets will be off.

Climate has more to do with progress than meets the eye. Since the Little Ice Age ended around 1850, earth's climate has been amenable to economic growth, food production, life extension, and long-distance transportation. The worst case of climate change could halt centuries of progress, and do this with the population fivefold larger than in 1850.

The other highly specific threat is a new naval arms race. During the decades when the US Navy had undisputed dominion on the seas, other nations saw little purpose in building expensive fighting ships, since the United States was the sheriff. Now a new naval arms race appears to begin.

Nations observe that China is laying down hulls in a frenzy, increasing production of both commercial liners and warships "more rapidly than any other country has in modern history," writes Andrew Erickson, a professor at the Naval War College.[3] Since 2010, China has added about two dozen destroyers, plus frigates and corvettes, along with three strategic nuclear submarines—the doomsday machines—and an aircraft carrier. That's roughly as many major fighting ships as acquired by the rest of the world combined in the period.

Nations see China growing fast in GDP and political heft. They see China launching droves of warships. India, Japan, Vietnam, and the United Kingdom conclude they had better launch warships too. Others may join the party.

In 2020, the United States began building advanced land-based antiship missiles, of the type that were banned from 1987 until 2018. China, which never signed the ban, has been fielding such weapons since around 2010. Noticing the number one and number two nations investing in land-based antiship missiles, other nations are likely to want them too.

This is the momentum of an arms race. The naval arms race that commenced in 1909 opened the door to global devastation.

A great-power war on land—the showdown at the Fulda Gap envisioned by a generation of NATO and Warsaw Pact planners—seems unlikely for a range of reasons, while great-power air strikes against each other probably won't happen, because they would carry the risk of nuclear escalation. Great-power fighting midocean, on the other hand, could occur with most of the foes' population never seeing a muzzle flash.

The momentum of a naval arms race, coupled with war at sea being the kind of great-power combat that seems imaginable, leaves the waters a damp powder keg—not easy to ignite, but hardly impossible. Which means the question of whether the blue age will continue comes down to this: whether the United States and China, the two most important nations of history, can get along.

DAVID HENDRICKSON, THE POLITICAL scientist cited earlier in the book, wrote in 2018, "The cartographic division of the world into good guys and bad guys makes it impossible for America to put itself into the shoes of others."[4]

Walking in another's shoes is the essence of human understanding. What is it like in China's shoes?

» For a century, from 1839 to 1949, Europeans, Americans, Japanese, and Russians forced their way into China where they oppressed, killed, and stole. If Chinese soldiers had oppressed Americans or Europeans or Japanese or Russians on their home soil, it would be outrageous for Beijing to claim the moral high ground. Yet the West does just that to China today.

» America, England, and France imported thousands of Chinese workers, subjected them to racism, double-crossed them on their promised payments. If China had imported thousands of American, British, and French workers and abused them, it would be outrageous for Beijing to lecture the West about human rights. Yet the West does that to China today.

» Austria, Belgium, Britain, Canada, France, Germany, Hungary, Italy, Japan, the Netherlands, Portugal, Russia, Spain, and the United States had "treaty ports" on China's coast—places from which all business profits left China. They had "concessions," which were not diplomatic enclaves, rather, towns where foreigners lived like kings, exempt from local law. In none of these nations did China enjoy any concession zone or special port.

» England engaged in a systematic initiative to get Chinese citizens addicted to dope, ruining millions of families while setting back national development. In some ways, the opium attack was worse than a military attack.

» The United States kept gunboats on the Yangtze River from 1902 to 1949, to protect US commercial interests and Christian missionaries. Had China put gunboats on the Mississippi River to protect Asian businesses and promote Buddhism, Americans would have been livid.

» The United States helped China win freedom from Japan and sponsored China for the United Nations Security Council. Those actions matter. But in 1915, when Japan imposed on China the degrading Twenty-One Demands, the United States made only pro forma objections.

» The United States created a naval unit called the Asiatic Fleet, based in the Philippines but often found at Qingdao harbor to remind the Chinese that America possessed a level of power they could not match. Had China created a Yankee Fleet home-ported at Veracruz and often calling at Savannah, the United States would be furious to this day.

» During the Dwight Eisenhower presidency, Secretary of State John Dulles supported an "Island Chain Strategy" in which the US military would ring China with force to choke off national development. This is the "encirclement" feared by Germany in 1914 and 1939, by the Soviet Union during the Cold War. If China had spoken of encircling the United States to strangle the American economy, would Washington now say let bygones be bygones?

» Beijing has declared a goal of military parity with America by 2049, centennial of modern China. In 2020, US Defense Secretary Mark Esper called that goal ominous because the Chinese military "does not serve the nation, as US armed forces do—their military serves a political entity, the Chinese Communist Party." This is the same Mark Esper who, alongside his top generals in battle fatigues, walked with the aspiring despot Donald Trump to a political campaign photo op as soldiers fired tear gas at orderly protesters. After Trump was defeated in his reelection bid, US Secretary of State Mike Pompeo—a West Point graduate and former army officer—told the world from the podium of the Department of State that the election outcome would be ignored and Trump would remain president.

» Esper the Secretary of Defense and Pompeo the Secretary of State swore oaths to defend the Constitution, and both went back on their word. Pompeo had the audacity to lecture China about democracy during the very month Trump was demanding Congress suspend the Constitution to reverse the 2020 election outcome. Had China's foreign minister or defense minister behaved the way Pompeo and Esper behaved, Washington and London would have been apoplectic.[5]

» China has done a reasonable job of administering the South China Sea—better than the West has managed the Persian Gulf. If circumstances of the South China Sea were the same but America were in charge, Washington would expect praise. All China ever gets is criticism.

» Renouncing the red-terror approach of Mao, China has since 1990 devoted itself to building, producing, and selling. A populace inured to poverty and ignorance is living better and longer, with rising education levels. China is doing things the right way. Why doesn't the West give credit where due?

Everyone should walk a mile in China's shoes.

Through its existence, the United States has had foreign attackers on its soil just once, two centuries ago. The last time hostile foreign soldiers walked on the British Isles was at Fishguard, Wales, more than two centuries ago. China has in living memory been invaded by many nations, with horrible consequences. Foreign warships have in living memory fired their guns in Chinese ports. Considering the multiple recent attacks endured, it is a wonder China is not more militaristic.

China has in living memory borne economic insecurity much worse than any experienced by America or the United Kingdom. From the Western standpoint, the Belt and Road Initiative looks like a ploy to exert market power across the Indian Ocean basin. From the Chinese standpoint, the initiative looks like a supply chain independent of nations that were hostile to China in the recent past—plus a way to move oil from the Persian Gulf to the Pacific Rim without the United States being involved at any step, considering the United States once cut off Japan's oil.

Any Chinese strategist who rotates a desktop globe sees that while the United States can put the Chinese economy into instant tailspin by blocking the Strait of Malacca or besieging the South China Sea, no navy could shut down the two long coastlines of the United States. The Chinese strategist thinks, *Maybe things with America will be fine, but we need a backup plan*. The Belt and Road Initiative is that plan.

Add to this the psychology of the contemporary Chinese state, a condition that is not America's doing but must be considered, in the same way that the wrath and resentments having their day in the United States are not China's doing yet must be considered by Beijing. For centuries the Han majority was oppressed by the Manchu minority. To be oppressed by a backward people on your own soil—that's humiliating. Only since 1911 have the Han controlled their country, and only since 1949 has a Chinese government ruled without foreign puppeteers pulling the strings. Collectively the Chinese Communist Party is repulsive, but individually its members are patriots who love China and want their nation to prosper. Rule by patriots is a recent development for the Middle Kingdom.

The Han Chinese are the largest ethnic group on earth. For the first time in centuries, they have cause to celebrate—major advances in public education, leading the world in infrastructure improvement, a spacecraft orbiting Mars. Centuries of grinding poverty and catastrophic annual flooding have at last begun to subside. Seventy years in power, the Han Chinese still are trying to stabilize the overall national situation. When America was the same age—that was 1860—perhaps you remember the instability.

Walking in China's shoes does not mean excusing failings, including oppression of the Uighurs and Tibetans, betrayal of Hong Kong, stifling of free speech, "labor camps" that are actually prisons, no constitutional rights, corruption top to bottom. In China there is plenty of disgrace to go around.

Above all these, 1.4 billion human beings are living close together in a place that's polluted and depleting its aquifers at an alarming rate. Modern China may not remain stable. Unstable societies may lash out. If China lashes out, the sea is the most likely setting.

Perhaps later in this century the situation with China will be different, perhaps auspiciously so. For now, the Washington–Beijing equilibrium is the essence of sustaining the blue age. Like it or not, if China and the United States stop getting along, no corner of the world will be safe, and no one will be happy.

CHINA IS "WELCOME" INTO the World Trade Organization structure, Senator Joe Biden of Delaware said in 2001, because "we expect this is going to be a China that plays by the rules." From the Chief of Naval Operations suite in the Pentagon to the harbor master's station at the Port of Los Angeles, I heard the same refrain—China must play by the rules. Do not steal intellectual property, respect exclusive zones, follow environmental and labor standards, and, when a line forms, don't cut to the front. Play by the rules.

Martin Dempsey, a retired army general who ran the Joint Chiefs of Staff during the Obama administration, then became a fellow at Duke University, is reported to have once told his counterpart, General Fang Fenghui, chief of the Chinese general staff, that China must play by the rules.[6] The reply Dempsey heard was that current norms for great-power behavior were expounded when China was absent from the world stage.

In 1949, after the worst of all wars, the United States and Soviet Union were becoming very strong and many other nations were achieving prosperity: China was a shambles. The 1950s and 1960s—best not to think about. In international terms, Beijing did not even answer the phone until 1972. How much of that was China's own fault may be debated. Regardless, norms the United States and Europe extol were established without Chinese participation. Now China has reached the point where Beijing gets a say.

In the period roughly from 1972 to 2010, China was weak and had to approach the West as a supplicant. If the United States gave orders, China had little choice but deference. Because China's GDP and military have gone through growth spurts, Beijing can look other capitals in the eye. Feeling for the first time in a thousand years the sensation of international strength, China expects to be listened to. This expectation is reasonable on Beijing's part. Brussels and Washington must listen—not necessarily agree, but listen.

If the Enlightenment frame for understanding the world eventually prevails in the Middle Kingdom, not only will China grow stronger and more prosperous and give honor to ancestors, the human prospect will be enriched. Before China will accept the Enlightenment frame, the West must show this nation the kind of respect that the West itself desires.

The Western view of the world—embraced by the United States, the European Union, the United Kingdom, Canada, Australia, New Zealand, Norway, and increasingly by Japan and South Korea—is the Enlightenment conclusion that the individual is more important than the state. The view is morally correct, is self-evident under natural law, is true in a metaphysical sense that exists independent of the empirical. The individual is more important than the state. That's five hundred years of Western thought in one sentence.

The Enlightenment frame is not just self-evident—it is pragmatic. Top officials of the Chinese government should be reminded daily that nations accepting personal freedom have become richer and more powerful than nations imposing state control. This does not happen some of the time—it happens *all of the time*. Oil and bauxite and silicon are not fundamental sources of power. Liberty is.

But the essential insight of the Enlightenment can succeed in China only if the Chinese reach the conclusion on their own.

BEHIND THE CURTAIN IN China is this: the ruling class has a deep-seated inferiority complex about the capital-C Communist system. Party officials know capital-C Communism has been a total failure everywhere. Capital-C Communism has not failed some of the time; it has failed *all of the time.* But the Chinese ruling class doesn't know how else to cling to power.

Party leaders of China already grasp that the Western system is superior to theirs—why else would they want so badly to send their children to college in the United States or Canada or France?

But knowing a thing and accepting it are different. A leading question hangs over the world: will China accept that freedom confers strength, or will China lash out instead?

BEHIND THE CURTAIN IN the United States is a deep-seated fear that China—and, down the road, India—will pass America as number one.

The United States has been number one for seventy-five years, and not coincidentally this is the period of peace on the waters. Being number one—baby, it's sweet. Washington, D.C., is the Rome of the modern world. Everywhere you go, an American passport is a bar of gold. Thousands of miles from American shores, people chant, "USA! USA!"

Nobody has ever rivaled American economic innovation. Nobody has ever won straight up against the US military. Nobody can match America's popular culture—or our colleges, research discoveries, business skills, medical advances, space missions, technological breakthroughs, even our literature and performing arts. For all of America's multitudinous faults, no nation has ever had a better story to tell—and no nation ever will.

Those seventy-five years of the United States being number one may be summed by the highly scientific formula America = Success.

But the United States will not stay at number one. The sooner Americans accept this, the better for everyone. Because Americans fear the loss of top status to China, we think China must be held back. Its commerce is viewed as a menace rather than as competition. Its military is viewed as an enemy, rather than a peer with which we must coexist and perhaps one day find common cause in some even-larger fight.

For China to keep getting stronger, more prosperous, and more influential seems, to America, terrible news. It's good news! The land of dragons is history's largest nation—though someday India may take that garland—and success for the largest nation is good. China's rapid progression from misery and feudalism to decent living standards and relatively up-to-date social culture is among the buoyant events of world history. For China, and perhaps India, to pass the United States in wealth and influence is not bad, as long as America is not diminished.

The British writer Rana Dasgupta, who teaches at Brown University, said in 2020, "The major economic process of the moment, after all, transferred mass prosperity from the West to Asia."[7] That's the zero-sum view: assets are being subtracted from one and added to another. Historically, zero-sum thinking is favored by those who presume economics has only predators and victims.

But what's happening now is not a transfer of prosperity; it is growth increasing faster in Asia than in the West. Asia is not taking what others possess: Asia is making and trading. Why should America object? If you and I each have a hundred oranges, and you grow a hundred more, I still have one hundred oranges. My store is not tapered; yours is enriched. The rise of China and India is not the same as the decline of the West. The situation is not zero-sum.

The United States and Europe can remain great even as China and India (later perhaps Brazil and Indonesia) advance in material well-being and global consequence. That's good! The West won't have less; the East and South will have more.

The American writer Robert Wright, who teaches at the Union Theological Seminary in New York City, calls this a "nonzero" result. Wright believes nonzero outcomes are the main current of history. The nonzero effects shown today in international economics are propitious for the human family.

It is vital the West resist the landlocked view of the world: that different cultures and new ways of doing things are threats, not opportunities; that trade, change, and new ideas should be stopped (always in some unspecified manner—it's far from clear preventing new ideas is even possible); that walls must oppose the outside.

Almost everyone is better off because of globalization: our future is brighter. The oceans are the mediator of this boon. The boon is nonzero. No aspect of the blue age need be zero-sum.

The United States would do well to recognize how many of its advantages are gifts of the sea. Keeping the waters peaceful, ecologically healthy, and open to every nation will bring benefits for generations to come. The world needs a hopeful narrative—of progress, however fitful, toward a place we want to be. Free commerce that reduces poverty and sustains living standards is one part of the hopeful narrative.

If we are careless, the blue age will end. This need not happen. To multiply the harbors does not reduce the sea.

ACKNOWLEDGMENTS

For the realization of this volume thanks are due to James Bennet, Patricia Boyd, David Bradley, Michael Carlisle, Diane Chandler, Whitney Dangerfield, James Fallows, Ruth Franklin, Pete Garceau, Nicole Girten, Tedd Habberfield, Kim Jaske, Jon Karp, Jaime Leifer, Nicholas Lemann, David Malpass, Marcia McNutt, Michael Mungiello, Peter Osnos, Charles Peters, Melissa Raymond, William Reilly, Clay Risen, Scott Stossel, Evan Thomas, Michelle Welsh-Horst, William Whitworth, Jeff Williams, Sarah Yager, and Mortimer Zuckerman; to my wife Nan Kennelly; to my children Grant, Mara, and Spenser.

I thank the US Navy officers James Adams, Nate Christensen, Eric Durie, Reann Mommsen, Jacqueline Pau, Mary Sanford, and Megan Shutka. That four of these seven are women is a leading indicator of change in the navy.

There were more interviews than the pages could reflect. I thank those CMA CGM, Evergreen Marine, Japanese Maritime Self-Defense Force, Maersk, and Royal Navy officers and sailors who took the time to sit—or to stand, or to shout above engine noise—for interviews that improved my understanding but did not lead to quotes.

I thank the US Naval Academy and Naval War College instructors who likewise were generous with their time but not rewarded with quotation. We live at a moment when the Pentagon's educational institutions exhibit more enthusiasm for the liberal-arts philosophy than do many private colleges and universities.

I thank my brother-in-law James Kennelly, who speaks Japanese and is attuned to the politics and culture of the Indo-Pacific. Jamie spent years scanning the Asian press to alert me about stories missed in the West but important to the Pacific Rim waterworld.

I especially thank the retired commander Don Sewell, a plank owner of USS *Wasp*, meaning he was aboard on the vessel's first day of commission. *Wasp*'s motto—"Honor, tradition, excellence" —may sound corny. During three decades at sea, often in pressure-cooker situations, the crew upheld this standard. If only all of us could say our standards were upheld.

RECOMMENDED READING

An academic treatise requires formal annotation; general-interest books may not. For general-interest books, deferring references to a bibliography and endnotes may allow the author to seem to have discovered everything himself or herself and to have conducted his or her own interviews. Only the determined reader squints at the reference grapheme, flips to the back, figures out what page that tiny number corresponds to, looks up the primary source and realizes the material and interview quotations originated with someone else.

A better way is to cite sources, thinkers and other writers in the main text, so the reader knows up front what comes from where. *The Blue Age* follows this practice. Here I repeat my earlier explanation of quotes in this book: *Quotations attributed to presidents or similarly well-known persons, or to organizations, are drawn from the public record. All other quotations are from interviews with me.*

In place of a traditional bibliography, what follows are some books on the subjects of *The Blue Age* that added to my understanding. I commend to readers these meritorious and rewarding volumes.

The Naval War of 1812, by Theodore Roosevelt. Published 1882, surprisingly readable today.

Monsoon, by Robert Kaplan. Random House, 2010. Kaplan, one of my generation's most productive researcher-writers, conveys the sense of contemporary Indian Ocean water cities being another world relative to the West.

Destined for War?, by Graham Allison. Houghton-Mifflin, 2017. Allison is a prominent academic who studies the historical problem of a rising power's coming into conflict with an established power. Athens and Sparta walked straight into a trap. China and the United States may or may not do so. Allison shows how what he calls the "Thucydides Trap" can be avoided.

Sea of Thunder, by Evan Thomas. Simon & Shuster, 2006. Leyte Gulf, October 1944, presented in vivid detail by a master of rich reporting. May it always remain true that Leyte Gulf was the final great naval battle.

Castles of Steel, by Robert Massie. Ballantine, 2002. Scholarly detail on how English and German mania for battleships engendered the Great War. Equal to Tuchman's *Guns of August*.

Sea Power, by James Stavridis. Penguin, 2017. A recently retired four-star admiral details the operational challenges of America's contemporary position on the blue water, leavening the serious subjects with engaging nautical anecdotes.

The Island at the Center of the World, by Russell Shorto. Doubleday, 2004. Ostensibly a history of how Europeans took over Manhattan, it is in many ways the story of the Atlantic Ocean, the English, and the Dutch in the seventeenth century. Wonderful factoid: Shorto lives not in New York City or Washington, D.C., or San Francisco but Cumberland, Maryland, an old-industrial railroad town, near West Virginia, that feels as if it were Brigadoon, thrown out of time.

When China Ruled the Sea, by Louise Levathes. Oxford University Press, 1994. Explores myth and fact about the fleet of treasure ships that plied the Asian coasts in the fifteenth century.

Forgotten Armies, by Christopher Bayly. Penguin, 2004. Everyone knows about Pacific island battles in World War II. There was also significant combat over port and road access in Burma, Malaysia, Assam, and what's now Bangladesh. Forgotten in the West, this fighting helped shape the contemporary worldview of the Pacific Rim and influences China's Belt and Road Initiative.

Seven-Tenths, by James Hamilton-Paterson. Faber & Faber, 2007. Literary-quality essays on the marine realm.

The World Is Blue, by Sylvia Earle. National Geographic, 2009. Comprehensive review of current factual understanding of the seas.

Accessory to War, by Neil deGrasse Tyson and Avis Lang. W. W. Norton, 2018. Much of the book concerns how ocean navigation by the stars during antiquity led to developments of the modern era.

Japan 1941, by Eri Hotta. Knopf, 2013. Hotta, who grew up in Tokyo, analyzes the culture and politics of her homeland in the year Japan made the worst maritime mistake in human annals.

The Fleet at Flood Tide, by James Hornfischer. Random House, 2016. The enormity of the ocean force that approached Japan in 1945 to retaliate for that mistake.

Downfall, by Richard Frank. Random House, 2001. Operation Downfall was the planned final offensive to annihilate organized life on the home islands of imperial Japan, a general bloodbath by air, water, and land obviated by atomic bombs at Hiroshima and Nagasaki. To an extent little appreciated in the United States, today's Chinese and Russian planners fret that the US Navy could do to them what it prepared to do to Japan.

The Box, by Marc Levinson. Princeton University Press, 2016. Well-done book on how the container shipping industry works.

Ninety Percent of Everything, by Rose George. Henry Holt, 2013. Life on a modern container liner.

The Perfect Storm, by Sebastian Junger. Norton, 1997. A fishing boat, a sailboat, and a Coast Guard cutter against the sheer power of the sea in a story that's all too real.

The Outlaw Sea, by William Langewiesche. North Point Press, 2004. One of today's leading writers on complex subjects (his 1998 *Inside the Sky* is the best book about flying) tackles abuses in maritime businesses. The chapter describing impoverished men on a beach in India engaged in arduous "shipbreaking" for a few dollars a day is particularly chilling.

The Outlaw Ocean, by Ian Urbina. Bodley Head, 2019. Nearly the same title, and the cover of this book is a ringer for the cover of the earlier *Outlaw Sea*. Urbina details harm to workers aboard unregulated vessels, especially trawlers.

The Rise and Fall of British Naval Mastery, by Paul Kennedy. Penguin, 1976. Look for the 2017 edition, which proposes a "new age of navalism." Considering the significance of fighting and commerce at sea, there ought to be many books of such import and stature. At least there's this one.

How Everything Became War and the Military Became Everything, by Rosa Brooks. Simon & Schuster, 2016. The enduring lesson of the American presence in Vietnam is that military power only solves military problems. In this book, a former Pentagon official details how that lesson is ignored by a contemporary Washington establishment wanting to treat everything untoward around the world as solvable with smart bombs.

Stillwell and the American Experience in China, 1911–1945, by Barbara Tuchman. Grove Press, 1970. Fathoming the tensions regarding China entails knowing what happened between the United States and the Middle Kingdom during the period this book covers. Contains a few passages about my great-uncle Ernest Easterbrook, a US Army major general who was Joseph Stillwell's adjutant in China, Burma, and India. After terrible suffering during World War II, Ernest lived a dreamlike retirement in magnificent Carmel, California, far from battle and anger, feeling the nearness of God. Fluent in several Sinitic dialects, Ernest's wife Nancy was a believer in the beauty and promise of Chinese culture. Well into her senior years, Nancy led groups of Americans on tours of the parts of China few Westerners see.

Log from the Sea of Cortez, by John Steinbeck. Viking, 1951. For my money Steinbeck and Willa Cather are the greatest American novelists. There was no way to work Cather's novels into this book (though the North Atlantic passage sequence in *One of Ours* . . .). It was a snap to work in Steinbeck, whose *Log from the Sea of Cortez* is among the best water books. Steinbeck was also concerned with the absence of water. His 1952 masterpiece *East of Eden* contains a long discourse on why cyclical drought and naturally occurring timber fires make most of California unsuited for development. Today there are four times as many people in California as when Steinbeck warned that more housing would lead ineluctably to devastating wildfire seasons.

The Allure of Battle, by Cathal Nolan. Oxford University Press, 2016. Long to excess, the book invites skimming. Central points about the illusion of "decisive battle" are great insights, as are pithy quotes such as "Hate is the conjoined twin of war."

The War Lovers, by Evan Thomas. Little-Brown, 2010. Not a romance! Details how prominent Americans of the late nineteenth century wanted to trigger the Spanish-American War to increase US sea power.

Vast Expanses, by Helen Rozwadowski. University of Chicago Press, 2019. Stretching backward many millennia, asserts water events meant as much to the human past as land events.

Sea People, by Christina Thompson. Harper, 2019. How ancient Polynesians were able to travel far across the Pacific despite lacking powered boats and compasses.

Nonzero, by Robert Wright. Pantheon, 1999. Wright argues that through history, nations and peoples have helped each other more than harmed each other—but we only remember the harm (battles, persecutions) because academics and journalists are obsessed with keeping everything negative. Wright's frame of understanding—much goes wrong, but as time passes, life mainly improves—fits the worldview presented in *The Blue Age*.

The Sea and Civilization, by Lincoln Paine. Knopf, 2013. One of the top works of history in our lifetimes, from an author and museum officer who lives in Maine. When *The Sea and Civilization* was published a smart guy (me) called it "magisterial." I am standing by that adjective. Paine memorably concludes, "All history is maritime history."

NOTES

This is a general-interest work, not a PhD dissertation. For that reason, I did not footnote every factual reference: after all, the book contains many hundreds. I offer notes on material specific to studies, reports, and original scholarship.

Generalizations usually describe the consensus of contemporary experts. Being the consensus does not ensure a contention is correct—experts are wrong more often than we care to ponder. But most of the time, the consensus of experts is the best call.

While books are considered arbiters of verity, many are not fact-checked. Sometimes publishers do not want to know if splashy unverified claims in books are true. A warning sign is a book whose front cover is a photo of the "author." One may assume a book whose front cover is a picture of a celebrity or politician masquerading as an author contains material that would never get past the fact-checking stage at *The Atlantic*, the *New Yorker*, or a good college newspaper.

The Blue Age was reviewed by a fact-checker. Any errors that remain are mine.

Chapter 1: A School of Big Fish

1. US Department of Defense, *U.S. Navy By Race, Gender and Ethnicity*, annual report, 2020.

2. "Best Colleges," *US News & World Report*, September 14, 2020.

3. The document was Center for Strategic and International Studies, *Is the U.S. Navy Too Small?* September 2015.

4. Interested readers can search online for "USNI News Fleet and Marine Tracker" for today's deployed-warship numbers.

5. Though the *Wasp* appears to the eye to be an aircraft carrier, it has no catapults. Assault vessels like *Wasp* employ jump jets, helicopters and tilt-rotor aircraft that take to the air unassisted. The commander in chief of the US military did not understand the difference between an aircraft carrier and an assault ship.

6. Congressional Research Service, *CVN-78 Background and Issues*, October 2020, details the status of next supercarrier.

7. The navy also has a guided-missile cruiser named *Chancellorsville*, memorializing a Southern victory over the Union. Confederate flags were in some years displayed aboard the *Chancellorsville*. In 2021, Congress asked the navy to rename the ship, ending the symbolism without having to reach any conclusion about whether it was wrong in the first place.

From roughly the late nineteenth century through the Vietnam War, Congress tendered the noncommissioned little in the way of wages or opportunity, which led to problems with recruiting. Southerners have shown themselves capable soldiers, sailors, and aircrew: the use of Confederacy names on military bases and warships was a way of expressing to potential Southern enlistees that regarding the Civil War, all is forgiven. In the most recent quarter century, Congress has offered enlisted personnel reasonable pay, benefits, and advancement. With the military now holding occupational appeal, the recruiting rationalization for honoring the Confederacy has expired.

8. Our World in Data, "Nuclear Weapons"; see *Stockpiles of Nuclear Weapons*. The nonprofit clearinghouse Our World in Data (ourworldindata.org), a project of the University of Oxford and created mainly by the scholar Max Roser, is an invaluable resource and places all its research in the public domain.

9. David Hendrickson, *Republic in Peril* (Oxford University Press, 2018).

Chapter 2: Is Sea Power Overrated?

1. Numbers that follow in this section appear in, or are computed from Stockholm International Peace Research Institute (SIPRI) *Military Expenditure Database* "Military Expenditure Database," SIPRI, 2018, www.sipri.org/databases/milex.

2. Interested readers should search for "Ethnographic and Archeological Evidence on Violent Death" to find a comprehensive Our World in Data study. A series of tables shows that in ancient Mexico, 5 percent of the populace died because of war; in Napoleonic France, 3 percent; in the United States and Europe from 1900 to 1960,

incorporating both world wars, 1 percent died because of combat; today, globally, 0.04 percent die from war or "one-sided violence" in which an armed group assails the unarmed. The contemporary battle death rate, 0.04 percent annually, is by far the lowest in human history. You'd never know from the mainstream media, would you? In the past, powerful forces tried to prevent talk of freedom. Today, powerful forces try to prevent talk of hopeful information.

H. L. Mencken wrote that wealthy elites want to "keep the populace alarmed by an endless series of hobgoblins." The *New York Times*, *Washington Post* (owned by Jeff Bezos, history's richest person), and CNN (owned by AT&T, one of history's richest corporations) participate with enthusiasm in keeping the populace alarmed, both by commission (overstatement of the negative) and by omission (ignoring the positive).

3. Interested readers can search online for "World Bank" and "Military Expenditure % of GDP" to obtain these or the most current figures.

4. James Stavridis, *Sea Power* (Penguin, 2017).

5. Donald Lankiewicz, "Alfred Thayer Mahan, Reluctant Seaman," *American History*, February 1997.

6. These institutions also read Julian Corbett, 1854–1922, a British naval theorist who placed pragmatism ahead of grand strategy and is in some ways the anti-Mahan.

7. Statistics in this section are from World Bank, *World Trade Summary*. Search "Trade Summary World Bank" to open the World Bank's data affiliate.

Chapter 3: Why Fighting on the Blue Water Stopped

1. See Arms Control Association, "U.S.-Russian Nuclear Arms Control Agreements at a Glance," April 2020, www.armscontrol.org/factsheets/USRussia NuclearAgreements, for latest status updates.

2. Interested readers should search for "Crop Yield" in the Our World in Data database (ourworldindata.org) for a detailed walk through how the human family overcame the greatest problem it ever faced—providing enough food as the family got larger. In *It's Better Than It Looks: Reasons for Optimism in an Age of Fear* (PublicAffairs, 2018), I wrote, "Farming has no sex appeal compared to miniature electronics or launching rockets, but if plants don't grow, little else matters."

Every map and graphic under "Crop Yields" in the Our World in Data shows a long-term positive trend: grains, cassava, legumes, bananas, rapeseed, citrus—name a plant. Americans and Europeans don't hear about success in agriculture, because hopeful tales do not advance the narrative of panic and fear. They do hear about implausible threats from trace chemicals in food, said to be super-ultra-deadly, though these compounds have no discernible impact on life expectancy.

3. Admiral Farragut was cursing harbor mines. In the nineteenth century, what are now called mines were known as torpedoes, named for a species of electric ray whose sting is not soon forgotten. Today mines and torpedoes are converging technologically. The navy's new Hammerhead antisubmarine weapon has the qualities of both, able to float passively like a mine for long periods then suddenly chase a target like a torpedo.

4. Studied as World War II is, many aspects of Yalta have been overlooked. Serhii Plokhy, *The Price of Peace* (Viking, 2010), details how Big Three military leaders refused to coordinate with each other. Plokhy, who grew up in Ukraine, is an old-fashioned historian who works from original-language documents.

5. I gave a lecture at the Naval War College in 2010, partly about an early version of the blue-age thesis. Officials of the college told me that while Chinese and Russian officers are not formally prohibited from the campus, they are never invited.

In early 2021, the president of the Naval War College was Rear Admiral Shoshana Chatfield, a former helicopter pilot. It has long been speculated that as women rise in business and government, behaviors of institutions will change. Women are headed toward the Joint Chiefs of Staff. Imagine it's 2050 and half the officers on the Pentagon's E ring are women. One can hope that having women at the top of military organizations will be a plus for human events.

Chapter 4: There's Always a Bigger Fish

1. Reagan's decision-making regarding ships is detailed in John Lehman, *Oceans Ventured* (Norton, 2018). Lehman, secretary of the navy for most of the Reagan administration, boasts among the world's most diverse CVs. Lehman was a naval aviator, flying the A6 off carriers, then served as an aide to Henry Kissinger, then left for Wall Street as an early adapter in the private-equity fad, then worked for Reagan. Lehman is the one who, in 2012, convinced Mitt Romney to raise the issue of the size of the US Navy in presidential debates with Barack Obama.

2. David Vine, *The United States of War* (University of California Press, 2020). Trained as an anthropologist, Vine studies the social impact of military installations. *The Blue Age* presumes the world is better off with a strong US Navy presence in many places, including the Indian Ocean island of Diego Garcia. David Vine, *Island of Shame*, (Princeton University Press 2009), recounts the mistreatment of native Diego Garcia islanders, who were driven out first by the Royal Navy then by the US Navy. The story does not reflect well on America.

3. Pew Research Center, "Generations Divide Over Military Action in Iraq," Pew Research Center, October 17, 2002.

4. An August 2018 page one of the *New York Times* proclaimed, "China Is Ready to Challenge U.S. Navy in the Pacific." Accompanying the prominent story was a photo of *Liaoning*, a Chinese aircraft carrier: the text suggested this vessel represents an unprecedented menace. The story was nuanced but did not explain *Liaoning* has about the capabilities of US aircraft carriers of the 1950s. The story further declared that twenty years ago, China possessed only three submarines, and now has eighty-three. Terrifying! A week later, the newspaper corrected that actually it was twenty years ago when China had eighty-three submarines; since then Beijing's underwater fleet has diminished in size, not expanded. The spooky report was prominent on page one, the correction a block of tiny type deep inside.

The accurate figure for Chinese submarines in 2018 could have been obtained by checking International Institute for Strategic Studies (IISS), *Military Balance 2018* (Routledge, 2018). On the day the *Times* story ran I checked this source, which said, "Actual size of China's operational [submarine] fleet appears to have remained remarkably consistent over the last 15 years." It is easy to make an honest mistake—trust me, I have experience! The point is that scary information was a big deal, reassuring information downplayed.

In 2014, the *Wall Street Journal* ran a page-one story expressing horror at news that Chinese submarines had traversed the Strait of Malacca. Not only are American warships in the Strait of Malacca regularly—as well they should be—but the vessels that unsettled the *Journal* had about the same technical qualities as French submarines from the period that Ronald Reagan was president. These qualifiers were not mentioned.

The Atlantic is the best general-interest publication in the world. In 2005, an *Atlantic* cover suggested impending naval war between the United States and Middle Kingdom. Any major article that offers a provocative thesis may turn out wrong—trust me, I have experience! But as someone who has loved *The Atlantic* for decades, written cover stories plus many other pieces for the magazine, I note that even this most thoughtful of publications may favor alarmism.

The cover illustration of the 2005 article was a Chinese sailor who had been false-color converted to appear intent on evildoing. Behind the sailor was an ominous Chinese warship. The hull number was visible: a quick check showed the vessel was equivalent to *Spruance*-class destroyers America had, in 2005, just retired. Boats the US Navy viewed as obsolete, *The Atlantic* implied, were ultra-powerful flying the Chinese ensign.

A structural problem in high-end journalism is that negative analyses draw attention and win awards, while there are no consequences for negativism that turns out false. In 2010, an *Atlantic* cover called Israel about to go to war with Iran. An autumn 2020 *Atlantic* cover declared COVID-19 "merely a harbinger of worse plagues to come," which could happen, but was presented as a certainty. Another 2020 *Atlantic* story proffered that a science-fiction premise called "cliodynamics" should be taken seriously because it predicts the world is "almost guaranteed" to experience "five hellish years" soon, very soon.

If doom-scrolling in the *New York Times* or *Atlantic* or similar prestige outlet proves wrong, there will be no reputational harm for the author or publication, because the current intellectual milieu does not subject alarmism to scrutiny. The result is that many authors and editors dwell on whatever's bad—and plenty is—while pretending good news does not occur.

5. In the same way real estate developers keep two sets of books—one to impress lenders claiming copious profits, the other to show tax collectors claiming dismal losses—Moscow contends *Kuznetsov* simultaneously is an aircraft carrier and a cruiser.

By calling the ship an aircraft carrier, the Russian navy gains status. Calling the ship a cruiser allows *Kuznetsov* to qualify for passage between the Black Sea and the Mediterranean under the convention that regulates the Dardanelles and Bosporus, choke points that have driven Russian leaders to distraction from the czars through Stalin to the present. That document, signed in 1936 as among the final acts of the League of Nations, says any merchant ship may use the Turkish Straits but no warship larger than a cruiser may. So if a British or an Indian aircraft carrier showed up requesting transit, entry would be denied. If the Russian aircraft carrier shows up, the vessel passes because Moscow's paperwork says that ship is a cruiser.

6. Interested readers can search online for "World Bank" and "Military Expenditure % of GDP" to obtain spending by nation.

7. Officers of two navies told me this anecdote. Not long after fighting Vietnam, Western militaries take something like fatherly pride in Vietnam's standing up to China. But I have no independent way of verifying the moods or intentions of the Vietnamese captains. The *Financial Times* reported the basic confrontation, which occurred in July 2019.

8. Martin Gilbert, one of the Bulldog's many biographers, contended Churchill said, "Meeting jaw to jaw is better than war."

9. Neta C. Crawford, "United States Budgetary Costs and Obligations of Post-9/11 Wars through FY2020: $6.4 Trillion," Watson Institute, Brown University, November 2019.

10. This and other statements regarding federal spending are supported in detail in *It's Better Than It Looks: Reasons for Optimism in an Age of Fear.*

11. During the virus lockdown, the Amazon stockholder MacKenzie Scott donated about $6 billion to food banks, civic organizations, and small colleges. This donation was hailed as great benevolence. Borrowing $5.3 trillion to distribute as COVID-19 emergency aid, the federal government gave 880 times as much as did Scott. The far larger sum was seen as mingy.

The gift giver in the former case will remain among the richest persons ever, since Scott retained almost all of her net worth—her donations were admirable but in no sense a sacrifice. The gift giver in the latter, far larger case was Generation Z, which will be handed the bill for long-term federal debt. Yet public opinion lauds the superrich as generous (few are), government as tightfisted (US federal government is consistently generous).

12. US Social Security Administration, *2020 Annual Report of the Board of Trustees of the Federal Old-Age and Survivors Insurance and Federal Disability Insurance Trust Funds* (Washington, DC: 2020), www.ssa.gov/OACT/TR/2020/tr2020.pdf.

13. US Department of the Navy, *Comprehensive Review of Recent Surface Force Incidents*, October 2017, available at https://news.usni.org/2017/11/02/document -navy-comprehensive-review-surface-forces.

14. Stand by for the XLUUV (Extra Large Unmanned Undersea Vehicle), which is described in Congressional Research Service, "Navy Large Unmanned Surface and Undersea Vessels: Background and Issues for Congress," CRS report R45757, updated February 25, 2021. Also, keep your eyes peeled for the US Army's NGOMFV (Next-Generation Optionally Manned Fighting Vehicle).

15. A pilotless tanker, the MQ-25 Stingray, has flown in tests. Crews call the new tanker T1, which was the robot in the first *Terminator* movie. In theory a T1 could spend hours at the edge of enemy airspace, fueling navy strike aircraft on their way in and again on their way out. For now, computers fly the tanker straight and level while the navy attack pilot does the tricky part, the rendezvous with the fuel drogue. Eventually computers will fly the fighter too.

Chapter 5: Marlin Brando
Would Not Recognize a Modern Port

1. Zhenhua Heavy Industries builds large steel structures such as cranes and bridge components, plus the unusual vessels that transport them. It is not directly related to Shenzhen Zhenhua Data Technology, an information-theft enterprise similar to Facebook. But given interlocking Chinese government control, it's not independent either.

2. Development of the General Electric low-emission locomotive is described in my book *Sonic Boom: Globalization at Mach Speed* (Random House, 2009).

3. In 1953, one year before the Brando movie, Congress chartered a Waterfront Commission "for the purpose of eliminating various evils in the ports of the New York area."

Racketeering influence at the New York area waterfronts has dropped in part because money flowing through local harbors declined when Los Angeles, Long Beach, and Baltimore took the lead in efficient gantry-crane operations. In 2018 Chris Christie, departing as governor of New Jersey, tried to withdraw his state from the Waterfront Commission, arguing its purpose had expired. No government agency ever ends! The commission still exists and tries to pretend the year is 1953. This vestigial source of no-show patronage jobs now calls itself "an instrumentality of the states of New York and New Jersey."

4. Baltimore location shoots for this season were filmed in 2002, when international water trade was just ramping up. In that year the Port of Baltimore handled less than half as many shipping containers as it would in 2019, and had fewer cranes. Scenes from that season of *The Wire* made the Baltimore docks seem a rusting, abandoned hellscape ruled by drunken stevedores and cackling mobsters. Regardless of whether that was really the case in 2002, today the Baltimore docks are bustling, efficient, and policed.

5. I drive an Acura that was built in Marysville, Ohio. I could have chosen an American-built BMW, Honda, Hyundai, Kia, Lexus, Mercedes, Nissan, Subaru, Toyota, or Volkswagen. During the 2016 and 2020 presidential campaigns, Donald Trump and Bernie Sanders both seemed unaware that most international-marque cars are now manufactured in the United States. Chauffeured everywhere, Trump and Sanders never deal with buying and maintaining cars, daily issues that torment the majority of Americans.

For his part, during the 2020 campaign Joe Biden filmed a commercial showing himself behind the wheel of a vintage 1967 Detroit muscle car and asking, "How can American-made vehicles no longer be out there?" The ad suggests he hasn't actually purchased an automobile in decades—cars are just provided for him. Biden seemed unaware that General Motors and Ford dominate the market for the two most popular vehicle classes, SUVs and pickup trucks, or that the hottest car of the moment is the mid-engined C8 Corvette, assembled in Bowling Green, Kentucky.

6. US Bureau of Labor Statistics, *New Vehicles in United States, 1995–2020.*

7. Changing trends in demand for US-made paper began decades before the globalized supply chain could have been the cause. The National Bureau of

Economic Research reports United States production of "fine writing paper" peaked in 1930, when the population was 40 percent of today's. Contemporary US production of writing paper is, on a per-capita basis, a fraction of the level of the 1930s. The reason is not that fine writing paper is "pouring in" from overseas. (Donald Trump found his third wife Melania when tall Slovene supermodels began pouring in.) The art of the handwritten personal letter has deteriorated, so sales of writing paper dropped.

In this generation, most transmission of news has shifted from paper to digital media, so sales of newsprint dropped, a change unrelated to international trade. At some future juncture, the market for binary hard drives on tablets and phones may drop. Politicians seeking donations will propose to ban imported digital media, interest groups in Silicon Valley will demand protectionism. Pundits will lament the good old days when data was stored on magnetic platters rather than in a floating tesseract or whatever comes next.

8. World Bank, *GDP Per Capita United States*.

9. Stephen Rose, *Growing Size and Incomes of the Upper Middle Class* (Urban Institute, 2016).

Chapter 6: From Ideal-X to the Megamax

1. China's Great Famine, from 1959 to 1961, killed at least twenty million people and was caused by Communist Party central planning. Yiyun Li, "The Man Who Eats," *New Yorker*, August 30, 2004, is a terrifying account of millions deliberately starved to death by Maoist incompetence and cult-of-personality. "Chinese Construction Firm Erects 57-Storey Skyscraper in 19 Days," *Guardian*, April 30, 2015, www.theguardian.com/world/2015/apr/30/chinese-construction-firm-erects-57-storey-skyscraper-in-19-days, includes a time-lapse video of large building construction, using market forces, in Changsha in the present day.

2. Shenzhen is the third-busiest port. In 2018 Shanghai was number one at 42 million TEUs shipped. That's *more* than a large container of goods every second, every day. See World Shipping Council, "Top 50 World Container Ports," www.worldshipping .org/about-the-industry/global-trade/top-50-world-container-ports, for the running box score. Many of the links on the websites of those facilities post their information in four languages.

3. Federal Reserve Economic Data (hereafter cited as FRED), "Federal Debt: Total Public Debt, https://fred.stlouisfed.org/series/GFDEBTN. FRED is a project of the Federal Reserve Bank of St. Louis. Clear, intuitive, comprehensive, the FRED resource is everything government information ought to be but rarely is. Although this source shows 2000 public debt at $5.7 billion, remember, this book adjusts all money numbers to 2020 values.

4. In December 2020, the Federal Reserve Board of Governors said it would pump the money supply in hopes of triggering "sustained inflation." That's what they are *trying to achieve*, not trying to avoid. This notion would have caused whatever remained of the brains of economists of the previous generation to fission down to the subatomic level.

5. See Stephanie Kelton, *The Deficit Myth* (PublicAffairs, 2020). Kelton was Sanders's economic adviser in 2016. She touts a series of conjectures that are far outside the mainstream. Among other things, Kelton argues that because the US dollar is "fiat currency"—money that lacks intrinsic value, the kind the United States has printed and minted since the gold standard ended in 1971—who cares how many zeros are added? Not only are huge increases in government spending okay, it's also okay for fiat currency to be nothing that is backed by nothing—no government revenue, no Treasury bills, no taxes, just more zeros. Establishment experts scoff at this assertion. But establishment economists have been unable to explain the 2000–2020 period of runaway debt without inflation.

6. Preparation of the vessel, with the dull bureaucratic name littoral combat ship, began in about 2000, when Pentagon and Wall Street analysts believed a second oil crisis was approaching. If American imports came from the west coast of Africa, tankers could sail directly into the open ocean, where the US Navy rules. That sounded better than oil tankers having to traverse the narrow Strait of Hormuz. The corvette was intended to guard tankers in the shallow littorals off Africa; once in the open ocean, deep-draft navy vessels with heavy firepower would take over.

Hydraulic fracturing, 3D seismology, and discoveries in the Permian Basin and Bakken Formation turned the United States back into the world's oil giant. With West African petroleum no longer essential, the fast corvette lost is mission—though not its contractor lobby, which continues to press Congress for more of these ships.

Chapter 7: Why Sea Trade Improves Lives

1. Robert Bryce, *A Question of Power* (PublicAffairs, 2020). His *Smaller Faster Lighter Denser Cheaper: How Innovation Keeps Proving the Catastrophists Wrong* (PublicAffairs, 2014), shows that as technology advances, it consumes fewer resources and generates less waste, the reverse of standard assumptions.

2. Hannah Ritchie and Max Roser, "CO_2 and Greenhouse Gas Emissions," Our World in Data, May 2017 (revised August 2020, https://ourworldindata.org/co2 -and-other-greenhouse-gas-emissions). I've used 2019 numbers, to subtract the impact of the 2020 pandemic lockdowns.

3. Numbers in this section computed from Max Roser, "Economic Growth," Our World in Data, https://ourworldindata.org/economic-growth.

4. Suppose we were asked to name the five foremost developments around the world since the Magna Carta. We would all have different answers. Mine would be the European Enlightenment (despite the moral horror of colonization), the US Constitution (despite the moral horror of the three-fifths clause), medical discoveries of the twentieth century (antibiotics, many types of vaccines, genetic origins of some diseases), the defeat of German and Japanese fascism just when all seemed lost ("light shines in the darkness, and the darkness did not overcome it," to quote John the Evangelist), and China's reduction of poverty from 1995 to 2020.

5. John Burgess, Lucia Foulkes, Philip Jones, Matt Merighi, Stephen Murray, and Jack Whitacre, eds., *Law of the Sea: A Policy Primer* (Fletcher School of Diplomacy, Tufts University, 2017).

6. FRED, "All Employees, Manufacturing," https://fred.stlouisfed.org/series /MANEMP.

7. Michael J. Hicks and Srikant Devaraj, "Myth and Reality in American Manufacturing," Center for Business and Economic Research, June 2015; David Autor, "Local Labor Market Effects of Import Competition in the United States," *American Economic Review*, October 2013.

8. David Autor, David Mindell, and Elisabeth Reynolds, "The Work of the Future: Building Better Jobs in an Age of Intelligent Machines," MIT Task Force on the Work of the Future, November 17, 2020. Noting superior conditions for wageworkers in European countries and Canada, which have more social cohesion then the current United States, Autor and his colleagues found that declining status for US labor is a deliberate political choice, "not an inevitable consequence of technological change, nor of globalization, nor of market forces. Similar pressures from digitalization and globalization affected most industrialized countries, and yet their labor markets fared better."

9. FRED, "Manufacturing Sector: Real Output," updated February 4, 2021, https://fred.stlouisfed.org/series/OUTMS.

10. FRED, "Manufacturing Sector: Real Output."

11. Max Roser, "Economic Growth," Our World in Data, https://ourworld indata.org/economic-growth.

12. United Nations Food and Agriculture Organization (FAO), *The State of Food Security in the World* (Rome: FAO, 2019).

13. Here is one of many examples. The 2005 volume *Collapse*, by the Pulitzer Prize and MacArthur grant winner Jared Diamond, received wide acclaim for a litany of depressing predictions, including that Asian poverty could not be overcome, that the US economy would fail soon—which should have happened by now—and that globalization would lead to economic breakdown (Jared Diamond, *Collapse: How Societies Choose to Fail or Succeed* [Viking, 2005]). Had Diamond in 2005 predicted rapid progress in China plus reasonable economic outcomes in the United States, he would have been analytically correct but scorned by award juries and the Aspen Institute set.

Why foundations and think tanks laud glumness is a question for history. Why writers and intellectuals cry doom is straightforward—it's good for their careers. They receive awards, grants, and academic advancement that way.

Predicting calamity and being totally wrong is a reliable path to praise in upper academia, among foundations, and at the soirées of Cambridge, Massachusetts; New York City; San Francisco; and Washington, D.C. Forecasting progress and being right is viewed in the same quarters with suspicion.

Chapter 8: Hey Look, a New Ocean!

1. This designation Great Green Fleet was a play on Teddy Roosevelt's battleships sent to circle the world. As what we would now call a branding device, Teddy had them painted white, to be visually distinct from other warships, and dubbed the Great White Fleet. In a similar PR move, in 1964, with every eye on the space race,

the navy staged Operation Sea Orbit, three nuclear-powered ships circumnavigating the world without having to stop for fuel. Across the deck of the carrier *Enterprise*, $E = mc^2$ was painted in huge lettering.

2. The media paid little heed to the Sea Launch project, though a decade later would laud Elon Musk's SpaceX. Partly this difference in interest reflects the entrepreneur's maxim that the first one to a new idea takes the losses, the second one gets the glory. (Netscape versus Microsoft Explorer, for example.) Another reason is that most SpaceX rockets blast off from Florida, where it's easy to arrange coverage, while Sea Launch operated from midocean. An exception to media disregard of Sea Launch was "Long Shot," *Atlantic*, May 2003.

3. In this chapter, factual statements about the high-north environment are drawn from Martin Siegert et al., "The Arctic and the UK: Climate, Research and Engagement," discussion paper 7, Grantham Institute, Imperial College London, June 2020, and from extensive presentations given to scientific groups by Fran Ulmer, chair of the US Arctic Research Commission. I thank Ulmer for sharing her files with me.

4. See National Oceanic and Atmospheric Administration (NOAA), "Arctic Report Card," 2020, www.arctic.noaa.gov/Report-Card.

5. National Academy of Sciences, *Climate Change: Evidence and Causes* (National Academies Press, 2014).

6. Carbon dioxide and methane are the primary gases associated with artificial global warming (water vapor causes natural global warming), but the ozone-depleting chemicals called CFCs and hydrochlorofluorocarbons (HCFCs) also cause warming, especially at high latitudes. CFCs have been banned, and HCFCs are being phased out. See Lorenzo Polvani et al., "Substantial 20th Century Arctic Warming," *Nature Climate Change*, January 20, 2020.

7. "Who Wins and Who Loses in a Warming World?," *Atlantic*, April 2007.

8. Susan Butler, *Roosevelt and Stalin* (Knopf, 2015).

9. Recounted at John 21. As day broke, the disciples were out trawling the Sea of Galilee, a freshwater lake. Jesus came to the water's edge to urge them on because he was hungry. Being resurrected sure sounds like it would give you an appetite! John 21:7 reports that realizing Christ had returned and was near, Simon Peter "put on some clothes, for he was naked." At that time it was common for fishermen to work nude, so the smells would not ruin whatever mean apparel they possessed. Then as now, bulk fishing using seines was a perilous, low-status task.

Chapter 9: The Next Stage Is to Govern the Seas

1. The magazine's peak came during the 1980s because its breadth and influence had never been greater—political leaders, academics, and literary writers quoted *The Atlantic* more than the other way around. But the web had yet to flood society with rants and factoids, while the 1987 federal rule allowing television and radio to be hyperpartisan had not taken effect, so national discourse had not yet begun the current downward spiral.

Like everything else, opinion responds to supply and demand. In the 1980s there were few sources of stimulating analysis, and foremost was *The Atlantic*: limited supply made the value high. Today the opinion industry is overcapacity; the value of analysis has plummeted. Another example of textbook economics.

2. Lynn Kuok, "China Can Learn from the Soviet Approach to the Law of the Sea," *Order from Chaos* (blog), Brookings Institution, March 27, 2018.

3. "Privatize the Seas," *Atlantic*, July/August 2009.

4. The Brundtland Report, formal name "Our Common Future," was released by the World Commission on the Environment. The Brundtland Report was thick with implications that climate change, smog, deforestation, and petroleum depletion would soon bring society to its knees. Which should have happened by now . . .

Easterbrook's Law of Doomsaying, enunciated in the *Washington Monthly* in 1992, specifies: Predict cataclysmic events ten years in the future. That's close enough that everyone will get upset, far enough that everyone will forget what you predicted. This law held firm during the 2020 election season, when Joe Biden, Elizabeth Warren, Bernie Sanders, and Alexandra Ocasio-Cortez forecast that global warming will destroy the world by 2030.

5. International Whaling Commission, "Total Catches," https://iwc.int/total-catches.

6. International Union for the Conservation of Nature, "The IUCN Red List of Threatened Species," www.iucnredlist.org.

7. Ranges of estimates of plastics in the seas vary widely. Probably most plastics reach the oceans via rivers. See Laurent C. M. Lebreton et al., "River Plastic Emissions to the World's Oceans," *Nature*, June 7, 2017.

8. News audiences have heard a great deal about propulsion innovator Tesla but little about CMA CGM, though the latter has three times the annual revenue of the Tesla, and its environmental improvements possess similar overall significance. Most American journalists would be hard-pressed so much as to guess which nation is CMA CGM's base. Don't you wish you too worked for a firm whose home office is along the waterfront at Marseilles!

9. Sönke Dangendorf, Carling Hay, Francisco M. Calafat et al., "Persistent Acceleration in Global Sea-Level Rise," *Nature Climate Change*, August 2019. Among other things, researchers found the extensive effort to build hydroelectric dams, roughly from 1950 to 1990, held back water that otherwise would have flowed to the seas. Now that dam building is largely complete, sea level rise accelerates.

10. Scott Kulp and Benjamin Strauss, "New Data Triple Estimates of Global Vulnerability to Sea Level Rise," *Nature Communications*, October 29, 2019.

11. See "Smart Weapons Need to Be Smarter," *Atlantic*, April 19, 2020.

Chapter 10: End of the Blue Age?

1. Begun in 1895, Slocum's voyage took three years. In 2017, François Gabart of France sailed around the world alone in forty-three days. Gabart used a modern trimaran with GPS guidance plus satellite radio updates on winds and currents. Slocum had no weather information beyond his own senses: for navigation he employed dead reckoning, gauging the sun position each noon or sometimes at night calculating the angle between the moon and a bright star.

2. FRED, "Real Median Household Income in the United States," updated September 16, 2020, https://fred.stlouisfed.org/series/MEHOINUSA672N. Inflation-adjusted household income fell from 2007 to 2012, creating a sense the country was going to hell. The year 2007 also saw the arrival of the iPhone and a big expansion of Facebook as it opened to public access and outside apps.

These two tech developments allowed feelings about the country going to hell to spread rapidly and directly among voters, and for scary claims and fake news to follow you around as people began to check their smart phones incessantly. In 2013, as economic graphs sloped upward—by the 2016 election, conditions were great—the sense of the country going to hell proved very "sticky," helping elect Trump.

3. Andrew S. Erickson, ed., *Chinese Naval Shipbuilding: An Ambitious and Uncertain Course* (Naval Institute Press, 2017).

4. David Hendrickson, *Republic in Peril* (Oxford University Press, 2018).

5. Accepting commission as an army officer, then becoming a Cabinet secretary, Esper took two oaths to serve and protect the Constitution. As an army officer, a member of Congress, the CIA director, and a cabinet secretary, Pompeo swore this oath on four occasions.

At the last, Esper resigned as secretary of defense to protest Donald Trump's demand that the 2020 election be overturned. In this Esper restored his honor, placing the public interest first as he had sworn to do.

Pompeo made no attempt to restore his honor, perhaps because he had none to restore. The day before Biden and Kamala Harris were inaugurated, Pompeo used the Department of State official account to send out a vicious social media post denouncing American multiculturalism—long one of the nation's proudest achievements. Pompeo openly violated the oath he took to uphold the Constitution, bringing shame to Foggy Bottom and shame to West Point. See "U.S. Diplomats Condemn Trump, Pompeo for Capital Riot," *Chicago Tribune*, January 10, 2021. The *Tribune* is a Republican paper!

6. Fang himself has some problems playing by the rules—in 2019, he was imprisoned for taking bribes.

7. Rana Dasgupta, "The Silenced Majority," *Harper's*, December 2020.

INDEX

ELIZABETH KENNELLY

GREGG EASTERBROOK is the author of twelve books, most recently *It's Better Than It Looks: Reasons for Optimism in an Age of Fear* (2018). He was a staff writer, national correspondent, or contributing editor of *The Atlantic* for nearly forty years. Easterbrook has written for the *New Yorker*, *Science*, *Wired*, *Harvard Business Review*, the *Washington Monthly*, the *New Republic*, the *New York Times*, the *Wall Street Journal*, and the *Los Angeles Times*. He was a fellow in economics and in government studies at the Brookings Institution. In 2017 he was elected to the American Academy of Arts and Sciences.

PublicAffairs is a publishing house founded in 1997. It is a tribute to the standards, values, and flair of three persons who have served as mentors to countless reporters, writers, editors, and book people of all kinds, including me.

I. F. STONE, proprietor of *I. F. Stone's Weekly*, combined a commitment to the First Amendment with entrepreneurial zeal and reporting skill and became one of the great independent journalists in American history. At the age of eighty, Izzy published *The Trial of Socrates*, which was a national bestseller. He wrote the book after he taught himself ancient Greek.

BENJAMIN C. BRADLEE was for nearly thirty years the charismatic editorial leader of *The Washington Post*. It was Ben who gave the *Post* the range and courage to pursue such historic issues as Watergate. He supported his reporters with a tenacity that made them fearless and it is no accident that so many became authors of influential, best-selling books.

ROBERT L. BERNSTEIN, the chief executive of Random House for more than a quarter century, guided one of the nation's premier publishing houses. Bob was personally responsible for many books of political dissent and argument that challenged tyranny around the globe. He is also the founder and longtime chair of Human Rights Watch, one of the most respected human rights organizations in the world.

·   ·   ·

For fifty years, the banner of Public Affairs Press was carried by its owner Morris B. Schnapper, who published Gandhi, Nasser, Toynbee, Truman, and about 1,500 other authors. In 1983, Schnapper was described by *The Washington Post* as "a redoubtable gadfly." His legacy will endure in the books to come.

Peter Osnos, *Founder*